I0797843

MORE THAN A PRESIDENT

Sundays with Jimmy Carter

MERCER UNIVERSITY PRESS

Endowed by

TOM WATSON BROWN
and
THE WATSON-BROWN FOUNDATION, INC.

MORE THAN A PRESIDENT

Sundays with Jimmy Carter

Edited by

Andrew Greer

MERCER UNIVERSITY PRESS
Macon, Georgia

MUP/ H1052

Published by Mercer University Press
1501 Mercer University Drive
Macon, Georgia 31207

29 28 27 26 25   5 4 3 2

Books published by Mercer University Press are printed on acid-free paper that meets the requirements of the American National Standard for Information Sciences—Permanence of Paper for Printed Library Materials.
Printed and bound in CANADA.
This book is set in Adobe Garamond.
Cover/jacket design by Burt&Burt.
Biblical texts taken from the NRSV unless otherwise noted.

ISBN   978-0-88146-974-5
Cataloging-in-Publication Data is available from the Library of Congress

For the members of Maranatha Baptist Church,

who helped a president teach the Gospel.

Religion, declares the modern man, is consciousness of our highest social values. Nothing could be further from the truth. True religion is a profound uneasiness about our highest social values.

—Reinhold Niebuhr, *Beyond Tragedy: Essays on the Christian Interpretation of History*

Contents

Foreword by *Barbara Brown Taylor* xi

Preface xv

Editor's Note xix

The 1970s 5

March 12, 1978: The Conflict of Being a Christian 11

April 29, 1979: A Cry for Justice 31

The 1980s 45

November 16, 1980: What Is Christianity? 53

March 8, 1981: Who Is the Church? 71

The 1990s 89

March 7, 1993: Responding to Honest Inquiry 95

October 9, 1994: Knowing and Loving 113

January 7, 1996: God's Covenant People 133

September 20, 1998: When All Is Said and Done 155

The 2000s 171

February 17, 2002: Reaching Out to People of Different Cultures 177

February 24, 2002: An Inclusive Gospel 191

December 9, 2007: The Call of God 207

August 24, 2008: An Admonition for Humility 223

The 2010s 241

June 22, 2014: Prayers of Lament 247

July 12, 2015: Seeking Wisdom Through Suffering 261

The Last Year 277
March 3, 2019: A New Way of Life 283
Afterword by *Jason Carter* 295
Notes 299
Acknowledgments 307
Selected Bibliography 313

Foreword

by Barbara Brown Taylor

One of my lasting regrets—both as a Georgian and a lifelong Democrat—is that I never made the 228-mile pilgrimage from my home in Clarkesville to Maranatha Baptist Church in Plains to study the Bible with Jimmy Carter. His Sunday school class was so famous that I knew I could watch recordings online or listen to them on Audible, but that wasn't the point. I wanted to be in the same room with him, where I could see the divine alchemy of the word-made-flesh happening right in front of me. I wanted to be in his presence.

In 2014, he flipped the script on me. Late that year, my husband Ed said there was an interesting message on our answering machine for me. "He says he's Jimmy Carter," Ed said, "and it sure does sound like him." With Ed standing over me, I leaned down and pressed "Play."

"Hello, this is Jimmy Carter," the familiar voice said. "I'm calling for Mrs. Taylor (he cleared his throat), I mean Reverend Taylor. If she would, please, um, ask her to call me back at this number at her convenience." Click. *What in the world?* When I dialed the number, a woman who sounded a lot like Rosalynn Carter answered with more than a touch of *what-now* in her voice, put her hand over the receiver, and called her husband to the phone.

He wanted me to consider nomination to the Board of Trustees at Mercer University. It was a fine group of people, he said, serving a fine institution, but women were somewhat underrepresented. He thought I would make a good addition. I thanked him more times than necessary before telling him I really wasn't the board member type. "Me either," he said, "but this one is different. You'll see."

I did the math while he told me a little more about Mercer. He was a 90-year-old former president and global humanitarian who had won the Nobel Peace Prize in 2002, taught Sunday school for nearly forty years, and still showed up in a beat-up leather tool apron to help build houses for Habitat for Humanity with his wife of 68 years. Though he wouldn't be diagnosed with metastatic cancer until the following year, it was already at work in his body. In sum, there wasn't a chance of telling this man that I was too old, busy, tired, or fragile to serve on a board, so I said yes instead.

The next thing I remember is standing behind a podium in the Board Room at Mercer giving the morning devotion to a wildly impressive bunch of people (who were definitely board member types) while former President Jimmy Carter sat directly in front of me, nodding and smiling like he was my favorite uncle. In this way I entered the great mansion of his heart, where the door was always open to welcome one more.

Now the script has flipped again, with this book full of *his* morning devotions. They date from the 1970's to the 2010's, bridging two millennia and speaking to the full span of some people's lives. If you place a timeline of world events beside the dates of these Sunday school lessons, you may be able to listen between the lines, hearing the teacher speak of humility, justice, unity, courage, and love (love wins in these lessons every time) over the drumbeats of the Gulf War, the collapse of the Soviet Union, the Oklahoma City Bombing, the Global War on Terror, Hurricane Katrina, the Great Recession, Sandy Hook, the Paris Climate Accord, Black Lives Matter and Me Too–to name just a few.

Thanks to Andrew Greer, the lessons come to us live, by which I mean they come to us with Carter's questions to his students intact, along with some of their answers, occasional asides to Rosalynn, and spontaneous bursts of wisdom or storytelling that defy all punctuation on the page. This means you cannot sleep through class. You will need to stay alert, tracking the teacher from thought to thought as a familiar piece of scripture heads off in an unexpected direction, or leads to a story of such shocking honesty that you can hardly believe your ears.

You may also have to forgive some dated understandings of first century politics, at least in the earliest lessons from the New Testament. Anyone who reads the gospels without taking Rome's vicious occupation of the Holy Land into account, or the bitter divisions that arose between different groups of Jews about how to live with that oppression, can forget that they are reading what Elaine Pagels calls "war literature."

By the time John's Gospel was written, the first of two Jewish revolts against Rome had failed spectacularly, the Temple in Jerusalem had been destroyed along with most of the city, Jews had fled in every direction with no consensus about what it meant to be Jewish under such apocalyptic conditions, and the early church had become predominantly Gentile. "The Jews" had become an easy target to blame for Jesus' death, though Rome had already crucified thousands of Jews before him and would continue the practice for another three hundred years.

No one ever taught me that in Sunday school, so even as a young preacher I embraced biblical stereotypes about Pharisees, the Law, and Jewish devotion to the Law without ever suspecting there was another side to the story. The devoted Christians I read about in the Bible belonged to a persecuted minority. Of course I was on their side! Their opponents came off as such villains that I never gave a thought to what they were defending or why, any more than I thought about what would happen to them when the tables turned and *they* became the persecuted minority.

Then, to cite President Carter, I started asking questions. "If we don't question," he said in his Sunday school lesson on March 7, 1993, "it indicates that we are satisfied with the way things are. We don't want to let our mind be active. We don't want to strain our mind. We are afraid what a changing concept might bring to us. We'll have to modify or endanger our comfort level if we open up our minds, our hearts, to new concepts, new ideas." In that same lesson, he spoke of Pharisees very differently than he had in 1978. He had strained his mind, changed his concept, opened his heart to new ideas. My hero.

Theological humility is a real mouthful, but it tops my list of human virtues. To be faithful to your view of divine reality without feeling compelled to attack someone else's is a true sign of spiritual maturity—and no one exemplifies it better than a former president and lifelong Baptist who says things like, "You have let me teach in a fumbling way…" or, "There has to be an ability to give and take, a non-domination of the others…" or, "The main thing is to recognize that above us all is a basic concept so great, and so important, that our human differences fade into insignificance."

If you become a student of these lessons for no other reason, do it to study how a great Christian mind works with a gallant heart—honoring the past while creating the future, loving the questions more than the answers, seeking the truth wherever it may lead, examining his private soul in public as an example to others, and seeking their welfare above the bandaging of his sometimes wounded own. Above all, notice how the teacher's life embodies his teachings so well that anyone can see the perfect fit, even with the sound turned down.

The book's dedication says it best: "For the members of Maranatha Baptist Church, who helped a president teach the Gospel." With this foreword I add my thanks to him, to them, and to Andrew Greer for allowing those of us who never made it to Plains to imagine ourselves in the teacher's presence as well.

Barbara Brown Taylor
Clarkesville, Georgia
April 2025

Preface

The morning air was warm for the close of December. The bare pecan trees were draped with a teary residue, a morning-after side effect from the unseasonable thunderstorms that had rattled and hummed throughout the night before. A dense fog blanketed the drowsy town, hypnotizing its inhabitants in a sort of early winter lilt. Rusty water, stained by the land's storied red-dirt clay, puddled on the empty streets.

I backed out of my driveway onto US Route 280, an old connector highway that rambles through rural Alabama into southern Georgia, where it drops off along the outskirts of Savannah, just short of spilling its tarmac into the Atlantic. Along the middle of the ambling road lies a quaint, peanut-farming town. This is where I live, in Plains, Georgia.

That morning, as I do every Sunday morning, I passed the sleeping downtown, a row of two-story buildings that have remained virtually unchanged over the course of the town's two-hundred-year tenure, and turned north on Highway 45 for my weekly half-mile pilgrimage to Maranatha Baptist Church. Nearly twenty years ago, I, like many others through the years, traversed this same off-the-beaten path as a tourist, intrigued to bear witness to a former leader of the free world delivering practical life lessons from the chronicles of Holy Scripture. You see, Plains is the lifelong hometown of the thirty-ninth president of the United States and former first lady, peacemakers Jimmy and Rosalynn Carter, and for nearly forty years, "Mister Jimmy," as the Plains folk call him, taught Sunday school at Maranatha for anyone willing to make the trek to the southwest Georgia village.

The church boasts an attractive red-brick structure worthy of its surrounding landscape. Nestled underneath centuries-old pecan orchards, the charming house of worship features a traditional entryway of ivory-painted wooden double doors inset with symmetrical square panels, and it is flanked by an even row of mint-and-lilac stained-glass windows and crowned with a subtly ornamented steeple, perpetually lit to serve as a beacon of acceptance to the local community, and to the world.

Maranatha's original flock began congregating in early 1977 after its mother church, Plains Baptist, refused to allow Black people to join the membership rolls. In 1954, more than two decades earlier, the United States Supreme Court outlawed segregation in *Brown v. Board of Education*, a landmark ruling in the nation's rapidly growing Civil Rights Movement. Yet communities in the Deep South still relegated Black Americans to the backseat of society, even as much of the country cried out for liberty and justice for all of her citizens. Plains was no exception in America's lingering conflict over race relationships.

In 1981, after being denied the opportunity to serve the American people in a second term in the White House, Jimmy and Rosalynn Carter and their thirteen-year-old daughter, Amy, returned home to Plains. The next Sunday, as was the Carter's custom, the former First Family planned to attend church, so, as town folklore records, their Secret Service detail drove the family to Plains Baptist, Jimmy's childhood church, and the same congregation that had denied membership to Black individuals just four and a half years prior, but, as the car approached, the Carters instructed Secret Service to keep moving on towards Maranatha.

The Carters' decision to move their church membership initiated a red-letter partnership with the congregation of Maranatha and the community of Plains to host a Sunday school class taught by Carter, a former United States president, to a spiritual seekers from around the world. The rest of the story is a history that only Jimmy Carter and the congregants of Maranatha could help write.

As I pulled into church that late December morning, only a few cars littered the parking lot. It was that lonesome Sunday squeezed between Christmas Day and New Year's Day, often coined "Low Attendance Sunday." Faithful churchgoers juggle out-of-town schedules typical of Christmastime travel, and the general population stays hungover from the mayhem of America's version of a holiday. The date, soon to be etched into our psyches forever, was December 29, 2024.

Kim Carter Fuller, Jimmy's niece, delivered a lesson from the Gospel of Matthew about Herod, the nefarious Hebrew king who ordered a ghastly massacre of Bethlehem's baby boys in a monstrous attempt to murder the long-awaited Messiah. The lesson suggested that we have very little, if any, control over the tragedies that inevitably color our lives, and Kim expounded upon the theme, stating that even within the advent of eternal hope, there lingers injustice, pain, grief, and even death. She offered that while the presence of God does not deliver us from our sorrows, the life of Jesus, the Christ, confirms that we are not alone. God is neither distant nor ignorant of our distress or our heartbreaks. The advent of Christmas marks the birth of the reality that God is, indeed, right here among us.

Sometime after Maranatha concluded her church services for the week, and before that late December day bowed its head for another long winter's night, Jimmy Carter drew his final breath on this side of life. At one hundred years of age, a family member, a neighbor, a confidant—and yes, a Sunday school teacher—took his turn in laying his body to rest and surrendering his soul to his Maker.

Jimmy Carter was more than a president. He was a human *actively* being who lived the best way he knew how the extraordinary example of Jesus. Jesus—this life of peace, of tenderness, of knowingness, of love, as recorded inside the books of Jimmy's beloved Bible.

Throughout the following pages, you will read Jimmy's words. You will learn from his lessons. You will explore his deep faith. And you will hear the Greatest Story ever told by anyone who has ever lived.

Andrew Greer
Plains, Georgia
December 30, 2024

Editor's Note

Jimmy Carter taught hundreds of Sunday school lessons throughout his lifetime. Possibly thousands. Most of the lessons he taught at First Baptist Church of the City of Washington, DC, and at Maranatha Baptist Church in Plains were recorded for posterity. In his later years, many were also filmed. So, to narrow down hundreds of lessons to only a dozen or so for this book, I had to listen. And listen a lot.

Thanks to Sara Mitchell at the Jimmy Carter Library and Museum and Lauren Gay Barber at the Carter Center, I was able to locate a comprehensive list of recordings, organized by date, lesson topic, and Scripture references. (Halfway through my research, Lauren also discovered a box of binders containing some of President Carter's handwritten teaching notes—one of which is pictured in this book—as well as lesson transcriptions he had ordered for his personal library, adding greatly to the development of the book!) I then selected several lessons that looked intriguing to me on the page. Since this book is organized by decades, I chose a few from each one.

Upon receiving an email from Sara with the requested audio or video files (some had to be digitized for the first time!), I listened carefully, paying close attention to the lesson content, President Carter's delivery, and the class's interaction with him. I did my best to discern which lessons featured all of the above admirably and then transcribed and edited those for inclusion in the book you now hold in your hands.

This is not a word-for-word historical account of those lessons. Carter's teaching style was casual and conversational, so some words and phrases don't always translate smoothly to the printed page. Filler words like "kind of," "anyway," "you know," and "you might say" can become clunky on the page, depending on how they're used. These words have been removed based on my editorial judgment. If any substantive content was removed to reduce word count or maintain focus, the deleted portion is indicated with an ellipsis. Rest assured, I did not change any of President Carter's words or add any of my own, aside from writing a brief introduction for each section to offer some "Carter context" for the period in which those lessons were taught.

President Carter loved to invite class members into the lesson. He asked a lot of questions, and he expected a response! To give you the feeling of being "in the room," much of his back-and-forth with the class has been included in these chapters. To make it simple, when a class member is speaking, it is notated in *italics*.

As a resident of Plains, a member of Maranatha, a longtime admirer of Jimmy Carter's, and a lifelong reader of the Scriptures, I approached my work on this collection with the utmost of personal care. Any and all mistakes are a result of my being human and are mine alone to assume.

The 1970s

It is the heron and I, under judging Sir John's elmed
Hill, tell-tale the knelled
Guilt
Of the led-astray birds whom God, for their breast of
    whistles,
Have mercy on,
God in his whirlwind silence save, who marks the spar-
    rows hail,
For their souls' song.

—Dylan Thomas
from "Over Sir John's Hill"

March 5, 1977. President Jimmy Carter, First Lady Rosalynn Carter, and daughter Amy Carter leave The First Baptist Church of the City of Washington, D.C. after attending Sunday School and church services. The newly minted First Family joined the congregation soon after Carter was inaugurated as President of the United States. Amy was baptized at the church shortly thereafter.

Courtesy Jimmy Carter Presidential Library and Museum

April 29, 1979. President Jimmy Carter and ministers of The First Baptist Church of the City of Washington, D.C. engage in conversation upon the conclusion of the Sunday worship services. Earlier that morning, President Carter taught a Sunday School lesson for the Couples Class entitled, "A Cry for Justice."

Courtesy Jimmy Carter Presidential Library and Museum

January 14, 1979. Upon receiving the Martin Luther King, Jr. Nonviolent Peace Prize Award at Ebenezer Baptist Church in Atlanta, Georgia, President Carter embraces Ambassador of the United Nations and confidante, Andrew Young, and former Morehouse College president and longtime friend and mentor, Dr. Benjamin E. Mays, while Coretta Scott King, Martin Luther King, Jr.'s widow, looks on. Young, Mays, and King were pioneers in the Civil Rights Movement.

Courtesy Jimmy Carter Presidential Library and Museum

January 14, 1979. The Carters and leaders of the Civil Rights Movement sing "We Shall Overcome" at the conclusion of the Martin Luther King, Jr. Nonviolent Peace Prize Award ceremony at Ebenezer Baptist Church in Atlanta, Georgia. Pictured (left to right): Martin Luther "Daddy" King, Sr., father of Martin Luther King, Jr., First Lady Rosalynn Carter, Ambassador Andrew Young, Coretta Scott King, widow of Martin Luther King, Jr., President Jimmy Carter, Dr. Benjamin E. Mays, Rev. Dr. Joseph Roberts, Jr., senior pastor at Ebenezer Baptist Church, and Jesse Hill, Jr., chairman of the Board of Directors of the Martin Luther King, Jr. Center for Social Change.

Courtesy Jimmy Carter Presidential Library and Museum

January 14, 1979. President Carter addresses an audience at Ebenezer Baptist Church in Atlanta, Georgia, upon receiving the Martin Luther King, Jr. Nonviolent Peace Prize Award from The King Center.

Courtesy Jimmy Carter Presidential Library and Museum

Introduction

From the beginning of Jimmy Carter's life, faith was the foundation. Equality was the offspring of his faith.

In the Deep Southwest Georgia that Carter grew up in, the pines grew tall, the soil ran red, and Black and White folks were all splintered up by segregation. The churches in Plains followed suit. White congregations built up along the north side of the rail ties, and the Black community stationed their houses of worship along the south side of the tracks. As Martin Luther King Jr. often said, and Carter often repeated, Sunday morning church services are "one of the most segregated hours, if not *the* most segregated hours in Christian America."

Jimmy's mother was a "whiskey-drinking saint," as Andrew Young, a civil rights icon and longtime confidant of Carter's, remembered. "Miss Lillian," as she was lovingly dubbed by the American public, espoused an earthy spirituality that, with a little cuss and a lot of compassion, preached and lived out the unpopular practice of integration. An unusual woman for her time, as a registered nurse and a member of the enlightened medical community, Jimmy's mother quite literally treated her neighbors as equals, delivering their babies and diagnosing their ailments with liberal concern and expertise, regardless of the color of their skin.

"She delivered every baby in a county that was eighty percent Black, and any baby she delivered she treated as one of her children," Young said of Lillian's indefatigable belief that all people are created equal in the eyes of God and so should be treated as such at the hands of one another. "Now, his daddy wasn't comfortable with that."

James "Earl" Carter Sr. was a man tailored by his times. Though his house and farm lay just on the outskirts of town in the majority-Black village of Archery, Georgia, Jimmy's father was a prominent member of the Plains community and the White congregation of Plains Baptist Church, serving as a deacon and teaching Sunday school classes for its parishioners. And though his cherished Scriptures included messages such as "thou shalt love thy neighbor as thyself" and "for ye are all one in Christ Jesus," Earl stuck to the strictly separate social structure often revered as "biblical" in the Deep South.

Yet we humans are a complicated bunch. In 1953, as Earl was dying from pancreatic cancer, Jimmy took leave from his burgeoning naval career as a nuclear submariner to attend to his dying father in the house he'd once called home in Plains. As father and son became intimately reacquainted, perhaps for the first time since Jimmy had become a man of his own, members of the community—both White *and* Black—streamed by his father's bedside to pay their respects and thank Earl personally for the many ways he had quietly, yet substantially, supported their families through the years. Jimmy was astounded by the profound impact his father's quiet benevolence had on his community, directly influencing Jimmy's decision to leave his career with the navy and return to Plains in hopes of having a similar connection with his hometown.

Though he subscribed to the customs of his time and place, one could argue that Earl's discreet generosity was a window into his soul—an attempt to move beyond his personal prejudices and to liberally live out his religious beliefs as scripted through yet another message from his Holy Bible, the message that "faith, if it hath not works, is dead."

But an accurate picture of Jimmy's early spiritual formation cannot be wholly illustrated without the mystical piety that Rachel Clark blended into the diverse color wheel of his flourishing faith. Rachel and her husband, Jack, worked as day laborers on the Carter farm and set up house in a small cabin close to the Carters' home in Archery. Whenever possible, Jimmy would spend the night with the Clarks in their sparse abode, expressing later in his life that during his childhood, outside of his own parents, he felt closest to Rachel, a Black woman he described as having the "aura of a queen."

When the chores of the fields slowed to an ambling pace, Rachel and Jimmy would peel off into the whispering woods that surrounded his family's land to answer the call of a creek and a fishing line in a shrine of Georgia wilderness. Once settled into the rhythms of nature, Rachel taught Jimmy about the sacredness of life, instilled in him the responsibility to steward and care for the environment, and, under the canopy of a Zion sky, guide him in opening his mind and heart to the grand adventure of a life lived within the mysteries and infinite love of God.

These rituals of faith that Lillian, Earl, and Rachel performed in their daily lives—these witnesses to a divine Spirit, witnesses whom the young Carter loved, and admired, and, even at times, worshipped—embedded a devout, personal faith that would follow Jimmy Carter for a lifetime.

Late in the year of 1978, President Carter opened up diplomatic relations with the People's Republic of China. Back in 1949, at the apex of the Chinese Revolution, the mainland of China fell to communist forces. For the next three decades, the United States, ever-fearful of the infiltration of communism into its freedom borders, kept China at arm's length, but a new emperor was in town, and Carter decided it was high time to open the lines of communication with the ole Red Dragon.

China's new premier, Deng Xiaoping, was an unorthodox autocratic leader, encouraging reform in the fashion of an open market commerce and individualism among the Chinese people. So, to further strengthen relations between the two countries, Carter invited the reform-minded leader to the White House in January 1979. Over the course of a few days, the two statesmen hashed out fresh agreements on a handful of issues that had stacked up as a result of the nations' estrangement.

During a state banquet held to celebrate the newly minted pacts, Deng, in a spirit of gratitude, said, "President Carter, you have been very helpful to the Chinese people, and I wonder if there is anything special that we may do for you." President Carter considered for a moment, and then replied, "When I was a little boy, my supreme heroes were Baptist missionaries who served in China, and I used to give five cents a week to help build hospitals and schools for Chinese children. Since 1949, missionaries, Bibles, and worship have been prohibited in your country, and my request is that these three things be permitted."

Freedom of religion is a bedrock of the American experiment, and President Carter's religious faith was enormously precious to him, so he decided to go for broke. Deng was surprised by Carter's request and told him he would need time to think about how to respond; Deng would let him know his final answer the following day.

The next morning, Deng informed Carter that he would reform the Chinese Constitution to include freedom of religion. He would also reinitiate the distribution of Bibles. He could not, however, permit Western missionaries to return to China, as they had disrespected Chinese culture and treated the people of China as inferior.

Deng made good on his promises, allowing autonomous practice of religion and the circulation of Scripture, and over the next decade, Christianity boomed among the Chinese. In fact, since Carter made his courageous request more than forty years ago, the Christian religion has grown faster in the People's Republic of China than in any other location in the world. Had Jimmy not observed his mother serving people of different races with dignity in the face of an undignified segregation, had he not fled to Plains to tend to his ailing father and unlocked the humble generosity of his father's private religion, had the majestic nature of Rachel Clark's spirit life not been poured into the heart of her young friend and inspired pupil, Jimmy, as President Carter, may not have had the courage or the wisdom or the experience or the directness or the meekness to request a cornerstone of freedom—the right to worship—for a people oppressed by Communist control.

❧

As a prelude to President Carter's inauguration in 1977, the First Baptist Church of the City of Washington, DC, hosted a pair of prayer services for the incoming president. On the following Sunday, January 23, President Carter transferred his membership from Plains Baptist Church to the capital's Baptist church, along with those of his wife, Rosalynn; his nine-year-old daughter, Amy; his son and namesake, James Earl Carter III ("Chip"), and daughter-in-law, Caron. One month later, Amy was baptized in the church.

Late that same year, President Carter would be invited to begin a sort of Bible-teaching residency at First Baptist DC. From the high and tucked-away balcony overlooking the gothic sanctuary, Carter taught Sunday school to the congregation's Couples Class more than a dozen times while occupying the most powerful office in the world. The following lessons from this collection confront the ever-present tension of a modern-day Christian pursuing justice in the shadow of the Prince of Peace, even when that Christian is America's commander in chief—the president of the United States.

March 12, 1978

The Conflict of Being a Christian

The First Baptist Church of the City of Washington, DC

Lesson Scripture

John 16:1–6, 20–22 (NRSV)

1 'I have said these things to you to keep you from stumbling. 2 They
will put you out of the synagogues. Indeed, an hour is coming when
those who kill you will think that by doing so they are offering worship
to God. 3 And they will do this because they have not known the Father
or me. 4 But I have said these things to you so that when their hour
comes you may remember that I told you about them.

'I did not say these things to you from the beginning, because I
was with you. 5 But now I am going to him who sent me; yet none of
you asks me, "Where are you going?" 6 But because I have said these
things to you, sorrow has filled your hearts.

20 'Very truly, I tell you, you will weep and mourn, but the world
will rejoice; you will have pain, but your pain will turn into joy. 21
When a woman is in labor, she has pain, because her hour has come.
But when her child is born, she no longer remembers the anguish because of the joy of having brought a human being into the world. 22 So
you have pain now; but I will see you again, and your hearts will rejoice, and no one will take your joy from you.'

This is a lesson I've been looking forward to for several weeks.... It's one that I think exemplifies, in a more personal way, the thing that afflicts us all.

We started out our life as an aware person. As soon as we could understand the English language–hearing fairytales. And there are two phrases that are typical in almost every fairytale.

Once upon a time.
And what's the other one?
Live happily ever after.

Live happily ever afterwards—that's right. It kind of gives us a false impression, but maybe it's good when you're two, three, four years old to think that eventually, after trials and tribulations and troubles, conflicts, testing, sorrows, dangers, that when that episode is over "they lived happily ever afterwards" always comes. And then, later on in life, we find that that part of the fairytale doesn't come true. This morning, we're going to study about the fact that "they lived happily ever afterwards" is something that's not easy to discern.

If you think about Jesus' life and his relationship with people around him, what would be the one word that would come to your mind? I know there will be a lot of different words, but just call out a few.

Love.

Caring.

Friendship.

Compassion.

Concern.

Servant.

Devotion.

Sacrifice.

All those are very good, inspiring, mostly pleasant words. Friendship, compassion, love, devotion. Can anybody think of a word that doesn't quite fit into that category?

Suffering.

Betrayal.

Sorrow.

Sacrifice.

Sought to kill him.

Getting close—nobody's gotten to the word that I want yet.

Joy.

No, that's not it.

Death.

How many of you studied your lesson? [*Congregation laughs*] There's a word that describes this lesson today—Jesus' relationship with the world around him, which is also the disciple's relationship with the world around them after Christ's death. It also is a word that describes the relationship between us as Christians and the world around us to the degree that we commit our lives to Christ.

Conflict.

When Jesus was encapsulated or surrounded by his own disciples who believed in him and who loved him, and who were blessed by God with some inspiration and some understanding, there was harmony, there was friendship, there was love. But when Jesus reached out and came in contact with the outside world, which was close to him but not part of his inner circle, the word that characterizes almost every time was "conflict." He created tension and he created debate and he created disharmony and he created misunderstanding and he created the opposite of love, which is what?

Hatred.

Hatred. It's hard for us, in the twentieth century, to look back on Christ's time, when he was living on earth as a man, to understand how anyone could have hated my Savior. How could anyone have hated Jesus Christ of Nazareth, whose life was epitomized by the words that came out first—love, compassion, understanding, friendship?

But hatred, as it focused on Christ among the broad populace, was probably a more accurate description of feelings toward Christ than the word "love." Jesus didn't respond with hatred, but he recognized that it existed, and he suffered because of it, as we know, to the utmost degree. Why?

Why did Christ's life bring out animosity and conflict and hatred? Jesus told us in this lesson.

A New Standard

Turn to John 15. And we'll read three verses, which are not a part of the lesson text—22, 23, and 24.

[22] *"If I had not come and spoken to them, they would not have been guilty of sin."*

Who said that?

Jesus.

We're all Bible students. We've been studying the Bible since we were three or four years old. How many of you understand what that means?

"If I had not come and spoken to them, they would not have been guilty of sin."...

It's easier to live by the admonition an eye for an eye and a tooth for a tooth than it is to live by the admonition, if someone slaps you on the face, turn the other cheek. And it's easier to live by the admonition thou shalt not kill, than it is to live by the admonition, you shall not hate or despise or criticize your brother.

Jesus presented to the world what? A new spirit, a new covenant, a new standard for what is right and what is wrong—what's acceptable in the eyes of God and what is not acceptable in the eyes of God. And he got away from the listing of all kinds of little, tiny things that you did on the Sabbath day, or exactly how you handled the tithing of mint and spices that grew in your garden, to the genuine significance of a life acceptable in the eyes of God.

And Jesus spoke with authority. There was something about Christ. When he witnessed to people either individually, like the woman at the well, or in vast multitudes, like the Sermon on the Mount, quite often, it says, they went away perplexed, because this man apparently spoke with authority. He apparently spoke directly from God. And what he said, although it was hard to believe, it was hard to ignore. There was a personal aspect of it that touched individual people's hearts. Even people like Nicodemus had his life transformed; he couldn't forget what Christ told him.

So, Jesus came into a kind of complacent religious world, where people prided themselves on their inner relationship with God's house, God's church, God's rabbis, and all of a sudden, their complacency was torn apart. It was destroyed. They had to reexamine the standards that they had set for themselves, and they were not willing to face God's facts in their own lives. Instead of a set of requirements very carefully molded to meet what you were willing to do, and then judging other people by those requirements, Christ said, "This is what it means to be a child of God. And this is what you must do to be accepted by God. And this is what you must do to have eternal life. You must repent. You're a sinner."

A lot of people said, "I'm not a sinner. You know, I follow all the little laws." Remember the Pharisees said "Lord, I thank you that I'm not like all these other people. God, thank you for letting me be acceptable in your sight," and Jesus said that man did not go away justified. But the recognition of one's own sinfulness is a shock. When Christ was alive, it was a shock when his disciples inherited the mantle of speaking for God, and it's a shock today.

Whether we like it or not, we tend to do the same thing that the people who lived around Christ did two thousand years ago. We tend to make for ourselves a set of rules that suit our own nature, our own incarnation, our own system of priorities. If we're not tempted by a particular thing, we elevate it to one of the most important requirements of God. If we have temptation and we yield to it, we tend to forget about that or move it from our minds. And so, we build for ourselves a definition of what is acceptable in God's sight that creates a sense of euphoria for us, or complacency for us, or assurance for us, that in God's eyes, we as Christians, we as Baptists, are acceptable.

When Christ talks about sinners, he's really not talking about me. I know it says all are sinners, but he's really not talking about me. Because I know what goes on in my own heart, and when I do sin, I know the reasons for it. I know the temptations that confronted me, and I know what that other person said that really made me so angry and filled my heart with hatred. And I know how it is because there are certain worldly responsibilities that I have that might be in conflict with a pure commitment to God, but I understand the circumstances that make me want to take care of my family first. And it's good for my business to be cutting a corner here and cutting a corner there. I understand, and I'm sure God understands also. But Christ said, "No."

And to the extent that we adhere rigidly to Christ's pure principles, we'll experience conflict.

We're a complacent church. We're a complacent denomination. We're complacent Christians, because we've modified the standards of God to suit our own lives. It's hard for us to apply to ourselves the phrase "for all have sinned and come short of the glory of God" and "the wages of sin is death." Surely this doesn't apply to us. We know all the good things we do. We know all the times we pray.

When Jesus said these words, his disciples couldn't quite understand because they had not suffered very much. Jesus had been the cutting edge of the new Spirit, the new setting of standards. His disciples were there with him, they gave him support, but I never have understood the reason they were not brought into all of the comprehension of what Christ was and what his ministry meant that they later learned. Jesus spoke to them in parables. He spoke to them in riddles. They didn't quite understand exactly what went on, and they were left out of the abuses that were heaped on Christ even when they walked the dusty roads with him. Later, they began to feel those problems during the last few hours of Christ's life.

The most vivid example that comes to my mind is Peter, who, when he was pressed with a possible condemnation of the political and religious authorities, he denied his own Savior, whom he knew was the son of God. Just because some serving maid came up to him as he was standing there by the fire and said, "Aren't you one of those people that was with Jesus of Nazareth?" "No, no, no. I've never heard of him before." He did it three times.

That was the first tangible experience of the pressures that fell on the disciples and Jesus is saying in this lesson, it's going to come to you. And he also said it's inevitable.

The Persecuted Christian

Read the twenty-third and twenty-fourth verses.

23 *'Whoever hates me hates my Father also.* 24 *If I had not done among them the works that no one else did, they would not have sin. But now they have seen and hated both me and my Father.'*

They hated Jesus without reason, and, in the process, they hated God, whom they professed to love and worship. Jesus came as a Savior, but he also came to judge, to condemn their way of life, and that made people uncomfortable and filled with hatred.

Turn to John 16:1–6. Do you have that, Rosalynn?

1 *"I have told you these things so that you won't be staggered by all that lies ahead.* 2 *For you will be excommunicated from the synagogues, and indeed the time is coming when those who kill you will think they are doing God a service.* 3 *This is because they have never known the Father or me.* 4 *Yes, I'm telling you these things now so that when they happen you will remember I warned you. I didn't tell you earlier because I was going to be with you for a while longer.*

5 *"But now I am going away to the one who sent me; and none of you seems interested in the purpose of my going; none wonders why.* 6 *Instead you are only filled with sorrow."*

Jesus is saying this is the inevitability or the certainty of conflict and sorrow and condemnation, and also went on to predict, very accurately, what was going to happen among people who were religious leaders.... Using the voice of God, the people who killed the disciples would say, "I'm doing this because of my faith." And Jesus said, this is what you're going to have to suffer. Now, what had occurred by the time all the Gospels were written?

The crucifixion.

Absolutely. When John wrote this, he knew that Jesus' prediction had come true. When Jesus said it, they couldn't quite understand, but by the time this was written—eighty, ninety, one hundred years later, whatever it was, I don't know—it had come true.

The Roman officials had outlawed the church, and the disciples had been excommunicated. They had been kicked out of the [Jewish] church. It was not an easy thing for them to accept. It was a heartrending thing.

And as you read through the Acts and through the messages of Paul to the early churches, you see how difficult it was for Paul and Peter and John to accept the proposition—we are no longer part of the synagogue, we are no longer part of the existing church. They did not cast away all of their historical religious beliefs. They wanted to have their intense faith in Christ transported into the existing church, but the existing church said, "No, this is incompatible with anything that we can accept." So, the disciples were excommunicated.

They did not consider themselves a pure, separate part of God's kingdom who were renouncing everything that had gone before; they wanted to be part of the existing church and to change the existing church to be compatible with Christ's teachings about love and compassion and understanding and friendship and sinfulness and redemption. But the church said, "No," and almost all of the disciples, I understand, were actually killed. They lost their lives because they believed in Christ and because they were willing to express their beliefs in spite of the condemnation or the hatred of the world around them.

Avoiding Conflict

We have a tendency to rationalize, and maybe it's a salvation for us. I don't know. It blunts the sharp edges of conflict.

I know quite often in politics the questions that come into the Oval Office are the ones that are most difficult to resolve. If a person has a problem and he can't resolve it, generally, it's handled by the family. Or if the family can't handle it, maybe by the city hall, or maybe at the county courthouse, or maybe at the state legislature. And if it can't be resolved any of those places, it eventually gets up here in Washington and gets on a desk of Congress members and gets on the desk of the president. And quite often, in my Oval Office there is finally focused the resolution or possible resolution of an intense conflict.

I've seen how hard it is for someone talking to me and for myself, to bring ourselves to recognize that difference in all its unadorned sharpness. We both tend to rationalize what we hear. We screen out the rough phrases and we try to find some compatibility there. We try to make things mesh in together when they actually don't mesh.

I've seen this happen in my dealings with foreign leaders and some of it's been publicized. The last time [Israeli] Prime Minister [Menachim] Begin came over, he presented a very complicated twenty-six-point program, without interruption, I might say, and then afterwards I said, "Well, I think that's a good step toward peace." He later went back to Israel and said that I had adopted his program in its entirety because—he wasn't trying to lie or mislead anyone—his hope was that the president of the United States would accept what he put forward. And my hope was not to alienate Prime Minister Begin so much that he would abandon the good offices of the United States in seeking a Mideast peace. We both wanted to hear the part of the conversation that confirmed our own position and minimized conflict or disagreement.

That's the way Christians are; we want to hear the part of the Bible, we want to learn the parts of Christ's teachings, that are not in conflict with the way we want to live. But Jesus said, you can only go so far with that. Eventually, there comes a time of decision or rejection—acceptance of Christ's teachings or turning away from them. And this created the conflict in the world.

The Humility of Following Jesus

Read John 15:19.

[19] *'If you belonged to the world, the world would love you as its own. Because you do not belong to the world, but I have chosen you out of the world—therefore the world hates you.'*

This is the only time that phrase "of the world" is used in the book of John. What does that phrase "of the world" mean to you?... What is our natural inclination as we build a life?

Selfishness.

We tend to build our life centered on what?

Ourselves.

On ourselves! And that's a human trait that Christ recognized. When we figure out how to build our lives and how to establish our priorities, the most powerful inclination is to build those priorities around what's best for us. What's best for me must be what's best because God created me a special person, an individual, and surely, he must have wanted me to have a good life. So, if I build my life around what's best for me and the ones that I love and depend on me, surely that's a very high and noble concept.

That's the way of the world. That's the way of the heathens. That's the way of those who despise other people. It's the way of those who've never heard of Christ. It's the way of Christians. All have sinned—that's the way of the world. And Jesus said, "When you're of the world, you can live in peace and harmony with your neighbors. But when you're not of the world, you're going to be hated, and despised, cast out, even killed."

What's the distinction now between those who are of the world and those who are not of the world? Those who are of the world build our lives around ourselves. Those who are not of the world build our lives around what?

Christ.

That's the difference. A self-centered life or a Christ-centered life.

This presents an almost hopeless distinction. How can you bridge this terrible chasm between me and Christ? A sinner and perfection? Jesus told his disciples, "That's what you have to do." And they despaired about the resolution. They knew already when this conversation took place that Jesus was going to die. He had already made that plain to them...

Jesus had just told his disciples, "I am choosing you out of the world. I have chosen you out of the world. I have made you separate from the world."

Now read John 15:20.

[20] *'Remember the word that I said to you, "Servants are not greater than their master." If they persecuted me, they will persecute you; if they kept my word, they will keep yours also.'*

... When Jesus was at the Last Supper, in the last few hours with his disciples, he got down on his hands and knees and did what?

Washed their feet.

And the essence of that was to show, what?

Humility.

And Jesus said that those who are servants are the greatest. He said that many times, and here, he's drawing another, different kind of relationship. He says, in effect, "I am the master, you are the servants."

What did he mean by this? It seems to me to be in conflict with what he had previously said. What did he mean?

... Jesus is saying being a servant makes you great. My greatness lies in my service to other people. And you should not be proud and seek an ascendant position when you get to heaven or argue about who's going to sit on my right hand, who's going to sit on my left hand, who's going to be the greatest among you. You're not better than other people simply because I love you and your sins are forgiven.

But "I am the son of God," Jesus said, "and my teachings you must repeat. There are things you don't understand. You're still in a questioning part of your life and you have to accept that my words come from God. And when I'm gone, I want you to remember what I said, because I am the master, I am the teacher, you are the student, you are the servant, and your loyalty to me, your love for me, should permit you to overcome these inherent conflicts between a self-centered life and a Christ-centered life. And let you act in accordance with God's teachings."

You can't, on your own initiative, as a fallible, sinful human being, create a theology or an explanation of what God thinks, what God means. You can't create your own God and put him in a box and say, "This is the God I worship because it's compatible with me." You've got to take God as he is and the perfect exemplification of what God is, is I, myself, Christ. So, Jesus said, "There's a limit to the equation of a disciple"—John, James, and others—"with me because the truth comes from my lips. It's given to me by God. And when I'm gone, you take my word," which is God's word, "and let that be the guiding light in your life," not create your own God to suit yourselves.

Now then Jesus goes on to give them some assurance. He said, "It's not going to all be negative. I've given you a bleak picture about alienation and being despised and being killed and being excommunicated, but it's not all going to be bad." He said, "Look, I was by myself, a carpenter from Nazareth and I spoke and I was despised and I was hated, but there were some who listened. You, my disciples, listened. Others who are not here listened. Part of the world hated me because they listened. And the word of God has been strengthened. What happened when you observed my life is also going to happen when other people observe your lives. Don't be hopeless, stand firm in your faith, and your voice will be heard." And to ensure that this is going to happen, what?

How will the disciples be strengthened?

The Holy Spirit.

The Holy Spirit, yes. Jesus said, "I'm going to be the one that goes to God and gets him to send the Holy Spirit. And with the Holy Spirit permeating your soul and your heart, preferably on a permanent basis, but certainly on a transient, temporary basis when it's crucial, your voice will be magnified as you speak my words. Don't be hopeless.

You'll be strengthened. You won't be abandoned. And you may suffer physically and you may be an outcast and you may be despised and you may be alienated and lonesome among men and neighbors, but you won't be alone. Because I will be with you through the Comforter."

The Comforter is an extension of whom? God himself. "God will live in you through the Comforter."

Speaking for Jesus

Let's read John 15:26–27.

[26] *'When the Advocate comes, whom I will send to you from the Father, the Spirit of truth who comes from the Father, he will testify on my behalf.* [27] *You also are to testify because you have been with me from the beginning.'*

... If you've actually known a great teacher, personally, when you speak that teacher's words, you're likely to be heard and people will give weight to your voice. "I was there. I know what happened. I heard him when he said this." People will listen.

I've been in many meetings with Andy Young, among Black audiences, and when Andy says Martin Luther King did this, or Martin Luther King said that, the audience listens. Because they know that Andy was there. And when King was thrown in prison, Andy was there. When he walked the streets, Andy was there. When he was stoned, Andy was there. It gives an authenticity to Andy Young's voice when he talks about the Civil Rights Movement, or what it means to be despised, or what it means to struggle for rights, that transcends what Andy has in himself had he not been with Martin Luther King Jr. during those trying days.

Well, Jesus is saying the same thing—that "because you knew me in the beginning, you can be assured that people will listen to your voice. Not because of your own strength of character, not because of your own oratorical skills, but because they will know that you speak for me."

Again, a parallel. "People listened to my voice because I was with God in the beginning," Jesus said. In the beginning was the word and the word was God, and the word was with God. In the creation of the universe, Christ was there. He spoke authentically because he was an extension of God, and the disciples who walked the dusty roads with Jesus were an extension of Jesus—as are we.

We are the present-day extension of Jesus. To the extent that our lives are Christ-centered. To the extent that our souls and our minds are permeated by the Holy Spirit. To the extent that we don't try to identify and worship a God that we create to be compatible with what we are and what we'd like to be. To the extent we've patterned our lives after the perfect example of Christ.

The disciples were sinners; so are we. Other people watched the disciples, listened to the disciples, saw them make mistakes. They watch and listen to us, as Christians, and they watch us make mistakes... But as the Holy Comforter, the Holy Spirit, sustained and strengthened the disciples, so the Holy Spirit and the Comforter sustain and strengthen us if we let him.

Pride, which comes from a self-centered life, can close the door on which Christ is knocking. If we think we're self-sufficient, there's no way, really, for God's spirit to combine with our own and give us a strength that's important in the eyes of God. We might be important in the eyes of our neighbors of the world, but without the Holy Spirit, without these very teachings that Christ is describing, our lives are insignificant in the eyes of God as a Christian witness.

The Pains of New Life

Read the twentieth verse of the sixteenth chapter...

20 *'Very truly, I tell you, you will weep and mourn, but the world will rejoice; you will have pain, but your pain will turn into joy.'*

That was kind of a riddle, wasn't it?... He said, "You will be sorrowful, and the world will rejoice at the same time. And then your sorrow will turn into joy." What does he mean by that?...

The world has triumphed. This radical has been destroyed. Our safe, secure life has been protected. We've rooted out this cancer in our midst that caused so much trouble and tribulation and disturbance, that shook up the church. We've gotten rid of him, finally, and the world rejoiced.

I imagine there were special prayers said in the synagogue that day: God, thank you for letting us get rid of this troublemaker. And his disciples were cast into the depths of despondency and sorrow. Then, what happened?

Christ was raised.

Then Christ was raised and the disciples rejoiced again.

They didn't understand this. They were still in a questioning mood. They hadn't got into the comprehending mood yet. And Christ said, in effect, "I'm teaching you in riddles right now. I know you don't quite understand, but later I'm going to speak to you in very frank terms so that you and the world can understand what's meant by these extraordinary happenings created by God."

Then he gave him one of the most vivid and easy to understand expressions that I've ever seen in the Bible. I'm sure there's not a woman here that won't understand this one.

21 *"A woman in labor is in pain because her time has come. But when the child is born, she forgets the anguish in her joy that a child has been born into the world."*

I don't think there's any more vivid description of the time of Christ's death and crucifixion, and then his being raised from the dead, then to draw the parallel with a woman in childbirth. It's something that a man can't understand. But the physical dread and torture and discomfort and intense pain that, I'm sure, almost creates a lack of faith and a rejection of one's husband and the family and responsibilities of motherhood, after the birth comes, and a new life is created, there's a flood of joy, and the pain is remembered, but not with rejection. The pain becomes, perhaps, a part of the pride and a part of the love: I went through suffering because of this little, tiny baby. It's part of me now and I'm part of it. That's what happened in the death of Christ. And then the world gave birth to Christ all over again, and a new life was created for him and for us. And the disciples' faltering faith was strengthened.

I'm sure they remembered John and all the rest of what Jesus had said: "You're going to be sorrowful. The world's going to be joyful. And later on, you're going to be joyful." And Jesus didn't say—he didn't create a perfect balance there. You notice that? He said, "The world's going to be joyful. You're going to be sorrowful." That's half of it. The other half is, "You're going to be joyful." Jesus did not say the world's going to be sorrowful, because with the disciple's life evoking in the rest of the world a renewed faith in the relationship between God and man, that could be bridged, the world was not cast into sorrow because Christ lives.

Mr. President, you told us once in a lesson that we will all bear a part of the crucifixion. Now you are telling us that we are all a part of the resurrection and the spirit that went forth from the tomb.

Absolutely... We are a part of both the resurrection and the death of Christ, and we know that part of the anguish of Christ on the cross was because of the sins of Jimmy Carter, and Fred Gray, John White, and others. Jesus was tortured because I sinned, and when he was raised from the dead, it gave me the assurance, not the belief, but the assurance that, in spite of my own sinfulness, I can also have eternal life.

Resolving the Ancient Conflict with God's Love

Let's read one more verse. The twenty-second verse, sixteenth chapter.

[22] *And ye now therefore have sorrow: but I will see you again, and your heart shall rejoice, and your joy no man taketh from you.*

Jesus said that you're going to have this joy after the resurrection, and you need not be worried about people taking it away from you because it was given to you by God and people cannot take it away.

One of the great things about Christ—God—is a means through which this conflict is resolved.

What characteristic of God resolves this conflict between a self-centered life and a Christ-centered life? Between hatred of the world and love of the world? Is it the power of God? It's not just the exertion of God's power to twist, but it's what?... What's the earliest Bible verse you ever learned?

God is love.

God is love. Divine love is more powerful than worldly hatred. It is the exemplification of what God is—not a punitive God, but a God that, through grace, gives us a redemption from our own sins.

Christ proved it with his well-described life, written down by John and Matthew and Peter and others. And the parallels that are drawn between Christ versus his disciples, and Christ versus you and me, is almost absolute. The responsibilities that Christ put on his disciples are exactly the same ones he puts on us. We are indistinguishable from Christ's disciples.

The one sobering thing today is that we don't experience the conflict and the punishment and the abrupt confrontation with the outside world that was created by Jesus' disciples two thousand years ago. And I'm afraid one reason is that we conform too much to the world. We don't draw the distinctions, we don't set the standards in our lives, and in our teachings, and in our public utterances that Christ told us to.

The instantaneous communication with the outside world tends to absorb us into it. A standing alone is much more difficult now, perhaps, or at least we say it is. Individuality is kind of sapped away. Even distinctions in speech that were preserved for hundreds of years in isolated parts of the United States or regions are now being filed away and those distinctions are being minimized. But Christ told his disciples, "Center your lives around me. Don't modify my teachings. Don't be afraid. Because the standards of the world are not important. The standards that I've given to you are important."

Well, I think this is a lesson that's both sobering and also encouraging, because the sum total of it is, the crisis, in the end, the conflict, will be resolved. Perhaps with personal physical suffering, perhaps with alienation and loneliness, oneliness. But with the presence of the Holy Spirit and with the knowledge of me and my example and my teachings, and with the grace and forgiveness and love of God, the ultimate consequence of a Christ-centered life is not suffering, but joy. Not pain, but peace. Not hatred, but love.

Let's bow our heads for a closing prayer.

April 29, 1979

A Cry for Justice

The First Baptist Church of the City of Washington, DC

Lesson Scripture

1 Kings 21:1–6 (NRSVA)

In our Sunday school text, the title of our subject is "A Cry for Justice," and the lesson comes from 1 Kings, the twenty-first chapter.

If you would open your Bibles there, we will follow along for a while, discussing Ahab, Jezebel, Naboth, and the prophet Elijah, and then later, we will talk about the lesson that we can derive from this text as we discuss these personal verses. I would particularly want you this morning, not to think about the time of Ahab...but to think about the United States, the Washington, DC, community, and, preferably, my life and your life and our actions in the eyes of God.

I will designate Ed Sunshine as our Bible reader this morning and ask him, if he would, to read the first verse, which is the second verse, really, in 1 Kings 21.... Ed, would you just read the second verse of the chapter?

Just that second verse?

Well, read two, three and four.

2 *And after this Ahab said to Naboth, "Give me your vineyard, that I may have it for a vegetable garden, because it is near my house; and I will give you a better vineyard for it; or, if it seems good to you, I will give you its value in money."* 3 *But Naboth said to Ahab, "The Lord forbid that I should give you the inheritance of my fathers."* 4 *And Ahab went into his house vexed and sullen because of what Naboth the Jezreelite had said to him; for he had said, "I will not give you the inheritance of my fathers." And he lay down on his bed, and turned away his face, and would eat no food.*

Why did Naboth refuse to give up his land?

It had been in the family for generations.

It was an inheritance or a heritage that was very precious to him. What else—what other reasons can anyone think of?...

There was a Hebrew law. The law of whom?

God, passed down to the Israelites through Moses, that said what?...

You couldn't sell land. And as you know there was a reason for it. What would be one of the reasons that would come to mind?

You get to pass it along to your children.

You had to pass it along to your children. But why?...

Part of the strength of God's Chosen People and their societal structure was that they be intact. That they strengthen one another. That they not be divided. That there'd be a clear teaching of God's word and that it would be passed down from generation to generation. For land, which was a basis for their presence, their ability to sustain themselves through earnings, their temporal or human work, and for the cohesiveness of the community itself and for the teaching of the word of God, it was important that the tribes not be completely intermixed or that land be sold to an alien who might come in with superior wealth or influence and take away this part of the inheritance. It was a very strict law.

Suppose a family got destitute and had nothing left and needed to sell the property, then what could be done? It could be sold under those circumstances, preferably within the tribe. But there was a special year. Does anyone recall what it was?

Jubilee.

The Jubilee Year.

The fiftieth year.

It was the fiftieth year. There were seven times seven, and that's forty-nine [years], and then the next year was a jubilee year. And if you had sold your land during that forty-nine or fifty-year period, at the end of that time, title reverted back where it was before, and slaves were freed, and debts were considered to be resolved. There was a kind of cleaning of the books every fiftieth year, but the point was that part of the cleaning of the books was a transfer of title to land, even though it had been paid for, back to the original owner. So, God's law was very clear in this instance.

And God, of course, monitored, through prophets, through teachings, through his Chosen People, the enforcement of this law and others.

Concern for Our Neighbor

When did God say, "Where are you?" Does anybody recall God asking someone that—"Where are you?"

Eden.

Yes, in the Garden of Eden. He asked Adam. There was another question asked, "Where is your brother?" Who remembers where that was asked?

Cain and Abel.

[God] asked Cain, "Where is your brother?" And there was a response given, "Am I my brother's keeper?"

All through the Bible, there are questions that God asked human beings that required them to give an embarrassing answer, or to search their own souls for an answer in the presence not only of God, but in the presence of the people. Even in Jesus' time, we have some very difficult questions asked by God and by people, but one of the most important ones was, "Who is my neighbor?"

And those four questions formed a pattern of God's relationship with human beings as we study this lesson, and as we think about its application in our own lives.

We tend to rationalize our own behavior. One of the easiest ways to rationalize is to say, "That doesn't apply to me. That was very embarrassing to Cain. How could anybody be so foolish as to ask Jesus, 'Who is my neighbor?'" But sometimes we should be required to answer the question, and to realize that we don't ask it with as heartfelt an inquiry as we should—"Who is *my* neighbor?"

...There are many Christians and there are also many non-Christians around the world who, compared to us, in material wealth and freedom and happiness, suffer severely. Are they just a transient, disturbing thought or realization every now and then when we read about a horrible deprivation of rights? Or are they a constant concern of ours every time we kneel to pray, or every time we assess our own blessings? My guess is that they are a transient concern. But God says, Christ says, in the Prodigal Son, and the Good Samaritan, and in many other parables, and directly, that our neighbors are those throughout the world about whom we should constantly be concerned.

It's difficult for us in a free society to obey God. Because, in effect, in our country we are encouraged under the law to obey God—"one nation under God." We know that the founding fathers of our country, we know that those who wrote our laws, we know that those who wrote the Bill of Rights, who wrote the Constitution, implied or directly stated that we should live our lives under the laws of God. So, we not only have God's law to support us toward righteousness and love, but we also have man's law. Patriotism, for us, is an inclination toward God.

It's easy for us, when you look at it. It's not easy, as proven by our own sinfulness, our own shortcomings, our own insensitivity, our own selfishness. How much more difficult would it be for us living in a society, knowing God's law but having every tiny, incremental part of man's law trying to seduce us from God? Convincing us in the schools, the kindergartens, the television, the radio, the news media, statements of respected officials, that it's sinful, in effect, to obey God. How much easier would it be then for us to turn against God's laws? Much easier.

A Quandary of Ethics

This is a problem that Ahab imposed upon Naboth.

Ahab was a strange man.... Where he came from, what he did. His effusive endorsement of God on one occasion, his selfishness and weakness on another. His abject admission of his sin, his repentance. He, indeed, goes from one extreme to another. He's kind of a weak man, avaricious, though. As we always have said in south Georgia, and in farming areas, he doesn't want all the land. He just wants the land that joins him. [*Congregation laughs*]

Ahab had great power, great wealth. Jezreel really was his winter palace—that's where he went to relax and kind of enjoy himself, and there was no doubt about his authority.

And he had a queen, Jezebel, who enhanced Ahab's image of authority because she was so ruthless. She had no commitment to God's law. In fact, she considered God's law to be an obstacle to the proper recognition of the rights of her husband and the authorities. God's law was something to be destroyed. God's law was something to be proven ineffective. When her Baal-worshipping priests were killed, she was extremely bitter, and undoubtedly looking for a way to come back and to prove that God's laws were impotent.

This awesomeness, not only of the power of Ahab and the fear that people suffered under him and his queen, was exacerbated by the fact that Naboth was an immediate neighbor living right under the observation of the king. And for the king to call him in and say, "Look, I want this little piece of land of yours for a vegetable garden," or herb garden. "I'm not going to steal it from you. I don't want you to give it to me. I'll buy it, give you an adequate price for it, or I'll give you even better land in exchange for it." It's a pretty good deal.

Naboth could very well have said, "That's good." Although it is a violation of God's law, surely God won't mind because this is a king who, ostensibly, is endorsed by God because the elders have laid their hand on him. He's even talked to God's great prophet. Naboth could very well have rationalized the transfer of that land in contravention to

God's law, but he decided not to. He said, "May God curse me if I give up this land, your majesty. I would be cursed by God if I gave up this land."

That was a very courageous thing to do. Although Ahab went back to his quarters, laid down on the bed, turned his head against the wall and pouted and grieved, I have no doubt that when Naboth got back home, he was extremely fearful. I'm sure as he discussed it with his own family, he recognized that dark consequences might result from his adamant refusal to obey what seemed to be a reasonable request of the king.

Jezebel Plots and Schemes

And then here comes Jezebel into the bedroom, and saw Ahab lying there grieving, and she said, "What are you grieving about?" He said, "I wanted the land next to me. I asked Naboth for it and he wouldn't even give it to me." He possibly even had tears in his eyes, and she said, "What kind of king are you?"

Jezebel had an attitude toward freedom or equality or basic human rights that was genuinely despicable. She had no thought that Naboth's rights should be preserved. They were of no concern to her. As a matter of fact, they further aggravated her. How could this commoner violate the rights of her husband, who was a king? Even, particularly, when her husband had given him a fair deal. So, the reaction against Naboth was very severe.

Jezebel, recognizing the weakness of her husband said, "Don't worry about it. Get up and have a good meal and enjoy yourself and be happy again. I'll get the land for you."

Ahab was one to uphold the law. He was the personification of God's law in his own country. That was the duty of the king, as supported by the entire church organization, as well as a secular organization was to uphold God's laws. Because almost invariably, down through history, the basic elements of law have been predicated upon religious law. Not only in the Judeo-Christian ethic, but within other similar ethics as well.

So, Ahab knew that, by right, he had no claim on that land. Had he detected the slightest, even devious way under the law that he could've taken the land, he would certainly have already taken it. When Jezebel said, "Don't worry, I'll get you the land," Ahab didn't say, "How will you do it?" And so as far as I know, Ahab never asked Jezebel any questions.

What did Jezebel do?...

Let's let Ed read the seventh through the tenth verses.

7 *And Jez'ebel his wife said to him, "Do you now govern Israel? Arise, and eat bread, and let your heart be cheerful; I will give you the vineyard of Naboth the Jezreelite."*

8 *So she wrote letters in Ahab's name and sealed them with his seal, and she sent the letters to the elders and the nobles who dwelt with Naboth*
in his city. 9 *And she wrote in the letters, "Proclaim a fast, and set Naboth*
on high among the people; 10 *and set two base fellows opposite him, and let*
them bring a charge against him, saying, 'You have cursed God and the king.' Then take him out, and stone him to death."

A Dissident Voice Quieted

Jezebel saw, quite clearly, that one of the ways to establish what I will call "uncontested temporal power" was to destroy religion. There was obviously a conflict between what she and Ahab saw as justice based on the enhancement of their own rights of the powerful, on the one hand, and justice in the eyes of God on the other. And the only way, when that conflict arises for those in political power, to deal with it, is to denigrate, or to actually destroy, or to distort the religious teachings. So, Jezebel, as I said earlier, was, in effect, killing two birds with one stone.

She also made a mistake, as it turned out ultimately, by considering the consequences of her act. She knew that in the eyes of the Jewish leaders, if not in the eyes of God—I don't know what her attitude was toward God—that her actions would not be judged proper. And she knew that there was one very important witness against her who had already demonstrated superb courage. Who was that?

Naboth.

So, what could she do?

This is not completely alien from our own experience in this generation—she decided to silence Naboth. There was no Siberia in Israel. So, she decided that Naboth would have to be destroyed.

And as Ed has just read to us, she wrote a letter, signed Ahab's name, put Ahab's seal on it, illegally, of course, and directed to her friends among the church elders a letter that was patently illegal saying, "Arrest Naboth. Put him on a pedestal so that he can be admired. Then, hire two scurrilous characters to testify against him and then stone him to death." There was a trial, ostensibly based on law and justice, but subverted because there was no truth. Deliberate lies were contrived under the guise of justice.

The law was a very good law. The so-called "constitution" of Ahab's nation was a very good constitution. Basic human rights were protected. The right to own property, the right to move, the right to speak, the right to worship were protected in the law. It's a good law.

You couldn't execute a person based on the testimony of one witness, because it might be false. You could only find someone guilty of a serious crime on the uncontested testimony of two or more witnesses, or if there was a contest, then the elder sitting in judgment would decide. But the whole system of justice was subverted by the state officials to get rid of a voice that spoke for God.

Jezebel was apparently very successful. Because the two men did come in and testify that Naboth committed blasphemy, that he cursed God, and also that Naboth cursed his own king. Naboth was convicted and he was stoned to death, and in 2 Samuel [*sic,* 2 Kings], the Bible tells us something that's quite obvious—his entire family was also eliminated.

It would not have been enough to eliminate Naboth and leave his wife and his sons alive, so, his whole family was exterminated, apparently very rapidly because even the next day, Ahab, who was then very happy, was out in his new land planning where he would grow his vegetables and herbs. I'm sure, as he looked out of the window of the palace in Jezreel, he could see his new property, and a feeling of self-satisfaction swept over him because he had achieved his goal. A dissident voice was quieted. A potential enemy or testifier would never be heard of again.

Circumventing the Truth

It's very difficult to find laws, even contrived by men, which are not apparently fair. They are always written in the guise of justice. No leader or group of leaders would ever write a constitution saying, I will deprive my people of human rights. That would be unacceptable. So, the laws are written with loopholes—very difficult to discern. Or they are written with a degree of vagueness that permits flexibility on the part of the officials when it's to their advantage to be flexible.

Jezebel could not have afforded to let the truth be known. Can you imagine headlines—"Two Liars Testify Against Naboth," or "Israeli Justice Subverted," or "Innocent Man Executed," or editorials calling for a further inquiry into the facts? That's inconceivable. So, in order to subvert man's law, there has to be secrecy and a deprivation of the rights of those governed to know the truth. And it was accomplished.

Why do you think the witnesses were willing to testify against Naboth falsely? What are some of the motivations Jezebel created or of which she took advantage? Can you think of one?

To gain favor with the king.

That's right—to gain favor with the king for possible future benefits. I don't have any doubt that Jezebel arranged, in ways that are not described in the Bible, to reward those who went along with her in the violation of the law because had they been detected, there would've been severe consequences. And so, there were undoubtedly some sorts of either privileged bribes or monetary bribes to those who cooperated in this deprivation of rights. Can you think of another reason?

They were men of low moral character.

That's right. They were men of low moral character to begin with. There [were] no conscience constraints on them.

Ahab was a dictator.

They were afraid to violate the interests of Ahab, and although Ahab didn't tell them what to do, they thought Ahab told them because his seal was on the letter, or they didn't much care.

They may have been more fearful of Jezebel than they were Ahab.

And there was another very subtle one that's difficult to detect. She told them to take Naboth and...put him on a pedestal. Why do you think she wanted to put him on a pedestal?

To draw attention.

To draw attention, yes, but, you know, when you put somebody on a pedestal, you kind of exalt them in the eyes of their fellow human beings.

It was deceptive.

It was deceptive. Or he may have deserved it. He may have been a very righteous man—we don't know about that. But why do you think Jezebel wanted to exalt Naboth before the trial?...

She may have been just laying a rationalization for herself. If anybody questioned, "Well, I told him to put him on a pedestal. I wasn't trying to hurt that guy. I didn't know he was guilty. I was trying to put him on a pedestal." But there's another reason that appeals to one of the human traits that are in the hearts of everyone here. What is that?...

Jealousy.

Jealousy! There was Naboth, a farmer—all of a sudden, the king exalted him. He was sitting on a pedestal above all of them, and there's a natural inclination to want to cut him down. So, when he was found guilty, and most of his neighbors probably knew that he was a righteous man, they had never heard him blaspheme against God, they had never heard him be treasonous against his own king, but by golly, it served him right. How could he possibly think he was better than they were?

So, I'd say, jealousy, fear, and various forms of bribery. The circumvention of the truth. The control of the knowledge. Those elements went into this trial. Elements still applicable in our time and day in some places in the world.

The Highest Ideal

God is not, in this episode, condemning government.... God said, honor those who lead you. Honor temporal governments. Because there can't be any realization of God's hopes, there can't be any protection of basic rights of human beings in an anarchy. When the power of the most mighty prevails over those who may be weak or timid or without influence, you have to have some structure of society to protect one another. But that temporal, or man's government, has got to be based on truth. It's got to be based on justice.

There have been times in our own country when we have not quite been willing to face up to this question, and I'm almost hesitant to bring it up because the press is here and I don't want to be misinterpreted, but one of our most famous sayings is, "My country, may it always be right," but what?

Right or wrong.

"My country, right or wrong." I doubt that God would approve that statement—"My country, right or wrong."

And the first time we ever had to face it, in my lifetime, was in the Vietnam War. If my president says bomb Cambodia, if my president says 500,000 lives or 50,000 lives should be expended, so be it. But the longer we were involved in the Vietnam War, the more we realized that our country's government may not always be right, and if not, it ought to be changed. It didn't mean that we were unpatriotic, but it meant that American citizens have not only a right, but a duty to constantly inquire into the righteousness of our nation's actions.

And that is not treason. And that is not in violation of God's law. And it has not always been easy in our own country to do so.

I'm a Southerner, as you know, and I remember the horror with which many White people observed Martin Luther King Jr. walking down the street without a permit. He was violating the law. And among many of us, he was condemned because of it. To violate the law in order to be proving a point is a difficult question, but when the point can be made that the law itself is unjust, or the administration of the law itself is unjust, then in God's eyes a human being has a right to question that law and sometimes to take the consequences even in a free society or democracy.

What's the salvation for this question? The best we can hope for in a society, under optimal circumstances, is to approach what? What does a government strive to achieve?

Justice.

Justice is the highest ideal that a government can hope to reach. Justice based on freedom. Justice based on truth. But justice is the highest possible achievement of a free society based on truth.

What is the highest ideal that a human being might achieve?

Love.

Love. Love's the word I want.

A government, a nation can provide freedom. A government, a nation can provide justice. A person can provide freedom, truth, justice *and* love, and God's relationship to us is one based on love. So, inherently, a human being, who comprises a tiny part of a nation, can have a higher ideal and can have a higher achievement than a nation during those moments, perhaps transient, perhaps relatively permanent, when we are close to God and when we represent what Jesus Christ is and what Christ said God is.

What did Jesus say that God is? One word.

Love.

Love. It's one of the first memory verses all of us learned—God is love.

So, a human being, the monitor of government, the monitor of a society, basing one's own influence on the highest possible ideal, which is God's love, can help to maintain a standard that will elevate society to a higher standard itself. Pure justice, pure truth, based on individual freedom and the cumulative influence of courageous human beings, can correct defects in government and can correct defects in a family or a community or a society.

...Ahab was sinful. Jezebel was sinful. The people who stayed silent were sinful—in the face of [in]justice. Naboth's neighbors. The Jewish council of elders who held the trial. Those who threw the first stones, which had to be those who testified against him. It's sinful to be silent in the face of injustice.

I would like to remind you, and be reminded myself, that the people of God, who know Christ, must represent the cause of justice on behalf of the oppressed everywhere.

The 1980s

And from the windy West came two-gunned Gabriel,
From Jesu's sleeve trumped up the king of spots,
The sheath-decked jacks, queen with a shuffled heart;
Said the fake gentleman in suit of spades,
Black-tongued and tipsy from salvation's bottle.

—Dylan Thomas
from "Altarwise by owl-light"

1980. President Jimmy Carter and First Lady Rosalynn Carter walking into the Maranatha Baptist Church to attend Sunday School. President Carter later attended church at the Plains Baptist Church by himself.

Courtesy *The Atlanta Journal-Constitution*; photograph by Calvin Cruce

November 16, 1980. President Jimmy Carter teaches his final Sunday School lesson for The First Baptist Church of the City of Washington, D.C. Couples Class from the sanctuary's balcony. Carter taught the class more than a dozen times while serving as President of the United States between 1977 and 1981.

Courtesy Jimmy Carter Presidential Library and Museum

October 3, 1982. Dan Ariail served as pastor of Maranatha Baptist Church from 1982 until his retirement in 2005. Here he is outside of the church with his wife and children and the Carters following his first service as pastor. Pictured (left to right): Nelle Ariail, Rosalynn Carter, Jimmy Carter, Danny Ariail, Robin Ariail, and Dan Ariail.

Courtesy Robin Ariail

Mid-1980s. The Millard Fuller family poses for a photo with the Carters after a service at Maranatha Baptist Church. Millard and his wife Linda are the founders of Habitat for Humanity. Their son, Chris, was ordained at Maranatha in 1986 with the Carters in attendance. Pictured (left to right): Faith Fuller, Georgia Fuller Leudi, Kim Isakson, Linda Fuller Degelmann, Jimmy Carter, Rosalynn Carter, Mike Thompson, Millard Fuller, and Chris Fuller.

Courtesy Faith Fuller

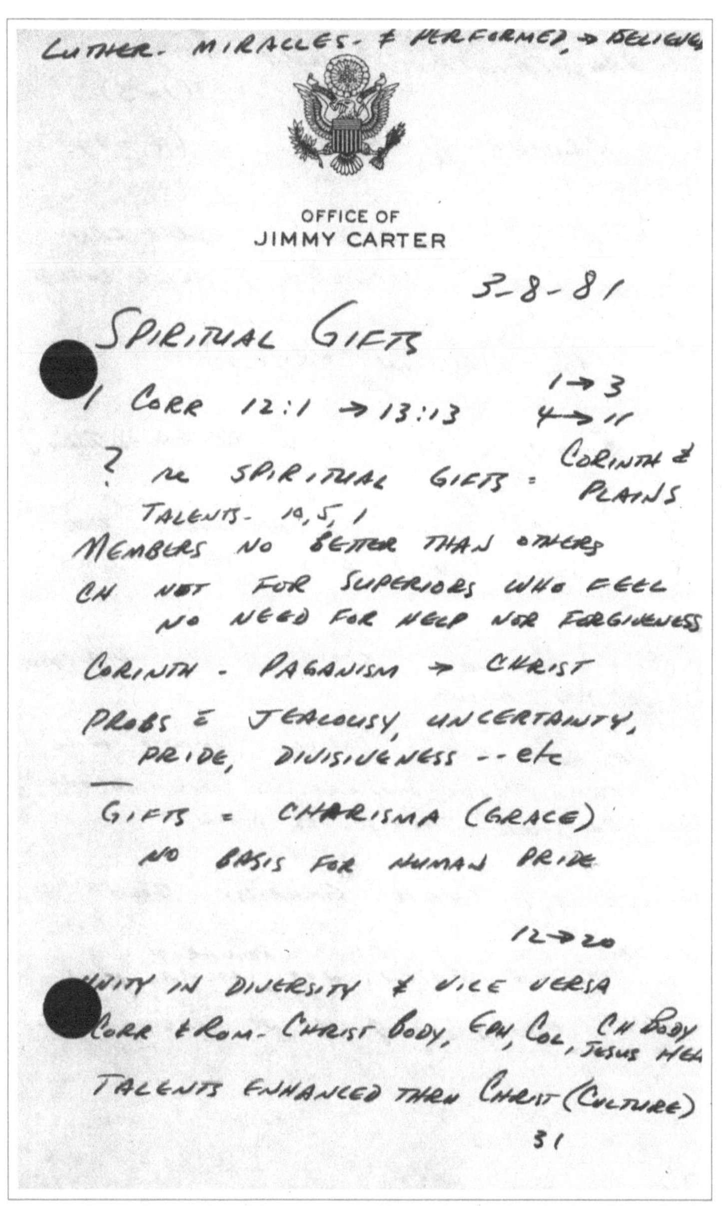

LUTHER- MIRACLES- & PERFORMED → BELIEVE

OFFICE OF
JIMMY CARTER

3-8-81

SPIRITUAL GIFTS

1→3
1 CORR 12:1 → 13:13   4→11

? re SPIRITUAL GIFTS = CORINTH & PLAINS

TALENTS- 10, 5, 1

MEMBERS NO BETTER THAN OTHERS

CH NOT FOR SUPERIORS WHO FEEL
NO NEED FOR HELP NOR FORGIVENESS

CORINTH - PAGANISM → CHRIST

PROBS c̄ JEALOUSY, UNCERTAINTY,
PRIDE, DIVISIVENESS --etc

GIFTS = CHARISMA (GRACE)
NO BASIS FOR HUMAN PRIDE

12→20

NITY IN DIVERSITY & VICE VERSA

ORR & ROM- CHRIST BODY, EPH, COL, CH BODY, JESUS HEA

TALENTS ENHANCED THRU CHRIST (CULTURE)

31

March 8, 1981. After leaving the White House, Jimmy Carter returned home to Plains, Georgia, to regroup and reenvision his future as a former President. He began teaching Sunday School at the newly formed Maranatha Baptist Church. These handwritten notes drafted on stationary from his White House office express an outline for a Sunday School lesson he taught from the book of 1 Corinthians at Maranatha in the early 1980s.

Courtesy Jimmy Carter Presidential Library and Museum

PAUL FAITH JOHN LOVE

(1-3)

NATURE of LOVE (4-7)

c̄ SELF CONFIDENCE = WE CAN LOVE ONLY c̄ SECURITY of BEING LOVED

PAUL WAS IN PRISON

CLIMAX: LOVE of G REVEALED THRU J

7- "CALL NOT HIM WORTHLESS FOR WHOM CHRIST DIED"

ST AUGUSTINE- "LOVE & DO WHATEVER YOU WISH"

PASCAL- WORLD DIVIDED: SAINTS WHO KNOW THEY'RE SINNERS VS SINNERS WHO CONSIDER THEMSELVES SAINTS"

WE ALL HAVE GREATEST GIFT

CHRIST FAITH NOT PRIMARILY MORAL LAW BUT ASSURANCE of DIVINE FORGIVENESS

On November 16, 1980, President Carter taught his second-to-last Sunday school lesson to the Couples Class at the First Baptist Church of the City of Washington, DC, the capital congregation he and his wife, Rosalynn, and young daughter, Amy, had called their home church since his inauguration as the thirty-ninth president of the United States.

Raised in the Plains Baptist church in his hometown, and having taught Bible classes for most of his adult life, Jimmy Carter had never been shy about his spiritual beliefs, but when he identified himself as a "born-again Christian" while stumping for the Democratic presidential nomination in 1976, Carter's spiritual beliefs captured the dedicated attention and allegiance of churchgoers across the country. By the time Election Day arrived, the majority of evangelicals placed their trust in the peanut farmer from Plains, helping to catapult the little-known former governor of Georgia into, arguably, the most powerful position in the world. However, by November 1980 the tides of the faithful shifted, and for the incumbent leader, the conversion was devastating.

Ronald Reagan, a former Hollywood actor and governor of California, pummeled the sitting president in his bid for a second term—a landslide victory achieved, in part, by the votes of evangelicals, and the baffling about-face of a faith-based constituency that shared Carter's deep Christian convictions and had vigorously supported him four years earlier. Considering the change of heart, one can assume that at least some of the members sitting under Carter's Bible teaching that Sunday had, just a few days earlier, marked their ballot in favor of Reagan and in opposition to their beloved Sunday school teacher.

It's true, the Carter White House administration was plagued by a series of serious domestic and foreign crises. A floundering economy, soaring energy prices that triggered massive fuel shortages, and the demoralizing Iranian Hostage Crisis—which dominated headlines and engrossed Americans for an agonizing 444 days—all contributed to the nation's increasing impatience with the government's lack of quick solutions. So, not surprisingly, Carter's approval ratings tanked.

But, as was characteristically Carter, for better or worse, he believed in the virtue of people, especially his fellow Americans. In an astoundingly apolitical speech, televised on July 15, 1979, President Carter implored the people of the United States to make short-term sacrifices in the interest of creating a more sustainable union for future generations. His piercing blue eyes steeled into the broadcast cameras as he spoke from his presidential perch in the Oval Office: "In a nation that was proud of hard work, strong families, close-knit communities, and our faith in God, too many of us now tend to worship self-indulgence and consumption. Human identity is no longer defined by what one does, but by what one owns. We've learned that piling up material goods cannot fill the emptiness of lives which have no confidence or purpose."

The address, entitled "A Crisis of Confidence," or the "Malaise" speech, as the sobering talk was more famously dubbed by the media, fell flat. Carter had a dogged ethical drive. He was a true public servant with an almost reckless disregard for his own political posterity when it came down to simply doing what was right and principled. But principles, especially in American politics, don't always pay off. The Republican Party recognized the widening gap between the desires of the public and the ideals of the sitting president, and they seized an opportunity to fill the void.

Deft political pundits of the Grand Old Party (GOP) dug deep into what most concerned modern evangelicals and then strategized how to turn those social concerns into "wedge" issues that would assemble Christians to vote Republican in 1980. By creating a platform on divisive political issues such as gay rights, women's equality, and abortion that aligned with the perceived values of evangelicals at that time, the GOP would ensure the votes of the faith-based bloc and win the ticket to the White House. The scheme worked.

Even more perplexing was the success of an emerging political movement called the Religious Right and the seemingly overnight growth of its organizational counterpart, the Moral Majority. Spearheaded by popular televangelist Jerry Falwell Sr., who in previous decades had encouraged his flock to be leery of politics and to stay focused on sharing the Gospel message as an agent for cultural change, he now encouraged his congregation, and soon a growing conservative constituency around the country, to become directly involved with governmental affairs in an effort to save America from what he believed to be a decline in traditional values. Over the course of a few years, Falwell and his Moral Majority counterparts effectively reversed one of America's foundational freedoms—the separation of church and state. While claiming to care about and represent the ideals of American Christians, in reality, the leaders of the Moral Majority used the capital earned from their alignment with conservative politicians to become powerful players in the nation's political landscape.

Randall Balmer, an Episcopal priest, historian of American religion, and professor of religion at Dartmouth College, writes, in *Redeemer: The Life of Jimmy Carter*,

> In rejecting Carter in favor of Reagan in 1980, evangelicals set aside the long and noble tradition of progressive evangelicalism. They abandoned the heritage that claims its warrant in the command of Jesus to care for "the least of these".... The leaders of the Religious Right, who worked tirelessly to deny Carter a second term, articulated a dramatically different understanding of the faith, one that celebrated nationalism, individualism, and free-market capitalism over community, human rights, and collective responsibility for those less fortunate.

A devastating upset for the Carters, who had hoped to serve the nation for four more years—Rosalynn was especially despondent over the country's decision to refuse her husband a second term—Jimmy Carter's return to civilian life eventually reinvigorated Rosalynn's and his passion for helping people. Over the next decade, the compassionate couple would establish The Carter Center, the innovative human rights hub housed out of Atlanta and designed to promote democracy, eliminate disease, and mediate peace in communities in conflict across the globe.

After accepting an invitation to participate in a Habitat for Humanity build in New York City in 1984, the Carters became the official spokespersons for the nonprofit housing project, helping to make Habitat a household name and establishing the Jimmy Carter Work Project, which hosted thousands of volunteers each year to build affordable homes around the world alongside the former president and first lady.

Perhaps most poignant in reconnecting with their down-to-earth roots, the couple returned to their beloved hamlet of Plains and joined Maranatha Baptist Church in an unprecedented partnership to facilitate a Sunday school class led by a former president. Nearly every Sunday for the next forty years, the small congregation of about fifty folks swung open the church's doors to host a diverse array of spiritual seekers and presidential history buffs from nearly every nation, tribe, and tongue who wanted to hear a message from the Bible as taught by Jimmy Carter.

These next few lessons witness President Carter's transition from an unannounced, periodic teacher for the Couples Class at Washington, DC's First Baptist Church to his famously frequent role leading Sunday school for students from around the world at Maranatha Baptist Church in Plains, Georgia.

On the same Sunday former President Carter taught his penultimate Couples Class—November 16, 1980—Dr. Robert G. Jones, a professor of religion at George Washington University and fellow Sunday school teacher at First Baptist Church of the City of Washington, DC, presented Jimmy and Rosalynn with a resolution he drafted and that was unanimously approved by the congregation. The resolution was entitled "A Message of Love and Support for President Jimmy Carter" and read aloud:

Almost four years ago, you became with us fellow members of the body of Christ in this place, although none of us could begin to realize the awesome burden of your public office as we all joined in a continuing fellowship of prayer for you and for our nation's First Family; for you and for members of our congregation.

This love and care continues even now. We have wanted to share with you the resources of faith and devotion to a cause which transcends all political parties—the kingdom of our Lord and of His Christ.

Being good Baptists, we have been aware that our freedom to differ politically has not destroyed that fundamental Christian commitment that we all share. To our diverse congregation, you have brought an appreciation for the presence of fellow Christians who have given themselves to political leadership in this nation.

Now none of us can imagine the feelings in your heart after the election; but still, all of us, devoted citizens of many political persuasions, understand the meaning of the commandment that we will bear one another's burdens and so fulfill the law of Christ.

Therefore, we wish to say to you simply and directly that our love and prayerful support will continue with you. Even those who may have differed from you in matters political shall treasure the association with you in these years together and pledge continually to work with you in the spread of the gospel of our Lord Jesus Christ.

We pray for you and for ourselves that we may attain the peace which passes understanding and the joy which can lighten every day in Christ our Lord.

Your friends and partners in the gospel,

The members of the First Baptist Church of the city of Washington, D.C.

November 16, 1980

What Is Christianity?

The First Baptist Church of the City of Washington, DC

Lesson Scripture

Luke 5:12–24, 27–31 (NRSV)

[12] Once, when he was in one of the cities, there was a man covered with leprosy. When he saw Jesus, he bowed with his face to the ground and begged him, 'Lord, if you choose, you can make me clean.' [13] Then Jesus stretched out his hand, touched him, and said, 'I do choose. Be made clean.' Immediately the leprosy left him. [14] And he ordered him to tell no one. 'Go', he said, 'and show yourself to the priest, and, as Moses commanded, make an offering for your cleansing, for a testimony to them.' [15] But now more than ever the word about Jesus spread abroad; many crowds would gather to hear him and to be cured of their diseases. [16] But he would withdraw to deserted places and pray.

[17] One day, while he was teaching, Pharisees and teachers of the law were sitting nearby (they had come from every village of Galilee and Judea and from Jerusalem); and the power of the Lord was with him to heal. [18] Just then some men came, carrying a paralyzed man on a bed. They were trying to bring him in and lay him before Jesus; [19] but finding no way to bring him in because of the crowd, they went up on the roof and let him down with his bed through the tiles into the middle of the crowd in front of Jesus. [20] When he saw their faith, he said, 'Friend, your sins are forgiven you.' [21] Then the scribes and the Pharisees began to question, 'Who is this who is speaking blasphemies? Who can forgive sins but God alone?' [22] When Jesus perceived their questionings, he answered them, 'Why do you raise such questions in your hearts? [23] Which is easier, to say, "Your sins are forgiven you", or to say, "Stand up and walk"? [24] But so that you may know that the Son of Man has authority on earth to forgive sins'—he said to the one who was paralyzed—'I say to you, stand up and take your bed and go to your home.'

...

27 After this he went out and saw a tax collector named Levi, sitting
at the tax booth; and he said to him, 'Follow me.' 28 And he got up, left
everything, and followed him.
29 Then Levi gave a great banquet for him in his house; and there
was a large crowd of tax collectors and others sitting at the table with
them. 30 The Pharisees and their scribes were complaining to his disciples, saying, 'Why do you eat and drink with tax collectors and sinners?' 31 Jesus answered, 'Those who are well have no need of a physician, but those who are sick.'

I'm not going to get emotional because we'll be here two more months, and I can't sustain it that long. It is always remarkable when Baptists pass something unanimously, [*congregation laughs*] and that makes the beautiful message in the proclamation even more dear to us because it's so rare...

I'm very grateful for a chance to be a member of this church. It's been an exhilarating and a calming and a satisfying, gratifying experience for us to make friends here who have accepted us, not as special people who live in the White House, but as neighbors and as fellow believers in Christ. You have let me teach in a fumbling way.... It has given me a chance to study, and to stay in touch with God's word and my own deep faith in Christ.

The Sundays that we are not here—we ordinarily are at Camp David or somewhere else—we always have church services. At Camp David, there's a chaplain who comes in from a nearby military base and he has a service for us—our family, and just a few people. And when we're out campaigning, or out traveling around the world, we always make a point to go to a church on Sunday morning to worship.

The Essence of Christianity

This morning, we have a lesson that I think is very interesting... "What is Christianity?" I'm not a theologian, I'm not preparing myself to tell you what Christianity is, but I think it's something that we ought to keep in mind, to question as we go through this lesson, and, maybe, at the end of the lesson we will jointly have some analyses of what does Christianity mean? What is Christianity?

If you were asked by the teacher, which you're going to be, what is one of your favorite verses that describes the essence of Christianity or your belief in Christ, what would you want to reply? Does anyone have a verse you'd like to mention?

For God so loved the world that he gave his only begotten son, that whosoever believeth in him should not perish, but have everlasting life.

Very good. That reply doesn't surprise me.

Let the words of my mouth and the meditation of my heart be acceptable...

...I think that came from psalms, doesn't it? Psalm 19?...

And yet, while we were all sinners, God proved his love...

Christ died for me, yes. Romans 5. Another one, anybody?

Jesus said, "Pick up your cross and follow me."...

What's one of the first ones you ever learned?

Jesus loves me.

God is love.

What is the verse for "God is love?"... Somebody read 1 John 4:8.

8 *Whoever does not love does not know God, for God is love.*

I was reading this morning a passage that describes Reinhold Niebuhr's favorite verse. Anybody know what it is? Look up Ephesians 4:32. I'd rather have the King James Version.

32 *And be ye kind one to another, tenderhearted, forgiving one another, even as God for Christ's sake hath forgiven you.*

I think that that verse, plus John 3:16, encapsulates as well as anything else the essence of Christianity. It's the connotation of love, mercy, the potential alienation of individual human beings, because of sin, from God, the recognition of that barrier that we ourselves build between ourselves and God, and the elimination of the barrier through Christ, and overall, or permeating that thought, is the worth of an individual human being. It's not a broad scope about society, or about war and peace, it's not philosophical dissertations, but it's that one human being, precious in God's sight, alienated because of sin, an acknowledgement of sin, and through Christ, who died for us, forgiveness and reconciliation....

The Environment of Christ's Early Ministry

We are studying from Luke, the fourth chapter through the ninth, Jesus' ministry in Galilee, and it gives a picture of Christ's life as he related to people around him. First of all, Christ started out an unknown person, acknowledged to be God's special son in the life of Mary and Joseph and Elizabeth and maybe a few other people—John the Baptist. He was not scorned or despised in Nazareth when he was growing up. He began to teach. And, eventually, he was known as a very famous person.

In the latter part of Luke 4, Christ was so pressed by the crowds around Capernaum that he was very eager to get away, and the people were clinging to him. He went out in the desert and said, "I'm going to go to another place." And the people who lived there in Capernaum, where Simon Peter lived, right on the edge of the Sea of Galilee, said, "Don't go. Stay with us. We need you. You've been healing the sick, you've been teaching us words of wisdom, we need you to stay with us." And Christ said, "My ministry is broader than Capernaum. I'm going to have to move further."

And then, of course, he had his first encounter with some fishermen.... He wanted to get on the boat and move out into the Sea of Galilee, enough distance so he could separate himself from the crowd and have a kind of podium from which to speak. And then he talked to the crowd.

When he got through, he said, "Take me back." He told the fishermen to catch some fish. They said they hadn't caught anything. They threw out their nets and caught more than the nets could hold. And

Peter and the others were convinced that Christ had a special authority, maybe because he caught a lot of fish, maybe because they were impressed at the crowd that surrounded Jesus—*If he's so famous, he must be great.*

But that's two elements: one is the press of the crowds, and the second one is the special relationship that Christ engendered with a few people who became his disciples. What is a disciple?

A learner.

A learner, a student. What else?

A follower.

A follower, a believer. One who reveres a teacher. One who looks on the teacher not only as a source of wisdom, but also as a source of guidance in one's life or a pattern that you would like yourself to emulate—someone you'd like to follow.

So, the discipleship, the recruitment of fame through his healing and words—but there was another result of Christ's ministry around Galilee. What was that? Another human relationship that became very important later in his life.

The Pharisees...

It was the relationship with power and authority in the church, but primarily what I wanted was the condemnation or the alienation or the struggle between them. Christ became despised and hated and feared and condemned by the church leaders. This is generating already in the lesson a very complicated relationship of teaching, healing, but a certain aloofness of Christ because he couldn't be captured by the crowds. His ministry had to be broad, it had to be generic in nature.

The special relationship that Christ had with individual human beings, whom he genuinely loved.... I won't go through all the parables that he taught about how important one person was. If you have one hundred sheep and lose one, that is special. If you have ten coins and lose one, that is special. But in many ways, Jesus said that the ministry that he personified was for a lost sinner and not the breadth of philosophical discussions that sometimes preoccupy us.

So, that relationship with the crowd in contrast to his love of individuals in the crowd, his need for aloofness and not being captured, his special dependence upon and love for a few disciples, and his alienation from the church leaders—all those things in Christ's early ministry began to form the lessons, or the environment within which he could teach the lessons to us.

The Pharisee in Me

What are some of the things about the Pharisees—what do you know about the Pharisees?... They were separatists. They thought it was sinful for them to deal with sinners.... They almost worshipped the law itself....

They had certain, very narrow definitions of what was acceptable and what was not acceptable. They had prescriptions for acceptability by God—what you must do to be accepted by God. And they had proscriptions—things that you cannot do. Very narrowly defined definitions of what is an acceptable person in God's eyes, and they made the definition.

They were traditionalists. They looked back on their study of God's word and they tried to preserve it, but they also expanded on it. There was a lot of human interpretation of what God meant in his teachings. They defined, in effect, "What is God?" and in order for someone to be accepted by God in their eyes, and in the eyes of the church, they had to comply with those human definitions. The personal aspect of God's love was secondary to them.

What did Jesus think of the Pharisees? They were devout people. They were sincere. They were very fervent. What did Jesus think of them?... Matthew 23—somebody read the thirteenth, and fifteenth verses. This tells succinctly what Christ thought about the Pharisees.

13 *"Woe to you, teachers of the law and Pharisees, you hypocrites! You shut the door of the kingdom of heaven in people's faces. You yourselves do not enter, nor will you let those enter who are trying to.*

[15] *"Woe to you, teachers of the law and Pharisees, you hypocrites! You travel over land and sea to win a single convert, and when you have succeeded, you make them twice as much a child of hell as you are.*

That gives you an indication of what Christ thought of the Pharisees. As a matter of fact, this encounter in the fifth chapter of Luke probably came before Christ said those words. As far as Luke is concerned, this is Christ's first encounter with the Pharisees and scribes—the first one he tells about.

Let's read Luke 5:12–16 as the first part of our lesson text this morning. Anyone, Luke 5:12–16. Fred, do you have it?

Yes.

[12] *And it came to pass, when he was in a certain city, behold a man full of leprosy: who seeing Jesus fell on his face, and besought him, saying, Lord, if thou wilt, thou canst make me clean.*

[13] *And he put forth his hand, and touched him, saying, I will: be thou clean. And immediately the leprosy departed from him.*

[14] *And he charged him to tell no man: but go, and shew thyself to the priest, and offer for thy cleansing, according as Moses commanded, for a testimony unto them.*

[15] *But so much the more went there a fame abroad of him: and great multitudes came together to hear, and to be healed by him of their infirmities.*

[16] *And he withdrew himself into the wilderness, and prayed.*

What was the status of lepers in those days? Outcast, despised. And what was the analysis of the leper's moral status in the eyes of God? He was not only an outcast because he had a contagious disease, but he was also an outcast because he was condemned by God in the eyes of the religious leaders. The reason he has leprosy is because God condemned him and because he's not worthy, and, of course, there was a morbid fear of leprosy.

If you had lived in those days, knowing what you would've known about medicine and so forth, just the approach of a leper anywhere near you would've been reason for great consternation. You would have guarded yourself, taken your children away. Lepers had to walk along, and cry out, "Unclean! Unclean!" to warn people about them.

What did the leper do when he saw Jesus? Fell on his face! Isn't that what it says, Fred?

Fell on his face.

Did Jesus knock him away? What did he do?

Stretched out his hand.

Touched him. With a feeling of condemnation or alienation? With Love.

It seems natural to us, doesn't it, to know that this is the way Jesus reacted. If you hadn't read this lesson and I had said, "What was Jesus' reaction when the leper approached him?" you would've said he reacted with love, wouldn't you? But in those days, Jesus had been looked upon by the crowds as a great religious teacher, and they said, "Since he's a great religious teacher, he's probably going to be like the other religious teachers."

So, it was a shock to people, when the leper approached Christ, fell on his face, and Christ responded with love, and affection, and physical contact. It was a radical departure from the religious ministry of those days. And the leper was healed, and Jesus told the leper to go to the religious authorities and have his soundness, or his cure, certified, because only then could the leper be accepted back in society. That lack of judgement of the leper as a condemned person in the eyes of God was more significant than his physical healing of the sores of leprosy.

This illustrates many things, but especially signifies Christ's care for those who are despised.

I don't know how a church would respond to those who are despised. We tend to think that people who are outcast in our society deserve it.

If somebody's a drug addict, we say, "Well, he brought it on himself. He shouldn't have fooled with it. Probably had bad friends.

Probably a weak person anyway. Thank God I'm not that way—weak, sinful."

If somebody's an alcoholic, we tend to say, "If they'd just follow the teachings of Christ—moderation, stayed away from alcohol, lived a sound life, come to Sunday school every Sunday, studied the Bible, they wouldn't be condemned to a loss of self-control." Because if a person's an alcoholic—probably wasn't good to start with. There's something basically wrong with them.

A prisoner—we look on a person in prison as someone that we can demonstrate, often publicly, our Christian compassion, but we really think that person's probably not quite as good as we are in the eyes of God. [That] person's committed a crime, been found guilty, sent to prison.

I visited all the prisons in Georgia when I was Governor. The average education level was fifth grade. Over 40 percent were [intellectually disabled] with an I.Q. below 70. The vast majority were Black, poor. And I've said many times that if my own son had committed the same act as those prisoners that I saw, my son would never have in prison. Because my family was known to be a respectable family and I had a lot of influence in a nice way, even before I got involved in politics. The local superior court judge and I both went to the Naval Academy, and I'm sure that if my son had been brought before the judge, in private chambers, probably, having committed some crime, say, stealing a car or something like that—thank God he didn't—I would've probably said, "Tom, my boy's a good boy, and if you send him to prison, his life will be destroyed. If you'll just let him go this time, I'll send him to a military school, or I'll exert more discipline, or I'll be personally responsible," I doubt if my son would ever have gone to prison.

We have a tendency to despise people, not actively, but kind of passively, who are different from us. Those who are poor, quite often, are looked upon as not very worthy. If they had worked as hard as we had, and studied as much as we had, they wouldn't be poor.

I've seen in my own earlier life, a strong, regional, even a national belief that because people were Black, or because people didn't speak English well, or because people hadn't been living in this country very long, somehow, they were not as good as us.

Homosexuality is looked upon as a reason for condemnation of a person in the eyes of God—a person who must be despised by God. People who commit adultery.

We read the Ten Commandments and if they don't apply to us, we tend to think other people are despised by God because they violate the Commandments, when we ourselves do. All have sinned and come short of the glory of God, and the wages of sin is death.

The point is, it's not just the Pharisees 2,000 years ago who excluded people from acceptability because they were different, and it wasn't just the Pharisees who thought that because somebody was afflicted that they didn't rank very well in the eyes of God. We tend to yield to the same temptation that afflicted the Pharisees. And that's the teaching of Christ—he went with this leper and healed him and saved him.

The Unsettling Ministry of Christ

Let's move on. The next few verses, Luke 5—let's read the seventeenth, eighteenth, and nineteenth first. Fred?

[17] *And it came to pass on a certain day, as he was teaching, that there were Pharisees and doctors of the law sitting by, which were come out of every town of Galilee, and Judaea, and Jerusalem: and the power of the Lord was present to heal them.*

[18] *And, behold, men brought in a bed a man which was taken with a palsy: and they sought means to bring him in, and to lay him before him.*

[19] *And when they could not find by what way they might bring him in because of the multitude, they went upon the housetop, and let him down through the tiling with his couch into the midst before Jesus.*

Read the next two verses—twenty and twenty-one.

[20] *And when he saw their faith, he said unto him, Man, thy sins are forgiven thee.*

[21] *And the scribes and the Pharisees began to reason, saying, Who is this which speaketh blasphemies? Who can forgive sins, but God alone?*

What's the significance of this act? Anybody? Fred?

The faith of friends enabled a man's sins to be forgiven.

The man's sins were not the concern of his friends, were they? His friends didn't put him on the pallet because he was sinful, or because he needed to be reconciled with God, but his friends loved him, to the extent that they climbed up on top of a house, tore a hole in the roof, and let him down. And they had some special awareness of Christ, because you would guess that even a Savior would say, "Don't tear a hole in that roof. These people are my hosts, they've let me in the house, and here you tear up the house." They had some special feeling that Christ would put that human being even above his friend's house.

Jesus knew the man was physically afflicted. There he was, lying on the pallet; he couldn't even walk, couldn't even move, couldn't even crawl. And Jesus didn't say, "Get up and walk." What did he say?

Your sins are forgiven.

Your sins are forgiven. He knew the Pharisees were there, and Jesus was not naive.

What is the significance of Christ saying, "Your sins are forgiven"? What makes it profoundly significant, even above and beyond anything he had done before, including healing a leper?

The Pharisees felt God alone was the only one that could forgive sins.

And that is accurate in that in many places in the Old Testament it points out that God is the one to forgive sins. There was a contrived way for reconciliation or forgiveness, and what was that in the church—in the synagogues? What was the way to be forgiven?

Sacrifices.

To offer a sacrifice to or give a major offering. And for certain kinds of sins and certain kinds of reconciliation you had to give a certain kind of sacrifice. I'm not condemning that, but the point was, when Christ said to that man on the floor, "Your sins are forgiven you," there was a justifiable reason for the Pharisees to believe that Christ had blasphemed God. Because this man, Jesus, was performing an act of God—forgiving a man's sins.

Even the Pharisees didn't claim they could forgive sins. They said God can forgive sins if somebody does certain religious rites. But Christ had forgiven a man's sins and I'm sure Christ knew that there was going to be a shockwave when he said, "Your sins are forgiven you."

He saw the Pharisees murmuring among themselves and said, "What are you talking about? What are you worrying about?," knowing what the answer would be, and then they accused him of blasphemy. He said, "If that bothers you, that I've forgiven sins, let me also let the man walk," and so, the man got up and took his pallet and walked away.

Do you think Christ would have healed the man if the Pharisees hadn't made a point?

Yes, he would have.

You're right. He would've healed him, because Christ loved that man. He wasn't trying to win a debating contest with the Pharisees by healing the man, he loved the man. He didn't say, "Your sins are forgiven you" to preach a sermon, he wanted that person to be reconciled with God. Christ loved that man.

And, as you know, several places otherwise in the Bible, Christ heals people because of the faith of someone else. He raised Lazarus from the dead because of the faith of Mary and Martha. And the Centurion had so much faith, that Christ healed [his servant]. But faith was there, and Christ healed.

And the Pharisees murmured among themselves. This was the embryonic beginning of the fear and the animosity of the Pharisees because they not only accused Christ of blasphemy, but they also saw the overwhelming power of Christ, the authority of Christ, the results of his words, and also the acceptability by the masses of Christ as a great religious healer. This is the beginning of the messianic age that was predicted in the Old Testament, that Christ could have preached a sermon on then, when sins can be forgiven.

...Read Luke 5:22 to 24. Anyone.

22 *But when Jesus perceived their thoughts, he answering said unto them, What reason ye in your hearts?*

23 *Whether is easier, to say, Thy sins be forgiven thee; or to say, Rise up and walk?*

24 *But that ye may know that the Son of man hath power upon earth to forgive sins, (he said unto the sick of the palsy,) I say unto thee, Arise, and take up thy couch, and go into thine house.*

Jesus uses the words, "Son of man," according to the lesson text, eighty times. And so far as we know, nobody else ever used it. His disciples—no one ever used the phrase "Son of man" except Christ. If you read this text in other places—I read a few of them this morning—you see there was a special connotation of it. If other people used the words "son of man," it was a kind of common expression just for a man. Christ may have been using this phrase as the Messiah, but there's no way to know...

When we hear Christ say, "Son of man," we think, in our minds, *the son of God, who was born a human being.* We know that Christ was the Messiah, but Christ, in order not to bludgeon people by saying, "I am the Messiah," would say, "I am the Son of man." It was a little obtuse, and his disciples interpreted it probably as we do, [but to] others, it was not very contentious.

Let's move on now to the final episode in this lesson.

People looked upon Christ, with this act, with fear, but fear doesn't mean a desire to run away. We use the meaning of the word "fear" as being—contemplating punishment for ourselves or some catastrophe in our life and we want to escape from it. But "fear" there meant an acknowledgement of purity, of holiness, an aspect of reverence. For them, fear meant, I want to kneel down rather than run away. Fear the Lord meant kneel down to the Lord, revere the Lord, accept his holiness, but we have kind of twisted the word fear around so that we mean escape from something—fear of punishment. When they said they were filled with fear, it meant an awareness of holiness.

Well, they were amazed at what had happened, and then their feeling was changed to one of hostility.

Let's read the next few verses. Fred, start with the twenty-seventh and read through the thirtieth right now.

27 *And after these things he went forth, and saw a publican, named Levi, sitting at the receipt of custom: and he said unto him, Follow me.*

28 *And he left all, rose up, and followed him.*

29 *And Levi made him a great feast in his own house: and there was a great company of publicans and of others that sat down with them.*

30 *But their scribes and Pharisees murmured against his disciples, saying, Why do ye eat and drink with publicans and sinners?*

Read thirty-one and thirty-two.

31 *And Jesus answering said unto them, They that are whole need not a physician; but they that are sick.*

32 *I came not to call the righteous, but sinners to repentance.*

It was not just the Pharisees that Jesus alienated when he went into eat with Levi (or Matthew). The eating of a meal with someone was a very intimate observance of friendship, and equality, and mutual acceptance, even more so than it is with us—it was kind of a ritual. Those of you who have visited in the homes of Jewish families on Holy Days, you know the observance of the meal has a special part in their lives. I had the Friday meal with Prime Minister Begin at Camp David one of the nights we were there, and there's a special religious quality about it.

And when Jesus sat down in the home of Levi, who was acknowledged to be a sinner, and I have no doubt that all of his friends—birds of a feather flock together—they probably drank a lot. I'm sure they didn't go to the synagogue, they were alienated from the community, the tax collectors were looked on as betrayers of the people of Israel—quislings who associated with the Romans, robbers of their own people—they were really outcast in more ways than one, and Jesus invited himself and went to the home of Levi. Apparently, the Pharisees and others were standing around kind of in an audience—I don't know exactly how it was; I've seen it in movies. But there was a table with them eating at it and these critics, the Pharisees and the good citizens of that community, were condemning Christ for associating with sinners. And Christ, again, said, "I came to seek and to save those that are lost. The righteous don't need me."

Christ's Ministry, Our Ministry

There are several lessons to be derived in closing. First of all, Christ ministered to human needs, material needs included, physical needs, yes. Because he saw that in a person's life, deprivation was harmful and needed to be corrected.

If a person's been given a talent by God, and societal obstacles prevent those talents from being nurtured and used, then that is bad, and Christ wanted to correct that badness. If somebody's deprived from an education or health, if somebody's not given equality of treatment, if someone is despised, if someone is an outcast, if someone is hungry, if someone is treated as inferior, if someone is deprived of justice, if someone is deprived of human freedom, if someone is sick and not treated, if someone is there and not loved, those human afflictions were the reason for Christ's ministry, and they should be ours.

Christ, also, was not concerned about religious custom or tradition as much as other leaders of that time. He saw the strict human creations of religious rules and regulations, prescriptions and proscriptions, as a substitute for "God is love."

And he saw himself as someone who was a teacher. Christ taught in the synagogues, he taught in people's homes, he taught on the streets, he taught in the countryside, he taught out of ships. He answered questions, he taught with his life, with his actions, with his words, with his suffering, with his death, with his resurrection—Christ was a teacher.

And I think in this day and age of ours, it's good for us to remember that the pharisaic approach is not a two thousand-year-old dead characteristic of people who profess to be Christians. The defining of what a Christian is, the defining of what is acceptable to God by human beings, the structure of complicated moral laws by human beings, is not Christianity. Which brings us to the original question we asked—what is Christianity?

Christianity—one definition—is the assurance of God's forgiveness toward those of us who acknowledge our sins because we believe in Christ. It's a reconciliation between sinful people—us—and God, through Christ's love.

In all these three episodes that I've covered this morning, Christ is teaching us that. And as we study what Christ did in these occasions, and the radical departure of Christ's actions from the religious teachings of that day, we should derive a lesson for ourselves. Love, compassion, concern, forgiveness, understanding, equality, human—those are the kinds of words that epitomized Christ's life. Humility. They are the ones that should permeate our own lives.

And as we depart from that and assume a pharisaic superiority, we depart from Christ. That's something we don't want to do.

March 8, 1981

Who Is the Church?

Maranatha Baptist Church
Plains, Georgia

Lesson Scripture

1 Corinthians 12:12–31 (NRSV)

12 For just as the body is one and has many members, and all the mem-
bers of the body, though many, are one body, so it is with Christ. 13
For in the one Spirit we were all baptized into one body—Jews or
Greeks, slaves or free—and we were all made to drink of one Spirit.

14 Indeed, the body does not consist of one member but of many.
15 If the foot would say, 'Because I am not a hand, I do not belong to
the body', that would not make it any less a part of the body. 16 And if
the ear would say, 'Because I am not an eye, I do not belong to the
body', that would not make it any less a part of the body. 17 If the whole
body were an eye, where would the hearing be? If the whole body were
hearing, where would the sense of smell be? 18 But as it is, God arranged
the members in the body, each one of them, as he chose. 19 If all were
a single member, where would the body be? 20 As it is, there are many
members, yet one body. 21 The eye cannot say to the hand, 'I have no
need of you', nor again the head to the feet, 'I have no need of you.' 22
On the contrary, the members of the body that seem to be weaker are
indispensable, 23 and those members of the body that we think less honorable we clothe with greater honor, and our less respectable members
are treated with greater respect; 24 whereas our more respectable members do not need this. But God has so arranged the body, giving the
greater honor to the inferior member, 25 that there may be no dissension within the body, but the members may have the same care for one
another. 26 If one member suffers, all suffer together with it; if one
member is honored, all rejoice together with it.

27 Now you are the body of Christ and individually members of it.
28 And God has appointed in the church first apostles, second prophets,
third teachers; then deeds of power, then gifts of healing, forms of assistance, forms of leadership, various kinds of tongues. 29 Are all apostles? Are all prophets? Are all teachers? Do all work miracles? 30 Do all
possess gifts of healing? Do all speak in tongues? Do all interpret? 31

But strive for the greater gifts. And I will show you a still more excellent way.

1 Corinthians 13 (NRSV)

1 If I speak in the tongues of mortals and of angels, but do not have
love, I am a noisy gong or a clanging cymbal. 2 And if I have prophetic
powers, and understand all mysteries and all knowledge, and if I have
all faith, so as to remove mountains, but do not have love, I am nothing. 3 If I give away all my possessions, and if I hand over my body so
that I may boast, but do not have love, I gain nothing.

4 Love is patient; love is kind; love is not envious or boastful or
arrogant 5 or rude. It does not insist on its own way; it is not irritable
or resentful; 6 it does not rejoice in wrongdoing, but rejoices in the
truth. 7 It bears all things, believes all things, hopes all things, endures
all things.

8 Love never ends. But as for prophecies, they will come to an end;
as for tongues, they will cease; as for knowledge, it will come to an end.
9 For we know only in part, and we prophesy only in part; 10 but when
the complete comes, the partial will come to an end. 11 When I was a
child, I spoke like a child, I thought like a child, I reasoned like a child;
when I became an adult, I put an end to childish ways. 12 For now we
see in a mirror, dimly, but then we will see face to face. Now I know
only in part; then I will know fully, even as I have been fully known. 13
And now faith, hope, and love abide, these three; and the greatest of
these is love.

This morning, we are talking about spiritual gifts. Paul wrote this letter, to the Corinthians—1 Corinthians—and we'll study this morning from chapters 12 and 13.

The Corinthian church had a special character or nature or environment within which it existed...the environment within which they lived, it was a Pagan community. They did almost everything just the opposite from what Christ taught, and the Corinthian church was small. And it was fumbling. They were struggling to exist, they didn't know how to get along with each other, they weren't naturally good people. They were somewhat proud of the fact that they were different Christians.

...They figured that once they became Christians, since Christ had treated women as equals, that they, themselves, in that new liberated environment, could act completely liberated, and they changed their way of dress and took off their veils, some of them cut their hair short, and they created a furor in the church because people saw them on the street and accused Christian women of being prostitutes—or accused them of being prostitutes. And those people, in those days, had accused Christ of being condemned. "The accursed one," many people in Corinth called Christ.

So, as Paul wrote this letter, where was Paul? Anybody, where was Paul? Rosalynn, do you know where he was?

Yes, in prison.

Paul was in prison. The Corinthians didn't quite know how to deal with these struggles within the church. The liberation, the freedom of being a Christian, the awareness that God loved them, equality of women—it was kind of a radical departure from the way people lived in Corinth.

How did the Pagans worship in Corinth?... Sometimes crazy sacrifices, but they combined the gratification of the body, sexual gratification, and so forth, with the worship service itself, and the Christians were trying to break away from this old debauchery and to show in their tiny church what Christ had taught. But as the church grew, it was isolated. It didn't have a big church next door to give it strength. It didn't have a parent church from which those Christians had learned a lot about the Bible, about Christ, about the Epistles, and so forth. They were really learning on their own.

Of course, they knew the name of James, and they knew the name of Peter, and they knew Paul, but they didn't have a constant stream of literature coming to them. They didn't have any printed Bibles. So, in a very human way, these other Christians felt isolated, and as they felt isolated, they weren't sure of themselves. They knew what Christ had taught, because they had heard it preached, but they weren't quite sure of it.

Maybe I misunderstood it. The world's just as bad as it ever was. I am tempted every day. I am still sinful. I don't get along with the other members of the church. Freedom is not as nice as I thought it was. I still have to work for a living. Somebody that I love just died. Has Christ forgotten us?

Those were the kinds of questions that the Corinthians were asking each other. And since they didn't have a spiritual leader there in Corinth, they would write letters to Paul, and I'm sure they waited, waited, waited, and waited, and checked every message, and said, "Did you bring us a letter from Paul?"

Finally, Paul wrote them back.

The Question of Spiritual Gifts

One of the questions they asked Paul was [about] spiritual gifts. Why was it that some members of the church were blessed with great talent, great abilities, even great financial wealth or social status or political influence? And other members didn't have quite as much?

This was not just an idle question; it was a practical problem. It created jealousy, because a meek, unselfish person in the church, quite often didn't see their effort recognized, and they thought, *Maybe the teachings of Christ that we are trying out for the first generation, really don't work.*

So, they asked Paul, "What about spiritual gifts?" And Paul, writing to them, tried to explain this very serious question of spiritual gifts.

Let's turn now to 1 Corinthians 12, everybody, either in a book or in a Bible. If anybody needs a book you can use mine. I'll ask Miss

Ida Lee Tillman, who is a much better teacher than I am, on the first row, to start. As you find the verses, we'll just read one verse at a time...

[1] *And, now concerning spiritual gifts brethren, I will not have you ignorant.*

Let's stop just a moment now. When Paul says "concerning spiritual gifts," this is pretty good proof that the Corinthians had asked him about spiritual gifts, and he said, "In answer to your question about spiritual gifts, I don't want you to stay ignorant."

[2] *You'll remember that before you became Christians you went around from one idol to another, not one of which could speak a single word.*

Very good.... The third verse.

[3] *Wherefore I give you to understand, that no man speaking by the Spirit of God calleth Jesus accursed: and that no man can say that Jesus is the Lord, but by the Holy Ghost.*

Let's stop here for a minute. He said, "You remember when you were Gentiles," that is Pagans, "that you worshipped idols." The King James says, "dumb idols." Whether he was condemning the idols, or saying they couldn't speak, we don't really know. "Even as you were led, this is the way you were taught; you are not to be condemned because of your ignorance, because once you learned about Christ, you formed a church." He said that no man speaking who says that Christ was accursed, was speaking with the spirit of God. "And no man can say that Jesus is the Lord without the spirit of God."

Some of the people around Corinth, looking at this strange little church, were saying that Christ was alienated from God; he was different from the religion which they had been taught since they were children. So, Paul's trying to put into perspective his answer to the people at Corinth.

To Love Is to Be Loved

Let's go ahead now and read the fourth verse all the way through to the eleventh verse. If you have a Bible or book, just read it and we'll go back and forth....

4 *Now there are diversities of gifts, but the same Spirit.*

5 *And there are diversities of administrations, but the same Lord.*

6 *And there are diversities of operations, but it is the same God which worketh all in all.*

7 *But the manifestation of the Spirit is given to every man to profit withal.* 8 *One is given by the Spirit the word of wisdom; to another the word of knowledge by the same Spirit;* 9 *To another faith by the same Spirit; to another the gifts of healing by the same Spirit;* 10 *To another the working of miracles; to another prophecy; to another discerning of spirits; to another diverse kinds of tongues; to another the interpretation of tongues:* 11 *But all these worketh that one and the selfsame Spirit, dividing to every man severally as he will.*

Very good, let's stop there. Now, what were some of the gifts that Paul described to the Corinthians as spiritual gifts? Wisdom, knowledge, healing, faith, prophecy, miracles, discerning of spirits, speaking in tongues, interpretation of tongues.

Let me ask you this now. What gift—think about your own life for a few minutes—what gift has God blessed you with?

Teaching.

Teaching. The dissemination of knowledge. Miss Ida Lee?

I don't know that I'm so gifted, but he certainly has given me the gift of wanting to go to church and learn God's word. But it doesn't say that thing in there.

...It doesn't have to be listed among these that Paul said. What kind of gifts do you think God has blessed your life with?

Good health.

Love.

Faith.

Jimmy, there's another place—this doesn't mean helpers, but there's another place that talks about the gifts and its helpers, and I think that's a wonderful thing.

That's true. Later on, Paul talks about teachers and ministers and helpers in the church, and so forth. But right now, we're just trying to point out that whether you're a famous person, or whether you've been involved with the public, like a teacher, or you've been an excellent Sunday school teacher for the last fifty years, God has given you certain gifts. It may have been physical gifts, like good health, but we are talking this morning about spiritual gifts, and one of the things that God has offered us all is faith.

Now, it's very hard to be kind and gentle and loving, it's very hard to be a good teacher, unless you are convinced that you have a place in life; unless your own life fits in somewhere; unless you think that you've got a role to play. That you're worthy. Or respected, or even loved. It's hard to love other people unless you feel like, at least, somebody loves you.

If you feel like you're isolated from everybody else, and you're despised and you don't have anybody loving you, the natural human inclination is to lash back, and to be filled with hatred. Sociologists know that this is one of the major sources of crimes; when young people living in the ghetto, Black or White people, or Spanish-speaking people, live in a ghetto and they don't think that anybody cares about them—they don't believe the mayor cares about them, they don't think the governor cares about them, they don't think the policeman cares about them, they don't think the corner grocery owner cares about them, they don't think the teacher cares about them, they don't think the social worker cares about them—their natural inclination is not to reach out with their arms and say, "I love everybody." Their natural inclination is to say, "I'm okay. The world is wicked. Those people are not worthy of my love."

So, one of the prerequisites of the foundations for loving others is to feel that you are, yourself, loved. This is a very important consideration in this lesson. These early Christians were not quite sure that they were loved or respected, and Paul is trying to reassure them that, no matter how insignificant you think you are in the church, you have spiritual gifts. Somebody might have been a great teacher, and have understood the gospel, understood Christ's word, and had met Paul in prison, and talked to Peter,... and may have been exalted—people might have sat at their feet and listened to them as they evoked the spirit of Christ. Paul says that particular person that you look up to is no better than you are because his gifts came where from? From the Holy Spirit.

Unity Within Diversity

Over and over in this series of verses, very strangely, he says, "from the Spirit. From the Holy Ghost." Diversities of gifts, but from the same Spirit; differences of administration, same Lord; diversities of operations, same God. But the manifestations of the Spirit is given to every man to profit from. To one is given wisdom, to another the word of knowledge by the same Spirit. To another faith, by the same Spirit. To another the gifts of healing where from? By the same Spirit. To another the working of miracles; to another prophecy; to another discerning of spirits; to another diverse kinds of tongues; to another interpretation of tongues.

What he's saying is that no matter how different those talents might be, they are not to be considered as a basis for pride or for the exaltation of those that might have more spiritual gifts than others, because all of them are given to them.

If there were three people in this room, all of them hungry, and I walked in with a loaf of bread, and I gave one person three slices of bread, and I gave another person two slices of bread, [and] I gave another person one slice of bread, would I consider the person that I had just given three slices of bread to be better than the other two because they had three slices of bread? No! So, Paul is saying that in God's eyes, the person that God has given three talents to is not better than the person that God has also given one talent.

Paul is trying to tell these people that there's a place for them to be self-assured. Because even if they are uncertain about the love of their fellow church members, and certainly uncertain about the other folks on the Corinthian streets, there is an overwhelming love demonstrated to them by God through Christ. Therefore, since they know they are loved by Christ, then they are in a position not to be proud, but to love other people.

The same question that the Corinthians asked Paul about spiritual gifts are the same questions that are in the minds of people in Plains, Georgia, in 1981. We have the same thing within our own church, within our own community. We've got two Baptist churches, a Methodist church, a Lutheran church—just among the predominant White people, and others among the Blacks. It doesn't mean that one church is better than the other—we have a tendency toward division, and misunderstandings, and hard feelings. We have a tendency to think that the folks in Maranatha are a little better than the folks in the Plains Baptist church. Paul says, "No."

In diversity there must be unity. We can be different, but we ought to be bound together. When we're unified, we've got to understand that we are going to be different—the two are not incompatible. Every human being is different, because God made us that way, but it doesn't mean that God thought one person was better than another. Paul says a church is for Gentile and Greek and Jew, for masters and slaves; equal in the eyes of God.

One Body, Different Parts

Let's read on a little further.... Let's read verses 12 through 20. That will pretty well wrap up the twelfth chapter....

12 *For as the body is one, and hath many members, and all the members of that one body, being many, are one body: so also is Christ.*

To emphasize the unity of the church, Paul used the word one three times in this verse; one Spirit draws persons to Christ, all believers are baptized to one body, and all believers drink into one Spirit. That is, they receive the gift of the Holy Spirit.

14 *For the body is not one member, but many.*

15 *If the foot shall say, Because I am not the hand, I am not of the body; is it therefore not of the body?*

16 *And if the ear shall say, Because I am not of the eye, I am not of the body; is it therefore not of the body?*

17 *If the whole body were an eye, where were the hearing? If the whole were hearing, where were the smelling?*

18 *But now hath God set the members every one of them in the body, as it hath pleased him.*

19 *And if they were all one member, where were the body?*

20 *But now are they many members, yet but one body.*

...Paul is using an example here to illustrate to these relatively ignorant people, like us, what should be the nature of the church. What should be the nature of believers in Christ? He said, "Because you are a foot," which is a vivid illustration, "and not a hand, should you not consider yourself as important a part of the body? And because you are the ear, and not the eye, should you consider yourself to be less significant?"

Paul is equating here, in his letter to the Corinthians and letter to the Romans, a body as being what? Christ. In the early letters of Paul to the Corinthians and to the Romans, when Paul described the body, he said all these parts of the body are the parts of Christ; we are a part of Christ. Later, when he wrote the Ephesians and the Colossians, he changed a little bit... later on, Paul said the body is a church and Christ is what? The head. So, this was kind of an evolution in Paul's teaching.

If the body was all one eye, it would be grotesque, wouldn't it? Or, if the whole body was a foot. It's kind of nauseating to think about the body being even a brain, or something that's beautiful. The body is coherent and useful and attractive to us because it's made up of diverse elements, like a church is made up.

Those of you who don't think much of a foot, if you hurt your toe, you immediately become aware of the importance of the one part of your body. Or, if you have an earache, or if a splinter gets in your eye, it's extremely painful, and for a few days you can become completely preoccupied with a relatively insignificant part of your body. Paul says this to prove to us...that every member of the church is important. Every human being is important. And those of us who are members of the church should not scorn those who are not members of the church.

A More Excellent Way

The thing that permeates Christ's teaching, more than any other single word, is "pride." Christ saw that the root cause of most of human sinfulness was pride. The exaltation of ourselves. The tendency of every person to think, *I'm a little bit better than others. I'm a little more honorable than others. I'm a little more self-sacrificing than others. I'm a little more knowledgeable than others. A little wiser. A little more devout. I have more faith. I'm a little purer. I'm more misunderstood. I suffer more.* We have a tendency to think excessively about ourselves.

I was reading last night an anthology about the Bible, and it told about the surgeons in London in the fifteenth century who were getting ready to dissect the body of a pauper that they had found on the street, and they wanted to do the dissection as quickly as possible to learn about science. The question, as they were going over this body, was, "What are we going to do with this worthless wretch?" According to the story, this person was not quite dead, and he spoke up in perfect Latin and said, "Call not him worthless, for whom Christ died."

Call him not worthless for whom Christ died.

We have a tendency to look down on someone else because they don't speak English well, or because their farm is not as big as ours, or because they might be Black. We should remind ourselves, Christ died for that person. The church is not a collection of superior people. We are a little more wise because we accept Christ as our Savior, and we are therefore better than others because of our faith—that is not what a church is. A church is not even an organization dedicated to the demonstration of moral law. Church is primarily a group of people who are bound together because of our assurance that God will forgive us for our sins through Christ. It's a collection of people who know we're sinful, but who also know that God will forgive us.

The philosopher Pascal said the world was divided into two kinds of people; one, saints who know they're sinners, and the other, sinners who think they're saints. Which are we? Do we think we're saints? Do we think we're better than the folks outside the church? Or are we here because we know we're sinful—we know we're no better than anybody else, and we know that God loves us in spite of our sinfulness and through Christ will give us salvation.

It's an important point Paul is trying to make to the Corinthians in the struggling church, and it's an important point that Christ, through Paul, and the Bible, is trying to make to us this morning. And Paul's vivid use of the human body teaches us a lesson: all the elements of the church are important. None is more important than the other....

What do you think, among all these things, was the greatest talent, greatest spiritual gift?... Forgiveness, you could say faith, but love is the one we're coming to. Let's read the thirty-first verse....

31 *But covet earnestly the best gifts: and yet shew I unto you a more excellent way.*

Paul said, search for the more excellent gifts. There's a tendency here for us to be satisfied. If you read the twelfth chapter, you can say, "Well, I don't have to do too much because Paul has said it doesn't matter if I'm not a teacher. It doesn't matter if I can't play beautiful music. It doesn't matter if I'm not a great speaker. It doesn't matter if I'm not wise. It doesn't matter if I don't interpret knowledge." That is not what Paul says. Paul wants us, and God want us, to take whatever opportunities we have to be wise, to be knowledgeable, to be a teacher, to heal, to love, to let our faith grow. He doesn't want us to be satisfied with the little, tiny talent.

I remember the most difficult part I had to understand in the Bible is the one about the person that had ten talents and invested it, and five talents and invested it, and one person had one little talent, and they didn't invest it—buried it in the ground. Christ condemned that person. It's been hard for me, all my life, to understand it, but I think this chapter tells us, if you've got one talent, don't sit back and say, "Well, Paul said one talent is just as great as ten talents." That is not what Paul says. Paul says in the thirty-first verse, "But covet earnestly the best gifts: and yet shew I unto you a more excellent way".

But the Greatest of These

And now comes a great chapter in the Bible.

...If somebody said, "Which one of the apostles of Christ, the teachers of the early church, would you associate most closely with love," you might say John. You might think, "What's Paul's strong suit?," and you might say faith. But now let's read a peculiar chapter.

If you read all the words of Paul to the Corinthians, to the Ephesians, to the Galatians, and others, sometimes it's hard to understand. Paul is not a poet. Paul is a theologian, or a philosopher. He can explain things sometimes in a very complicated way, but it seems to me that when he got to the first verse of the thirteenth chapter, 1 Corinthians, he kind of turned into a poet. There is a rhythm to the thirteenth chapter that's not typical of the rest of Paul's writings.

...Let's read the first three verses, first.

1 *Though I speak with the tongues of men and of angels, and have not charity, I am become as sounding brass, or a tinkling cymbal.* 2 *And though I have the gift of prophecy, and understand all mysteries, and all knowledge; and though I have all faith, so that I could remove mountains, and have not charity, I am nothing.* 3 *And though I bestow all my goods to*

feed the poor, and though I give my body to be burned, and have not charity, it profiteth me nothing.

There really is no reason to divide the thirty-first verse [of chapter 12] from the first verse [of chapter 13]. Paul is saying, all these gifts that I have described to you, all these little, tricky things I have given you about the body, are worthless as far as our own lives are concerned, without love. Even if I make the greatest sacrifice of all—give my body to be burned—if I don't have love, it profiteth me none. If I take everything I have in the world and give it all to the poor, and don't have love, in the eyes of God it doesn't mean anything. So, Paul is exalting love.

Let's start with the fourth verse, read to the seventh.

4 *Charity suffereth long, and is kind; charity envieth not; charity vaunteth not itself, is not puffed up,*
5 *Doth not behave itself unseemly, seeketh not her own, is not easily provoked, thinketh no evil;*
6 *Rejoiceth not in iniquity, but rejoiceth in the truth;*
7 *Beareth all things, believeth all things, hopeth all things, endureth all things.*

...What Paul is doing now...is outlining for us, and the Corinthians, the characteristics of love. It suffereth long. In our minds, instead of charity or love, substitute another word—Christ. Christ suffereth long and is kind; envieth not, vaunteth not himself, is not puffed up, doth not behave himself unseemly, seeketh not his own, is not easily provoked, thinketh no evil, rejoiceth not in iniquity, but rejoiceth in the truth; beareth all things, believeth all things, hopeth all things, endureth all things. Try to substitute the word Betty, or Ida Lee, or Hugh, or Jimmy, and see if the words fit you or me.

Paul was not trying to condemn the Corinthians. Because he said in the first verse up there, "Though I speak with the tongues of men and of angels and have not charity." It was a generous thing to do.. If he wanted to condemn the Corinthians, he would have said, "Though you speak with the tongues of men and angels," and "you don't have charity," but Paul didn't do that. He said, "I don't have love." I think it's good when you read the thirteenth chapter, not to just think how beautiful it is, or the price of love or charity or Christ, but that it be a measuring stick against ourselves. "I suffereth long. I am kind."—just looking at the fourth verse—"envieth not, vaunteth not myself, not puffed up, doth not behave myself unseemly, seeketh not my own, not easily provoked, thinketh no evil, rejoiceth not in iniquity, rejoiceth in the truth, bareth all things, believeth all things, hopeth all things, endureth all things." That is the purpose of the Bible—not to think about this in non-personal ways, or applying to somebody else—Paul, the Corinthians, other people, preachers, or even Christ—but to put ourselves in the role of saying, "How does this chapter, or this verse, or this word, apply to me?"

We all know that Christ is not puffed up. We all know that Christ doesn't envy. We all know that Christ doesn't vaunt himself. That's no great achievement when we remind ourselves of that. But the achievement is when we recognize our own sinfulness and we say, "I am envious. I do puff myself up. I do participate in iniquitous things. I don't always tell the truth. I am not always kind. I'm not always filled with love. I am a sinner. But I know God loves me, and I know he'll forgive me, and I know Christ died for me." That is the message Paul is trying to impart to you this morning. It's not an idle exercise in an ancient letter to a tiny church in Corinth. It's a message from God, through Christ, through Paul, through the Bible, to me and to you, today, in Plains.

Let's read one verse at a time.

8 *Love never fails, but if there are gifts of prophecy, they will be done away; if there are tongues, they will cease; if there is knowledge, it will be done away.*

9 *For we know in part, and we prophesy in part.*

10 *But when that which is perfect is come, then that which is in part shall be done away.*

11 *When I was a child, I spoke and thought and reasoned like a child does, but when I became a man, my thoughts moved far beyond my thoughts of childhood, and I have put away a child's things.*

[12] *In the same way we can see and understand only a little about God now as if we were peering at his reflection in a poor mirror, but someday we will see him in his completeness face to face. Now all that I know is hazy and blurry, but then I will see everything clearly, just as clearly as God sees into my heart right now.*

Now we'll all read together the thirteenth verse: *And now God is faith, hope, charity, these three. But the greatest of these is charity.*

This lesson this morning is really thought-provoking because it covers three basic elements. One is a description of the various talents that we have, a reminder that all those gifts come from God through grace—a free gift. It's not a payment to us because of our worthiness, or because of our goodness. Secondly, in his illustration of the body of Christ, the fact that all of us are important. And third, that all these gifts, and all of our relationships with one another or with the church itself, pale in [significance] when we compare those other gifts, even faith and hope, even knowledge and wisdom, when we compare them with love.

Christ said "God is love." St. Augustine said, "Love and do anything else you want." If you love, you don't have to memorize a long list of rules and regulations, but it's not easy to love. It's easier to love if we know we're loved. That's one of the roles of a Christian church—a body of people so full with thanksgiving to God because he loves us, that we love one another, and don't condemn anybody else, don't look down on anybody else. Filled with humility, not because we can say pridefully that we are humble, but because we recognize that we are humble, and Christ said that the greatest among these is a servant of all.

As you struggle through this complicated interrelations of words that Paul gave, there is a simplicity that can help you with the complication. And that's the thirteenth chapter about love.

If you have a prayer this afternoon or tonight, let it be a review of the twelfth and thirteenth chapters of 1 Corinthians and remove everything else from it except you. And say, Christ through Paul is talking to me. How am I going to make my own life better in the eyes of God? By acknowledging my mistakes and my sinfulness and my unworthiness and letting that be an avenue toward a greater, more fulfilling spiritual life, utilizing the talent that God gives us and the love that the Holy Spirit, by God, demonstrated by Christ's death for us.

The 1990s

The
Born sea
Praised the sun
The finding one
And upright Adam
Sang upon origin!
O the wings of the children!
The woundward flight of the ancient
Young from the canyons of oblivion!
The sky stride of the always slain
In battle! the happening
Of saints to their vision!
The world winding home!
And the whole pain
Flows open
And I
Die.

— Dylan Thomas
from "Vision and Prayer"

December 14, 1997. Jimmy Carter teaches Sunday School at Maranatha Baptist Church during the Advent season. Advent refers to the four weeks leading up to Christmas Day during which many Christian communities reflect upon the importance of Christ's birth.

Courtesy Todd Stone Photography

Situated in the middle of an old pecan orchard along rural Georgia Highway 45, Maranatha Baptist Church became a symbol of the most famous Sunday School teacher in the world—Jimmy Carter.

Courtesy Library of Congress, Prints & Photographs Division; photograph by Mark Harrell

An avid woodworker, Jimmy Carter handcrafted four offering plates to collect donations from the congregation during each service at Maranatha Baptist Church. The plates are still used today.

Courtesy Madison Hernandez Photo + Art

Jimmy Carter often used a simple black leather-bound Bible when teaching his Sunday lessons. His name was imprinted on the lower right-hand corner in gold.

Courtesy Andrew Greer

To love our enemies is no small thing. To relate to a person or a group of people whose ideals are so far removed from our own can be downright intimidating. Not to mention complicated. And when our neighbors threaten our peace with acts of terrorism, atomic warfare, violent rioting, and bloody lawlessness, the gospel instruction to "love our neighbors as ourselves" seems, frankly, unfair. So, when Jesus turns the tables on our so-called godliness to deliver an upside-down moral code in the Sermon on the Mount—blessed are the poor in spirit, blessed are the merciful, blessed are the peacemakers, blessed are those who mourn—we freeze.

In our exacting, modern-day version of justice, there is so little margin for humility. The notion that we are no better than members of Al-Qaeda, no more deserving of a place at God's table than Hamas extremists, no less guilty in the eyes of God than the pimp or the prostitute, flies in the face of our well-tended self-righteous spirits. In the fifth chapter of the Gospel of Matthew, Jesus teaches us that everyone is worthy of love, of forgiveness, of a second chance. Mercy is so counterintuitive to our human nature, to the way we treat ourselves and the way we love—or judge—one another.

In these next few lessons, all taught at Maranatha Baptist Church, Jimmy Carter mines the pages of Scripture and endeavors to help us students find courage to meet our prejudices face forward, and in doing so, to discover our own proper placement in the wildly all-are-equal frontier of God.

~

In 1994, Jimmy Carter made history, but this time not as an elected government official. Granted, his former rank continued to provide him with unusual access into tentative world situations, but his function was no longer as president of the United States, it was as a common, and often concerned, citizen. In an action of renegade diplomacy, Jimmy and Rosalynn crossed the demilitarized zone that separated the constitutional democracy of South Korea from the oppressive stratocracy of the heavily nuclearized North Korean regime. The Carters' purpose for such a dicey expedition was to conduct productive talks about nuclear arms controls with North Korea's imperious despot Kim Il Sung. As America lashed out criticism, the Carters civilly negotiated with a vilified dictator.

But I say to you, Love your enemies and pray for those who persecute you, so that you may be children of your Father in heaven; for he makes his sun rise on the evil and on the good, and sends rain on the righteous and on the unrighteous. (Matt. 5:44)

The Carters' peace-keeping mission to North Korea was controversial. The Clinton administration was indignant at Carter's self-appointed authorization to negotiate with one of the world's most tyrannical adversaries. Rightly or wrongly, President Carter did not feel beholden to a man-made government; rather, he was inspired by the instruction of a higher power to recognize Kim Il Sung as more than his policies—a personal conviction that he chose to follow despite political pressures.

Jimmy Carter felt secure in his spiritual identity, a closeness with his Creator, who sets "a table before me in the presence of my enemies." His deep Christian faith infused him with a transcendent courage to humble himself to sit down at the table before those whose ideals and philosophies opposed his own, and to yield to the native worthiness of their human lives. This supernatural grit in loving the person in front of him, regardless of how egregious his or her sins were, reflected his spiritual resolve to pattern his life after the countercultural character of Jesus. And as a result, Carter had a profound impact on the lives of millions of people, from the most decorated to the most destitute, in thousands of communities across the world.

Put simply, Jimmy and Rosalynn Carter were pillars of peace in a modern world gone mad. They were unashamed, unafraid, even, to fail. When they founded their nongovernmental human rights hub,

The Carter Center, in 1982, the tenacious couple's willingness to try, win or lose, fueled the fire of their humanitarianism and mounted an army of peacekeepers to fight disease, foster democracy, and mediate conflict around the globe. Their principled passion for defending life resulted in The Carter Center's worldwide crusade to eradicate Guinea-worm disease. The ancient parasitic infection contracted by drinking water contaminated with Guinea worm larvae, primarily in rural villages in Africa, resulting in an afflictive blister. When the blister breaks, a worm that can measure from between two to three feet in length gradually emerges over the course of several weeks. This process is extremely painful and often disabling for the host affected by the Guinea worm.

Since the campaign to annihilate the disease began nearly forty years ago, the number of cases has nearly disappeared, from an estimated 3.5 million cases in 1986 to just fourteen in 2024. Those "cases" are people who have names and children and dreams and desires and the Carters saw them as human beings, and, as such, people worthy of a little help. This concerted effort to cure people who look, and think, and, in many ways, believe differently than the Carters is yet one more touchable expression of how they attempted to channel the energy of Jesus into their everyday work and everyday lives.

I wonder how many wars could have been avoided, or curtailed, or altogether eliminated if those who wear crowns and suits would take a knee, see each other as people with varying perspectives, talk through their differences, and reach a compromise that could bring peace for everyone else. Jimmy Carter was willing to sit down at a table with his enemies, and because he did, lives were saved.

~

In these next lessons, all taught at Maranatha Baptist Church, our open-and-honest Sunday school teacher prods us to break out of the self-prescribed "safety" of our comfortable and convenient lives to enter an expanded and adventurous and joy-filled life in pursuit of the ideals of God. A life marked by service to, and sacrifice and love for, others.

March 7, 1993

Responding to Honest Inquiry

Maranatha Baptist Church
Plains, Georgia

Lesson Scripture

John 3:1–17 (NRSV)

1 Now there was a Pharisee named Nicodemus, a leader of the Jews. 2 He came to Jesus by night and said to him, 'Rabbi, we know that you are a teacher who has come from God; for no one can do these signs that you do apart from the presence of God.' 3 Jesus answered him, 'Very truly, I tell you, no one can see the kingdom of God without being born from above.' 4 Nicodemus said to him, 'How can anyone be born after having grown old? Can one enter a second time into the mother's womb and be born?' 5 Jesus answered, 'Very truly, I tell you, no one can enter the kingdom of God without being born of water and Spirit. 6 What is born of the flesh is flesh, and what is born of the Spirit is spirit. 7 Do not be astonished that I said to you, "You must be born from above." 8 The wind blows where it chooses, and you hear the sound of it, but you do not know where it comes from or where it goes. So it is with everyone who is born of the Spirit.' 9 Nicodemus said to him, 'How can these things be?' 10 Jesus answered him, 'Are you a teacher of Israel, and yet you do not understand these things?

11 'Very truly, I tell you, we speak of what we know and testify to what we have seen; yet you do not receive our testimony. 12 If I have told you about earthly things and you do not believe, how can you believe if I tell you about heavenly things? 13 No one has ascended into heaven except the one who descended from heaven, the Son of Man. 14 And just as Moses lifted up the serpent in the wilderness, so must the Son of man be lifted up, 15 that whoever believes in him may have eternal life.

16 'For God so loved the world that he gave his only Son, so that everyone who believes in him may not perish but may have eternal life.

17 'Indeed, God did not send the Son into the world to condemn the world, but in order that the world might be saved through him.'

It's not easy for us to reexamine our way of life if it might mandate change in our way of looking at things or setting of priorities. Because we have carved out for ourselves, in a competitive world, as best we can, a convenient place for ourselves—a convenient status for ourselves. Our lives are shaped by our family heritage, or by our gender, whether we are man or woman, or our class in society, whether we are upper class or middle class or lower class, or our race, our economic status, our geography, where we happen to live. And most of our lives are shaped by those factors and we don't often question the result.

In a constantly changing life that we live, we are competitive, we give and take, we modify our habits as little as possible to accommodate changing circumstances, and we try to be comfortable with our prejudices, with our achievements, with our goals, our purposes in life. But it's not easy to correlate the way we want to live with the teachings of Jesus Christ.

Jesus never advocated comfort or security or dominance or achievement through the competition of a superior position or power or influence or prestige or reputation. He always told us not to be satisfied with the way we feel or the way we are. He preached mostly against pride or self-satisfaction. He said constantly, "Search for a way to improve yourselves," and he shocked people.

But quite often we are reluctant to explore, through Christ, answers to questions that are perplexing to us. Who am I? Why was I created? What is the purpose of my life? What have I achieved? What are my priorities in comparison with those that Christ himself set for me? We don't want to ask questions like that because it might shake up the sinecure, or the comfort level, or the security or self-satisfaction of our lives, but we are urged through Christ's actions and words, and through theologians that came after him, to explore new ideas.

The Courage to Question

One of my favorite authors is Stephen Jay Gould. How many of you know who Stephen Jay Gould is? Gould is a paleontologist who teaches at Harvard University. He writes an article every month in *Natural History* magazine, and then every three or four years he takes those columns and puts them together in a book. Stephen Jay Gould explores in a very intriguing way...how scientific discoveries interrelate with our concept of the world as it relies, say, on the Bible, or on our own circle of knowledge.

I write back and forth with Gould because sometimes I disagree with what he puts in his books. I thought my letters were private, but I noticed in one of his books he quotes me—quotes my letters—and then goes on to prove how mistaken I am in his book. He didn't give me a chance to debate with him. [*Congregation laughs*] But he's a wonderful person and he's becoming increasingly well known.

How many of you know who Carl Sagan is? A lot more. He's a very famous astronomer who has credentials on his own as an astronomer, but he's more famous by having PBS series and writing books, giving lectures, as well. But those are the kinds of scientists who are exploring ways for us to examine what are our beliefs as compared with what we actually observe, and it shakes up sometimes our preconceived ideas.

For instance, as Bishop Ussher said, the earth was created at 12 noon, October the 25th, in 4004 B.C. That's a presumption that was assumed by Christians for many, many years, that the earth could not have existed prior to that. And that at noontime on October the 25th, 4004 B.C., God created the heaven and the earth and the people and so forth. And Bishop Ussher wrote a thousand-page volume to explain why he arrived at that precise figure, and it was adopted by the pope and by many others. In fact, most of the King James Version Bibles early on had the Creation—you remember Genesis 1, it had up at the top "4004 B.C." Then when Moses lived it had "1500 B.C.," or whatever it was.

Anyway, we are urged through these scientists to explore ways to find the truth. Many people feel that it's sacrilegious to question what the pope said in 1535 A.D. about the earth being created in 4004 B.C., but Christ urges us to ask questions about anything that is disturbing to us and our reluctance to question is a restrictive and counterproductive decision.

Why do you think that's true, anybody? Why is it wrong not to question or not to explore any doubts that are in our minds? Do you think I'm wrong?

We stay the same.

If we don't question, we stay the same. It indicates that we are satisfied with the way things are...

We become lazy.

We don't want to let our mind be active, and we don't want to strain our mind. Not only are we lazy and don't want to carry things or clean up the house or sweep the house, and so forth, but we don't want to stretch our mind.

We fear what that change will bring.

We are afraid what a changing concept might bring to us. We'll have to modify our comfort level, or endanger it, if we open up our minds, our hearts, to new concepts, new ideas.

If we are afraid to change and refuse to change, we become dangerous to others because we're so sure we're right we don't want to look at other ways and we're dangerous to other people.

True believers are dangerous, because a true believer, which might include some of us, says, "My way of thinking is absolutely right. I have no doubt about it, so everybody that disagrees with me must be wrong, must be inferior."

We sometimes lack courage, too.

We lack courage. We don't want to test our own ideas in a debate with facts or with a source of information. It might be embarrassing to us to find out we've been mistaken. We don't want to test ourselves.... We put a lid on our lives, and we build a cage around ourselves—a very small cage. A cage of knowledge of God's world. And also a cage that prevents our expanding our hearts with increased opportunities for what? Love, concern, knowledge about other people.

And you see, both of these concepts are contrary to the teachings and actions of Christ. Christ constantly expanded his heart to encompass people who were unlovable, who were despised, who were different... Christ reached out to them.

Nicodemus and Jesus

Jesus had a lot of conversations with people who were identified by name. Who knows what the most extensive conversation Christ had in the Bible with anyone? Anybody have any idea?

It's today's lesson. [*Congregation laughs*]

Yes, it's today's lesson.

Nicodemus.

Nicodemus! The most extensive conversation Christ had with anyone who was named was Nicodemus. Who was Nicodemus? Tell me one thing about him.

He was a ruler of the Jews.

He was a very learned man.

He was a teacher of Israel, the Bible says.

He was a member of the Sanhedrin.

A member of the Sanhedrin, which was the ruling body under the Romans. The Sanhedrin was given the authority and the responsibility of caring for the Jewish law and the administration of law, justice, keeping order among the Jews themselves. What was his religious faith or sect?

He was a Pharisee.

I was surprised to know that most Pharisees were laymen; they were not full-time preachers. They worked for a living, and they occupied positions of authority, but they worshipped in a very devout fashion. They honored meticulously the laws of Moses.... The Pharisees studied the entire book of what we know as the Old Testament. Whereas the Sadducees only studied the first five books in the Bible. So, the Pharisees were a dominant group of leaders in Israel....

What did Nicodemus do later, after this episode?

He sold everything he had.

No, he didn't sell everything he had.

He came and claimed the body [of Jesus].

Nicodemus provided the spices for Jesus' burial. And one other thing he did—what happened when Jesus was brought before the Sanhedrin for his trial? Nicodemus spoke up for him and the other Sanhedrin members ridiculed Nicodemus by saying, "Are you from Galilee, too?"

Galilee was looked upon as an ignorant place, not nearly so sophisticated in theology and law as were the people who lived in Jerusalem. So, Nicodemus, while he faded out after the fifteenth verse, I think it is, later Nicodemus indicated that he had derived some benefit from this conversation by defending Christ at his trial and providing, the Bible says, about one hundred pounds of spices for Jesus' burial itself.

Let's start with the first three verses of John 3.

[1] Now there was a Pharisee named Nicodemus, a leader of the
Jews. [2] He came to Jesus by night and said to him, 'Rabbi,'

which is an address of honor,

'we know that you are a teacher who has come from God; for no one can do these signs that you do apart from the presence of God.'

Why do you think Nicodemus came to Jesus in the first place?

Curiosity.

He was a student. He was eager to learn. He was willing to ask questions, which we admitted a few minutes ago that we're sometimes reluctant to do so.

He knew what the law of Moses was. He was very familiar with the Scriptures. And to question anything that might conflict with the Scriptures was a courageous act. So, in a way, he was admirable in his willingness to stretch his mind, to use a phrase we used a few minutes ago.

Why do you think he came at night?

Secret.

He didn't want to be seen with Jesus. Just recently before this, in John, Jesus had created a great disturbance in the temple, which was a sacrilegious act punishable by death, by the way. So, for a leader of, you might say, the Supreme Court and the attorney general all rolled in one, to visit someone who was guilty of a crime that could be punishable by death was a cause for caution. He didn't want to be seen.

Another reason he might have been a very busy man. He had to earn his own living, and it was convenient for him to come after working hours. I doubt that that's a fact.

Do you think he took it on as a challenge?

I think he took it on as a challenge, yes. I think he had an inquisitive mind, maybe even a scientific mind. He wanted to know, what is it? Because he knew, obviously, from these first two verses, that Christ had performed miracles. He knew that Christ had given signs that he was indeed relating directly to God.... But I thoroughly think that, most likely, he didn't want to be seen with this strange person.

3 Jesus answered him, 'Very truly, I tell you, no one can see the kingdom of God without being born from above.'

Or again, or anew. I like born again, or born anew. The most precise interpretation among modern scholars is "born from above," but the word can also mean "anew." I don't want to get into semantics, I'm not qualified to do that. But obviously, as you'll see from Nicodemus's response, he thought it meant to be born one more time. To be born again. Or to be born anew....

How did Nicodemus think a person could see the kingdom of God? What was the belief of the Pharisees?

Keeping the law.

And what they thought was perfection in complying with the hundreds of laws that were written down in Deuteronomy and Leviticus, and so forth. Exactly how far you could walk on a Sabbath day. Exactly what you could do to cleanse yourself. Exactly how much you had to give in tithing. Exactly how you performed a religious service. So, they very carefully delineated all these little rules, and if you could keep all the little rules, then you were looked upon as someone qualified to be in the kingdom of God.

The kingdom of God is the environment within which a person lives and dwells if they accept the domination of or the principles put forward by God. And Jesus said, "Nobody can come into the kingdom of God without being born anew or being born from above."

Inconvenient Truths

Let's read on now—the fourth through the ninth verse.

4 Nicodemus said to him, 'How can anyone be born after having grown old? Can one enter a second time into the mother's womb and be born?'

You can see that Nicodemus was restricted in his comprehension by his previous life experiences. When you say, "born again" or "born anew," "born" for Nicodemus only meant coming out of your mother's womb. So, in many ways, this morning, we should put ourselves in the position of Nicodemus.

We don't comprehend a lot of the truths about life because we have a limitation on what words we want to accept. We've got our own definition that has been carved out and frozen in our consciousness, because it's convenient for us and we don't want to change. We know what truth is, we know what justice is, we know what democracy is, we know what human rights means, we know what peace means, we know what power means, and we don't want to take any chances on revising our definition. It may not be so convenient.

I used to argue vociferously with the Soviet leaders, when I was in the White House, about human rights. I would say, "You don't honor human rights," because most Americans have a very convenient definition of human rights. Freedom of speech—we have freedom of speech, right? Freedom of religion, we have freedom of religion. Freedom of worship, freedom of the press, freedom to own weapons—those are our freedoms. They're in the Bill of Rights. But in most countries on earth, "human rights" means a place to live or medical care or a job.

It's very disturbing to us, it was, to me, when I was president, to hear [Andrei] Gromyko, the foreign minister of the Soviet Union, say, "Everybody in the Soviet Union has a place to sleep, has a home. Everybody in the Soviet Union has medical care. Everybody in the Soviet Union has a job." Obviously, they were assigned a job, they had to live where they were told. But it was not easy for me to accept any new definition of human rights.

I had a very convenient definition of human rights. It didn't cause me any pain or problems, it didn't even put any real responsibilities on me as president, but when you start talking about a homeless person who doesn't have human rights, that's kind of disturbing. Walk down the streets in New York, day or night. Walk around our fellow citizens sleeping on the sidewalk. Do they have the human rights?

The problem is the definition of words is a very biased commitment that we have. So, we don't want to really think about new definitions, and this is the way with Nicodemus this morning in this lesson.

Water and Spirit

And then Christ's response to him in the fifth verse.

[5] 'Very truly, I tell you, no one can enter the kingdom of God without being born of water and Spirit.'

There's quite a lot of argument about the meaning of "water." It doesn't mean that you have to be baptized. "Water" probably means the birth from your mother.

How about "Spirit"? What does that mean?

The soul.

Yeah, your soul; the spirit of God. You have to be born of your mother. You also have to be born through the spirit of God. Christ is trying to explain to Nicodemus what it means to be born of the spirit of God. That's the point of this lesson this morning.

I have a program on my word processor called Bible GodSpeed and can punch in any combination of words, one word or ten words, and it gives you every verse in the Bible where those words appear...I punched in "God" and "Spirit" this morning, and it came up with 111 verses in which those two words apply. By far, most of them are in the Old Testament. So, the point is Nicodemus was familiar with the spirit of God, he knew about spirit, but this is a little bit of a different interpretation from what he had been accustomed to understanding.

To go on, and Jesus said:

[6] 'What is born of the flesh is flesh, and what is born of the Spirit is spirit. [7] Do not be astonished that I said to you, "You must be born again,"'

Or anew, or from above. Then, he goes on to explain this very interesting, little simple thing.

[8] 'The wind blows where it chooses, and you hear the sound of it.'

And I'll add here, you see the trees sway back and forth.

'But you do not know where it comes from or where it goes. So it is with everyone who is born of the Spirit.'

Jesus tried to give a very simple explanation. And by the way, I understand in both Greek and Hebrew, the word for "spirit" and "breath" and "wind" has the same derivation. It's something that you know is there, but you can't see it. You can feel the impact of it, but you can't see it, so Christ is trying to expand Nicodemus's mind to encompass the real meaning of the spirit of God.

And then Nicodemus in the ninth verse says to him:

9 'How can these things be?' 10 Jesus answered him, 'Are you a teacher of Israel, and yet you do not understand these things?

And then Jesus goes on in the eleventh verse:

11 Very truly, I tell you, we speak of what we know and testify to what we have seen; yet you do not receive our testimony.'

By "we," Jesus means he and his disciples. Jesus has been active in his ministry since he was baptized. He's been demonstrating the power of God. He's been calling people to repent. He's been showing his ability to perform what was considered to be miracles in the name of God. And he knows Nicodemus has observed him carefully because of what Nicodemus has already said. But Nicodemus still doesn't quite grasp what it means because he's still clinging to the way he has lived, to the way he has been taught, the way his life has been shaped by the characteristics of his environment, his family, his status in life, his wealth, his early studies....

12 'If I have told you about earthly things and you do not believe,
how can you believe if I tell you about heavenly things? 13 No one has

ascended into heaven except the one who descended from heaven, the Son of Man.

That's Christ himself.

[14] And just as Moses lifted up the serpent in the wilderness, so must the Son of Man be lifted up, [15] that whoever believes in him may have eternal life.'

How do you draw a parallel between Moses holding up the serpent—you remember, as long as he held it up his people were saved—and how do you equate that with Christ? How was Christ later lifted up?

On the cross.

He was lifted up to what? Death, human death. But through that sacrifice of himself to save us, Christ saved the people for whom he cared. And Jesus is telling Nicodemus, and I can tell in an incomprehensible way—there was no way that Nicodemus could understand what Jesus was talking about, not being able to anticipate the cross or the resurrection—but these words are not designed only for Nicodemus. But for whom?

For me.

For me and for you...

Exploring Our Questions

Let's review...how this lesson does apply to us because it would be fruitless for you to come here and fruitless for me to try to teach if we just considered Nicodemus or things that happened two thousand years ago. What's the point of the lesson so far?

Keep your mind open and be willing to change.

And if you have a question in your mind, do what? Explore it! You're not going to change God by asking a question.

If you live through life with a question in your mind that troubles you about the status of God, or the nature of God, or what Christ meant, or what your life should be, and never ask the question, and never explore and find the answer, you're circumscribing your life. You're setting a limit on what you can be as a human being, and you're submitting yourself in a cage of existence. Without even thinking about it, you're building a wall around yourself as far as the number of people you will know and understand, and with whom you will relate, and with whom you will love. You're denying yourself knowledge about other people and about God's world—about science and history and astronomy and paleontology and the earth's truths.

I studied astronomy in college. I did my graduate work in nuclear physics. I'm intrigued with scientific discoveries. I really love to read about them even when I can't quite understand them. And when scientists explain the Big Bang Theory, that twelve billion years ago, or whatever it was, the universe was created in an instantaneous explosion, to me this does not conflict with the Bible. To me, this proves that there has to be a Superior Being who created it.

Where did the substance come from that now comprises a hundred billion galaxies, each one having a hundred billion stars, almost all of them as big as our own sun? The enormity of it, the complexity of it is just mind-boggling. How could this have occurred without a Creator?

The fact that we evolved—not trying to create dissension here because some of you may be very strict in your interpretation that God created everything in six days, I don't think so, but you can think so if you'd like—but I don't see that evolution conflicts with the teaching that God created us. He chose his own way of having us evolve.

And the fact that women were not created, perhaps, by a rib from Adam doesn't cause me any concern. If you want to believe that, fine. But I don't find an inconsistency with scientific discoveries and theories and the fact that God Almighty is even more awe-inspiring and worthy of worship and exploration than I thought when I was a child.

But here there is freedom for us to think and question and ask and learn and stretch our lives.

Salvation Is a Relationship

Now we come down to the essence of it, where Nicodemus, in a way, fades out of the picture and we come down to Jesus giving a summary, in one verse of the entire New Testament—of the entire Bible. And we all know this verse: "For God loved the world so much that," what?

That he gave his only begotten Son.

His only son, who was there at the Creation, John says. "In the beginning was the Word, and the Word was with God, and the Word was God." The Word is Christ. Christ was there when the universe was created, and now, in the form of a child or man, God himself came on earth to condemn the world? To do what?

"For God so loved the world that he gave his only begotten Son, that whosoever believeth should," what?

Should not perish.

Should not perish but have everlasting life.

We have to remember, kind of in a parenthetical way, that Christ was talking to Nicodemus, perhaps who was the only person there, but his words resonate or echo down through the ages and forever, after we're gone, throughout the whole world. And the conflict between this explanation and what Nicodemus thought couldn't be more profound. Nicodemus was dealing in little, tiny details, wasn't he? Semantics.

[The Pharisees] would argue for weeks, for centuries as a matter of fact, about what a particular little word in Deuteronomy meant. People are getting killed in Israel right now on the definition of a Jew. I've been reading, with some concern, the last two or three weeks, that devout Jews, who observe the Sabbath, and who observe all the laws, and all the jots and tittles of the law in Deuteronomy and Leviticus, and so forth, who wear skullcaps all the time and have sideburns, whose mothers and fathers were Jews, are now being expelled from Israel, why? Because they believe that Jesus Christ is the Messiah. The Jews await the Messiah. But the point is, when they meet all the other standards that the Jewish laws have set down, the Israeli laws, for the definition of a Jew—to meet all those standards but believe that the Messiah has already come, they're being expelled from Israel. They're now appealing to the Israeli high court. My guess is that they're going to be expelled.

So, you see, that what Jesus is telling us here is that all those little minutiae or definitions or self-contrived explanations of the Word of God for salvation, for realization of the kingdom of God, are relatively insignificant.

For God so loved the world that he gave his only begotten Son, so whosoever should believe in him should not perish but have everlasting life.

And Christ is saying that God doesn't condemn us as sinners and then let us slowly but laboriously work our way up to acceptance by God through observing the detailed laws of Moses. That's what the Pharisees believed—everybody's condemned; the only way you can be saved is by observing all these laws and only then will God love you. Jesus reversed that a hundred percent.

He said God loves us so much to start with, free of charge—through God's grace we are blessed with God's love—that he sent Christ, his only son, to explain to us what is God, what is truth, what is justice, what is compassion, what is service, what is humility, what is love. And through that knowledge we receive the blessings of God that is salvation.

Not what we do, not how many houses we build, not how many…try to find a new life, that's not what brings us into a proper relationship with God—it's through our faith in Christ, and the application in our lives of what Christ demonstrated or taught. And that is search, search, search in our own minds for a better life. Correct, correct, correct our own failings. Stretch our minds, stretch our hearts, ask questions without fear of the answers. Search for the truth.

One of my favorite theologians, Paul Tillich, said that...religion is the search for the truth about ourselves, our relationship with God and our fellow human beings. And Tillich goes on to say, when we stop searching, when we think we know all the answers and we think we've got it made, we lose our religion. That may be an extreme theological statement, I'm not trying to vouch for it, but it's quite applicable to our lesson this morning.

We should constantly strive to live in continence with the teachings and the words of Christ. And encompass in our hearts, not a restricted number of people to be loved, but an expanding number of people to be loved. To demonstrate the characteristics of our Savior, whom we profess to follow.

It's not a comfortable change. It takes a lot of personal courage to take a chance on changing our convenient way of living. It causes us to share what we've got instead of keeping it for ourselves. It causes us to look beyond our own family, to a broader family to be understood and cherished and served and loved. It's not an easy thing. So, we are in the same boat as Nicodemus, who was disturbed but who had the courage to come, at least, and ask.

The World of Christ

The seventeenth verse is the end of our lesson for today.

Indeed, Jesus says "God did not send the Son into the world to condemn the world, but in order that the world might be saved through him."

You see how clear that is. For all of us who believe, we have our world. The world of Jimmy Carter. The world of John Jones. The world of Mary Smith. There is an alternative world—the world of Christ. Filled with the things that we cherish. Filled with peace and truth and justice and harmony. That wipes away the problems of our daily existence where we are worried about competing with others, and being successful, and being rich, and having a lot of things we don't have, and being obsessed with a world that we have defined since birth because of the environment within which you live. Christ says, “Look at another world. A world of compassion, understanding, harmony, unselfishness.”

I think it’s a good lesson. It’s one that is disturbing to us.

Is it possible to combine the idealistic concepts of Jesus Christ with the real world in which we have to live? Is it possible? Can we be a human success if we apply Jesus’ standards of unselfishness and sharing? That’s part of the questions to which we should seek the answers.

And the answer that we know, theoretically, is that, yes, it is possible to be compatible, to combine a Christian life with a life in the real world. We might have to give up some things we don’t want to give up, but invariably, as we give them up, we get rewards that we couldn’t anticipate that are much greater than what we gave up. When we think we’re making a sacrifice, it turns out to be an enormous, new, unanticipated blessing.

That’s what Jesus teaches us. The blessing may not be in a bigger bank account, or a more beautiful home, or even a better reputation on the front page. It may be quiet things. That’s what we hope will come from our searching for answers that in the past we have not wanted to explore.

That’s the lesson that we get from the conversation between Jesus and, I think, an admirable figure, Nicodemus.

October 9, 1994

Knowing and Loving

Maranatha Baptist Church
Plains, Georgia

Lesson Scripture

1 John 4:1–21 (NRSV)

1 Beloved, do not believe every spirit, but test the spirits to see whether they are from God; for many false prophets have gone out into the world. 2 By this you know the Spirit of God: every spirit that confesses that Jesus Christ has come in the flesh is from God, 3 and every spirit that does not confess Jesus is not from God. And this is the spirit of the antichrist, of which you have heard that it is coming; and now it is already in the world. 4 Little children, you are from God, and have conquered them; for the one who is in you is greater than the one who is in the world. 5 They are from the world; therefore what they say is from the world, and the world listens to them. 6 We are from God. Whoever knows God listens to us, and whoever is not from God does not listen to us. From this we know the spirit of truth and the spirit of error.

7 Beloved, let us love one another, because love is from God; everyone who loves is born of God and knows God. 8 Whoever does not love does not know God, for God is love. 9 God's love was revealed among us in this way: God sent his only Son into the world so that we might live through him. 10 In this is love, not that we loved God but that he loved us and sent his Son to be the atoning sacrifice for our sins. 11 Beloved, since God loved us so much, we also ought to love one another. 12 No one has ever seen God; if we love one another, God lives in us, and his love is perfected in us.

13 By this we know that we abide in him and he in us, because he has given us of his Spirit. 14 And we have seen and do testify that the Father has sent his Son as the Savior of the world. 15 God abides in those who confess that Jesus is the Son of God, and they abide in God. 16 So we have known and believe the love that God has for us.

God is love, and those who abide in love abide in God, and God abides in them. 17 Love has been perfected among us in this: that we may have boldness on the day of judgement, because as he is, so are we in this world. 18 There is no fear in love, but perfect love casts out fear;

for fear has to do with punishment, and whoever fears has not reached perfection in love. [19] We love because he first loved us. [20] Those who say, 'I love God', and hate their brothers or sisters, are liars; for those who do not love a brother or sister whom they have seen, cannot love God whom they have not seen. [21] The commandment we have from him is this: those who love God must love their brothers and sisters also.

This morning we're going to be studying what I think is a very intriguing lesson called "Knowing and Loving." It discusses the interrelationship between those two factors in our lives. And we're going to use the letter of 1 John as an example of the biblical application.

What is the disparity or incompatibility between knowing and loving? Or the relationship—we won't even say a negative thing. Do you feel like knowing more about somebody causes you to love or not love that person?

I think it works both ways.

It can cut both ways. When we look at a generic group, we might think that they are, basically, good people, primarily because they are like us. For instance, if we look at a nation that looks almost exactly like us, we'd say, "Well, they are probably pretty good folks." If we look at people who have a little bit different appearance, or different styles or customs, we're probably inclined to say they are not quite as good as us, or "I don't think I know them individually, and if I did, I wouldn't like them very much."

But the point to understand this morning is, what is the common ground on which we can build an almost certain increase in our affection for someone or some organization or some group as we get to know them? And that's what John was referring to in this epistle, or this letter that he wrote to a church. There has to be some common basis on which to build an understanding relationship, an improved relationship, as we get to know someone.

I was thinking about three or four examples on an international scale. [Israeli Prime Minister Menachem] Begin, [Egyptian President Anwar] Sadat, [Palestinian Authority President Yasser] Arafat, [Somalia's] General Aidid, [North Korean leader] Kim Il-Sung, [Haitian military ruler] General Cedras, [Cuban President] Fidel Castro, [Iraqi President] Saddam Hussein. What do you think might be common to those names?

[*Congregation laughs*] Come on, Come on. Don't be hesitant.

They're all dictators.

Leaders.

Infamous.

Family persons.

They are not Anglo-Saxon names.

They're all men.

They're not Democrat. [*Congregation laughs*]

You can see, though, that as you discuss people who've been in the news, some favorably, perhaps, most unfavorable—I don't believe that most people here would look upon both Begin and Sadat as unfavorable. Although, there was a time when almost all Arabs, from the point of view of American citizens, the vast majority of us, were looked upon as terrorists, or incompatible with us, or not understood, and I think it was Anwar Sadat who turned the American public around almost overnight. As we got to know him, we realized that there were two sides to an issue. And as we've gotten to know Arafat lately, most of the opinions about him have changed. It's almost inconceivable that thirteen months ago, Arafat was on the South Lawn of the White House shaking hands with Bill Clinton, shaking hands with Yitzhak Rabin, and now is looked upon as someone in whom we invest hopes for peace in the Middle East.

So, as we've gotten to know these people and understand their backgrounds, their philosophies, their points of view, we have begun to think more of them. I am not saying that we have yet reached a point of agape or Christian love in our attitude towards them.

Let's go a little bit further. How about some of the others in that group. How about General Cedras?

Distrust.

Distrust? Okay.

His wife called me yesterday morning to tell me that he had just told General Shelton that he was going to step down—I think tomorrow—as he promised me he would do two or three Sundays ago. As he promised, he's doing it.

I met with him, with his wife, with his three kids in their home, and I saw a different person from what I had seen through the American news media, or through the speech that President Clinton gave Thursday night, two or three weeks ago.

When I departed from him Sunday morning about two-thirty, I told him that I would like to meet his family. He said, "I would, too. I haven't been home in several days." [*Congregation laughs*] He said, "My little ten-year-old son had a birthday yesterday. I haven't even been able to wish him a happy birthday." So, the next morning, he invited us to come by and meet his family—a seventeen-year-old son, I think a thirteen-year-old daughter, and the little boy was ten years old. But in their front living room, in a home environment, they became not just a scorned and despised and hated person from the verbiage that we hear on TV and in the newspapers, but also human beings—a family.

I have only met Fidel Castro once. He and I both happened to attend the inauguration of Carlos Andrés Pérez when Pérez became president, the second time, of Venezuela, and I talked to Fidel about thirty minutes. But he has my phone number; he calls me on occasion to converse with me. I don't know enough about him to say what my opinion of him is, but I do have a cautionary hang-up in my mind not to believe everything I hear coming from, say, the more conservative members of the Cuban American community in Miami. Because there are two sides to most issues.

And how about Saddam Hussein? I'm stretching the point here, I know. [*Congregation laughs*] What do you think?

Terrible.

Untrustworthy.

Well, we helped him at one time.

Yeah, he was in the same boat with us at one time. When President Reagan came into office, we established diplomatic relations with Iraq. We gave them a lot of free food, we gave them a lot of loans, we sold them a lot of weapons, and then all of a sudden, he became an ogre again.

The same thing happened with President Assad in Damascus, but the other way around—he used to be an ogre and, all of a sudden, he became our buddy. Same thing with Noriega, who was in the same boat with President Reagan's administration helping the Contras, then, when he quit helping the Contras, he became a criminal.

You can see, though, that there are changing opinions whether you agree with anything I've said or not, you can see they are changing opinions of people depending on our own perspective and how they relate to us.

I've written a poem that'll be published in December. I hope all of you will buy my book of poetry when it comes out. [*Congregation laughs*] It's called *Always a Reckoning*. And this poem is "With Words We Learn to Hate."

"With Words We Learn to Hate"
We take lives in times of peace
for crimes we won't forgive
claiming some have forfeited
the right to live.
We justify our nation's wars
each time with words to prove we kill
in a moral cause.
We've cursed the names of those we fought—
the "Japs" instead of Japanese,
German Nazis or the "Huns,"

and "Wops"—when they were enemies.
Later, they became our friends,
but habits live in memories.
So now, when others disagree
we hate again, and with our might
war by war, name by dirty name,
prove we're right.

How many of you remember the Japanese during the Second World War? Did we call them Japanese? No, we called them all kinds of ugly things. "Jap" was the nicest thing we said about them.

How about the Italians during the war, when we were fighting against Mussolini?

Wops.

But after the war was over, we got to know them, got to understand them, visiting back-and-forth, and, all of a sudden, they are human beings like us. But we have an ability to depersonalize those whom we do not understand or with whom we have a difference.

I hope that in the near future there will be a good faith effort made to bring Iraq into compliance with the United Nations resolutions so that we can lift the embargo from Iraq.

We [The Carter Cener] have a very strong connection with the Centers for Disease Control and the World Health Organization. Before the war started, Iraq had an infant mortality rate of thirty-two [per thousand babies]. It's now gone up to 135 out of every thousand babies born in Iraq, under the economic restraints, 135 babies die. So, set Saddam Hussein aside for a moment. Quite often, when we try to punish a leader like Noriega, like Castro, like Cedras, like Saddam Hussein, we wind up punishing the very people under them who are already suffering from a dictatorship.

The point I want to make here is that in our international scope of things, how we know someone has a direct interconnection with how we feel about that person. Knowledge and love are closely related.

Would you agree with that? I'm not trying to draw any conclusions at this time. We're going to shift in just a minute to the biblical text that's the basis for our lesson today.

But in our our own personal attitudes, we also have this burden to bear because there are, undoubtedly, people in your life against whom you have a grievance, or at least whom you look upon in an unfriendly fashion, or about whom you make derogatory remarks—maybe just to your own spouse in your own home. It might even border on direct animosity or hatred, because of something that happened in the past between you and that person, or something that person did, and that can be a canker within a person, like a cancer, that gnaws away at the essence of our Christianity.

We know in Revelations 3:20, "Behold I stand at the door and knock. If anyone will open the door, I will come in and sup with them." The Holy Spirit would like to be in us, but with a small core of hatred burning inside us that flames up every time we hear that person's name, or see that person's picture, or see that person in person, that tends to alienate us from Christ, from the Holy Spirit, from a good relationship with God. This is what John is going to be talking about this morning.

The Transcendence of Common Belief

I happen to be a Southern Baptist, and I've been grieved the last few years at the division that's taken place in my own denomination. It's been a terrible thing for us.

And for a hundred years or more, 150 years almost, we got along fine in the Southern Baptist Convention. We had our differences; we'd go to the convention—I used to be invited even. No more—they don't invite me anymore. [*Congregation laughs*] But I used to be invited to the Southern Baptist Convention as a delegate, twice as a speaker, and we would debate and argue and vote, and however the vote came out, that was what the Southern Baptist Convention did or recommended.

Then we'd come back home to our home church and have a conference—that's the way Baptists do—and it was a great pleasure to say, "We agree or disagree with what the Southern Baptist Convention said," and we took a lot of pleasure in rejecting anything that the Southern Baptist Convention voted that the local congregation didn't like. This is the way the Baptists have always done.

But about...ten, fifteen years ago, it wasn't that way anymore. We've always believed in the autonomy of the local church, and even the local believer. And we had differences inherently on philosophy or theology or interpretation of certain Scriptures in the Bible, or on some controversial social issues of the day.... But there was, above that or below that, as a roof or a foundation, an environment within which we could live together.

Why? How could we live together in an environment when we are no longer able to do so, I hate to say? What was it that existed then, that doesn't exist now? Even non-Baptists can speak up. [*Congregation laughs*] What do you think?

And it applies to a lot of your own denominations. Episcopalians, Presbyterians, Methodists also are finding it more and more difficult to have a united front. What is it that is required?

Tolerance.

Love.

Education

Faith.

Trust.

I think a sense that we are all members of the Body of Christ.

All right. We're all members of the body of Christ. A sense that we are brothers and sisters.

We know that within a family environment...within a home like I grew up out in Archery, Georgia, two and a half miles from here, my sisters and I—Billy didn't come along until I was thirteen, I didn't know him as a young boy—we would have our differences, but there was a commonality among us that presented a united front to the outside—to others who might challenge our own family entity. And I don't mean that in an antagonistic way. But there had to be an ability to communicate with each other with mutual respect. With a willingness to accommodate different points of view and without any ability or desire for one group to dominate the other. And that means that the majority can't dominate the minority.

That's one of the problems in Haiti. Every time someone won an election, the ones who lost the election had to go in hiding because they were very likely to suffer, even to give their lives or to lose their property and so forth. It was a winner-takes-all proposition. There has to be an ability to give and take and a non-domination of the others. And the main thing is to recognize that above us all is a basic concept so great, and so important, that our human differences fade into insignificance. Do you see what I mean?

We obviously have differences in opinion on homosexuals in the military, or the death penalty, or abortion, or whatever. You could go down a list of things and I know within this group we would have sharp differences of opinion. But here we are, all in the same auditorium. We come here from very different points of view because of our faith in Jesus Christ. And that faith transcends whether we are immersed in baptism or sprinkled in baptism, whether we have a hierarchical church with pastors and a bishop, and maybe even the pope—some of you are Catholic. We transcend that as we deal together as Christians, as common believers.

So, in the relationship even with unsavory leaders, there has to be a sense of understanding, of searching for a common roof under which we can work. And I would say one of those is a desire for peace, a desire for economic progress, a desire to see citizens of a country have jobs and decent housing and medical care and food to eat. I'm talking about the world economic stage now and non-domination by one country over another.

These are the kind of things that relate to us in a secular, nonreligious way. Although religion can be a very important factor in how we address these secular issues—our own religious faith.

A Shift in Perspective and Priority

Let's turn to 1 John now the fourth chapter. Let me remind you first that the book was written the last part of the first century, probably. Maybe the early part of the second century. And what did this mean about the original disciples?

Paul [and] Peter had already passed away. This was a second generation, you might say, of leaders in the Christian church. We don't know the exact identity of the author of 1 John. He's sometimes called "John, the Elder."

But here, the early Christian church had reached a point of...change. What do you think had changed about it? What was one of the characteristics of the early Christian church in the time of Peter and Paul?

They welcomed everybody into the church.

Welcomed everybody in. There were some squabbles about whether you had to be circumcised or not, those kinds of things, but there was an overriding memory, history, experience with Jesus Christ himself.

Paul met Christ on the road to Damascus. Peter walked side by side with Paul in the dusty roads of the Holy Land. And they would say, "This is the way Jesus did it. This is what he told us. His whole life was permeated with love for us. He forgave us when we made a mistake."

We know how terrible were the mistakes that Peter made. We know how terrible were the mistakes that Paul made. But they knew about God's forgiveness and God's love from a very personal relationship, and this was an overarching roof under which the early church started. Then later, there were some more things injected—human interpretations of what Peter said, human interpretations of what Paul wrote—and they became foundations for a struggle for power and influence in the church.

Sixty percent said Peter meant so-and-so, 30 percent said the opposite, and 10 percent had no opinion. [*Congregation laughs*] So, the 60 percent took over.

And what happened in John's church? The 30 percent split! That's probably the foundation of the Baptist Church. [*Congregation laughs*] We split, form new churches, and both churches grow quite often. That's the way the Baptists have gotten to be so numerous, maybe too numerous to suit some people. But anyway, that's what happened in John's church.

John's church had just split because of a difference in theology. They had let the overarching concepts of love and forgiveness be brought down on an equal basis, or even a subservient basis, with interpretations of exactly what was written, or said, or remembered about past history. Does that sound familiar? It is familiar, because the same thing happens now. Perhaps it's even more vivid in the time of the author of 1 John.

Let's see what he has to say here. This is a very interesting letter. John's not writing to the folks that stayed in the church, he's writing to the people that left.

Love—God's Guiding Principle

First John 4. We'll start with the seventh verse.

Look at the first word in the New Revised Standard Version. "Beloved." This is the way he starts his letter. Don't you think that's interesting already? You don't look very interested. [*Congregation laughs*]

He starts out writing these split-off people who have turned against him because of some difference. We don't know what the difference was. And he's calling them "beloved."

Beloved has an implication of reciprocity. It means a sharing of love. And so that's the way he starts the seventh verse.

[7] Beloved, let us love one another, because love is from God; everyone who loves is born of God and knows God.

John is already connecting love and knowing, but as he addresses the people with whom there's very little love left, because of a secular difference in the church, he immediately refers back to what? Human love?

God's love.

God's love. And that's what we're going to talk about the rest of our lesson this morning, is God's love and how God's relationship with us individually can be translated into our relationship with others—even Saddam Hussein, even General Cedras, even Yasser Arafat. It's going to be difficult. It wasn't easy for John.

[2] By this you know the Spirit of God: every spirit that confesses that Jesus Christ has come in the flesh is from God, [3] and every spirit that does not confess Jesus is not from God. And this is the spirit of the antichrist, of which you have heard that it is coming; and now it is already in the world.

I'll read on down to the seventh.

[4] Little children, you are from God, and have conquered them; for the one who is in you is greater than the one who is in the world.

God's greater than the antichrist.

[5] They are from the world; therefore what they say is from the world, and the world listens to them. [6] We are from God. Whoever

knows God listens to us, and whoever is not from God does not listen to us. From this we know the spirit of truth and the spirit of error.

John is, in fact, saying that we are so diverse—so set in our ways, so heavily affected by our culture and our family influence and our own environment and our profession and our commitment, our obligation, our fears, our dreams—from one another, that it's very difficult to understand another person. And the difference is greater in our understanding, or our ability to understand, depending on how different those cultures and race and history and songs and environment are.

It's very difficult for us to accommodate one another with these inherent, unique differences that exist between us. It may be self-evident what John is telling us, but he's reminding people who didn't get along with the remaining members of the church. And it's a very good lesson for us to look upon.

We tend to think that we Americans are superior to others in the world. And I would agree with anyone that says that we have the best nation in the world—with freedom, democracy, respect for human rights. With our fallibilities, with our faults, we're still the best, I think—I feel that way—but that doesn't make us, in God's sight, better than others.

We are not better than Ugandans or Sri Lankans or Chinese or Haitians or Ethiopians. We White people are not better than Black neighbors, and we Baptists are not better than Methodists, or vice versa. In God's sight we are the same. Paul made this very plain when he said, "There is no Jew or Greek. There is no male or female. All of us are the same in Christ Jesus."

That's not an easy thing for us to accept because we have a natural human inclination to feel superior, to feel that I am right and anyone who disagrees with me is wrong. That's a natural human trait—I have it myself, all of us do. And there's nothing wrong with that, in my opinion, unless it's carried to extremes. The extreme state of that is when we elevate that feeling of superiority above God's teachings. A realization of God's forgiveness. A realization of God's love.

And that is what John is telling these people who split off from the church, who might be filled with animosity, certainly alienation. "Beloved," he says, "let's remember God's forgiveness and God's love." He also says, by the way, that love and knowledge of one another grow together, and we must be guided by God's love and forgiveness for us....

[8] Whoever does not love does not know God, for God is love. [9]
God's love was revealed among us in this way: God sent his only Son into the world so that we might live through him.

He's reminding us of Christ's presence and Christ's transcendent importance.

[10] In this is love, not that we loved God but that he loved us and sent his Son to be the atoning sacrifice for our sins.

This is a repetition, in a beautiful way, of John 3:16.

[11] Beloved, since God loved us so much, we also ought to love one
another. [12] No one has ever seen God; if we love one another, God lives in us, and his love is perfected in us.

[13] By this we know that we abide in him and he in us.

What is there about the word abide?

Trust.

Constant.

Yeah, permanence. There's an element of permanence in the word "abide."... It means something continuing, something permanent.

[15] God abides in those who confess that Jesus is the Son of God,
and they abide (*Or rest or dwell or live*) in God. [16] So we have known
and believe the love that God has for us.

There are some people, many of whom I have known, that cannot believe that they are forgiven by God for their sins, or their crimes, or their inherent character defects. But we cannot really have spiritual or emotional health—listen to this—unless we believe that God forgives us. If we live with permanent guilt, feeling that we cannot be forgiven, then we are spiritually and emotionally crippled.

The extreme case of this is someone who goes into depression and commits suicide. *I just cannot believe that I'm forgiven. I am an unworthy person. I have committed terrible sins which cannot be forgiven. My life is no longer worth living.* That's an extreme case.

One of the crucial elements of the New Testament teaching of what Christ brought is that all of us can be totally—not partially, totally—forgiven through Christ who gave his life for us. And God demonstrated in the most vivid and memorable way, the most beautiful way, his forgiveness by letting Christ take the punishment for our sins—a perfect entity. God took my punishment on himself and through that act I am forgiven.

So, I can constantly renew my relationship with God. I can constantly be reconciled with God. I can break down the barriers between me and God knowing, absolutely, that God will forgive me. No matter how bad I may have acted.

Forgive Us, As We Forgive Others

There's another element to it, and it's not the subject of our lesson, and that is reconciliation.

If we have sinned and hurt someone else, God expects us to be reconciled with that person. When we say the Lord's prayer, God will forgive us as we forgive—provided we forgive. And forgiveness is a mutual thing.

I think it's a very beautiful thought—that we have to realize we can be forgiven before we can, in turn, forgive others. We have to realize that God loves us in spite of what? In spite of all our defects.

Does this make it easier for us to forgive someone else in spite of all their defects? That's exactly what John is reminding us of—he said it's not possible for one human being, with all of his fallibilities, just to go out and forgive somebody because you have different opinions and they may have hurt you, and so forth. But if we remember that God forgives us and loves us in spite of all our faults, that's the perfect pattern to use as we relate to other people.

That's what he's saying to these folks that have broken away from the church. He's not condemning them. He's forgiving them.

I'm sure they were shocked when they opened up John's letter and saw he was calling them "beloved." That's a word not often used in the Southern Baptist Convention between the fundamentalists on the one hand and the moderates on the other. But it's a word that needs to be used. In both ways, by the way.

But I don't know how long it's going to take us before we get back to the point of forgiving each other, communicating with each other, accepting differences among us, and going back to the transcendent elements of God's forgiveness, and love, and the brotherhood and sisterhood that binds us together in that common faith. That's not easy to do, because quite often those human animosities or differences become so important we can't even think about "insignificant" things like God's love or his forgiveness. We twist our lives around that way.

16 So we have known and believe the love that God has for us. God is love, and those who abide in love abide in God, and God abides in
them. 17 Love has been perfected among us in this: that we may have boldness on the day of judgement, because as he is, so are we in this
world. 18 There is no fear in love, but perfect love casts out fear; for fear has to do with punishment, and whoever fears has not reached perfection in love. 19 We love because he first loved us.

That's a verse we learned when we were four years old.

[20] Those who say, 'I love God', and hate their brothers and sisters, are liars; for those who do not love a brother or sister whom they have seen, cannot love God whom they have not seen. [21] The commandment we have from him is this: those who love God must love their brothers and sisters also.

Reinhold Niebuhr said that the ultimate goal of any society, any group, any church, any government has to be what? Justice. That's the maximum you can hope for.

When I was president, I never tried to go beyond justice in the high ambitions that I had in the White House, but for an individual there is a transcendent goal—what is that? Agape love. Forgiving love. Love without recompense. Love of someone who is not lovable.

And John is saying here, we have to grow into that perfect love. We can't just automatically think that we've got it just by saying, "I'm a Christian." It doesn't make us adopt forgiving love as a basic philosophy of our lives.

Do you follow what John is saying here? We have to work at it.

How do we work at it? By remembering, as a guide, as I relate to that person, I'm going to remember how God relates to me through Christ. And that's going to be the pattern for my decisions. That's going to be the common foundation on which that person and I can relate or the roof under which we can live together.

I think John has really put his finger on an important problem that human beings have to face: how do we combine getting to know someone with loving that person?... If I find them just like me, I'm going to love them. If I dig deeper into their attitudes or their philosophy or their religion or whatever and find them different from me, "I ain't going to love 'em."

John is saying, "Don't let that be the pattern of your life." You have to have a basis on which to relate, and that basis is the realization of the Holy Spirit in our hearts and the memory of God's forgiveness and love for us through Christ. And then, we can build knowledge of other people without seeing love for that person cast aside....

We Are Standing on Level Ground

I think it'd be a serious mistake to think that John is only talking about our fellow Baptists, or our fellow Methodists, or our fellow Christians. I think he's talking about any human being.

To repeat myself, Paul said, there is no Jew nor Greek. There is no master or slave. There is no male or female. We're all one in Christ. So, I think God loves all people everywhere. We're all the same at the foot of the cross, we're on level ground, so, we shouldn't think that we just forgive people who measure up to our own standards. Christ said several times, "Judge not that ye be not judged."

When I go to meet with Arafat, or with Kim Il-Sung, or with Cedras, or with Begin and Sadat when they were enemies—there had been four wars in twenty-five years—they were incompatible with each other. At Camp David, we were there thirteen days. I kept them in different cabins. They literally never even saw each other for ten days because they were so incompatible. But when we finally found common ground on which they could build a relationship, they had a respect for each other. They embraced each other, they exchanged kisses on the cheek, and they signed a treaty 15 years ago—not one word of which has been violated, but they had to find a common ground.

John is telling us, find a common ground. The basis might not be the peace agreement with the Sinai Desert demilitarized and with United Nations observers there to make sure the treaty terms are carried out, but the common ground, as far as John is saying, is our faith in Jesus Christ and our belief, through that faith, that God forgives and loves us. Therefore, we should forgive and love other human beings—not in a dormant way, but in an active, reaching out way.

A neighbor that you might think is a selfish community irritant—I'm sure all of you have neighbors like that, and some of your neighbors might think they've got a neighbor like that [*congregation laughs*]—but that may be just a lonely person who, in order to conceal his hurt, pretends that he doesn't want friends.

I don't have any friends. I don't want people to think it's my fault. I'll just make people think I don't want any friends.

Inside that person might be a burning need for a friendly word, or a knock on the door, or a piece of cake that you just baked, or an invitation to go to a movie or baseball game, or just to stop by in the yard, if you see him out mowing his lawn, or a discussion about some common interest, maybe puppy dogs or pets or something. But there's little, tiny things we can do to practice what Christ taught us, and that's what John is telling us to do.

So, within our own marriage, within our own family, within our own church, within our own country and international affairs, there are some common grounds on which to build understanding, knowledge, forgiveness, even love, recognizing that we'll never have total compatibility in beliefs or philosophy or religion or government organizations or even interpretation of the Bible. We'll never have that. That's inherently out of our hands, as John has said. But just accept it. And then find a way to stop being hypocrites when we say "I am a Christian" and begin to demonstrate that I am a Christian.

I think it's a very good and provocative and interesting lesson.

January 7, 1996

God's Covenant People

Maranatha Baptist Church
Plains, Georgia

Lesson Scripture

Isaiah 42:1–9 (NRSV)

1 Here is my servant, whom I uphold,
my chosen, in whom my soul delights;
I have put my spirit upon him;
he will bring forth justice to the nations.
2 He will not cry or lift up his voice,
or make it heard in the street;
3 a bruised reed he will not break,
and a dimly burning wick he will not quench;
he will faithfully bring forth justice.
4 He will not grow faint or be crushed
until he has established justice in the earth;
and the coastlands wait for his teaching.
5 Thus says God, the LORD,
who created the heavens and stretched them out,
who spread out the earth and what comes from it,
who gives breath to the people upon it
and spirit to those who walk in it:
6 I am the LORD, I have called you in righteousness,
I have taken you by the hand and kept you;
I have given you as a covenant to the people,
a light to the nations,
7 to open the eyes that are blind,
to bring out the prisoners from the dungeon,
from the prison those who sit in darkness.
8 I am the LORD, that is my name;
my glory I give to no other,
nor my praise to idols.
9 See, the former things have come to pass,
and new things I now declare;
before they spring forth,
I tell you of them.

What do you know about Isaiah? What does Isaiah mean to you? Millard?

Suffering servant.

Suffering and servant. A prophet of about five hundred years before Jesus was born. Yes, what else?

He had all the promises of the future Messiah.

He had the promises or predictions or prophecy about the future Messiah....

The book of Isaiah is divided into three parts, and the scholars—I'm not one of them and I'm not going to start an argument this morning—think that Isaiah, personally, only wrote the first forty chapters, or so.... My preference is to think that Isaiah wrote the whole thing. If anybody wants to think different, you can do it. I'm not here to tell you about the history of the Bible.

But I think one of the very wonderful things about Isaiah is that he was able in his lifetime, in the time that Isaiah, at least, was written, to look at the current situation—what was the situation, by the way, when he wrote this book? Where were the Israelites?

Exile.

They were in exile. Where?

Babylon.

In Babylon and they were hoping to come back. [Jerusalem] had been destroyed and there was a prediction that they would come back, a hope that they would come back. They needed a leader, but they were under oppression, and then along came whom? That helped to save them and bring them back? King who?

Cyrus.

King Cyrus. King Cyrus had mercy on the Israelites, or he was inspired by God, or he had a belief in Jehovah—we don't know—but he opened up the opportunity for some of the Israelites to go back to Jerusalem and begin a very horrible ordeal of rebuilding the city walls, and so forth, under very difficult circumstances.

What was the status of the Israelites in Babylon? They had a good life. They had been assimilated into the society, they had intermarriage, they became very successful merchants, so they had a relatively good life of success—economically, financially, and also a life of ease. They were not persecuted there, so far as we know.

It was a very big problem for them to decide to go back to Jerusalem and to face hardships that were totally unpredictable. But Isaiah writes about King Cyrus kind of pushing them, at least a few of them, back toward Jerusalem, and when they got there, they had a very difficult time. They were supposed to rebuild the temple; it was destroyed, and they looked around after they had been working for, we don't know, many months, maybe several years, and what did they say? "We don't have the temple of Solomon, we've got a what? We've got a butler building for a temple, and we are not even proud of our own construction work." So, there was great disparagement there, a great discouragement there among the Israelites.

Who Are the Chosen, According to Isaiah?

Isaiah really wrote these verses, in Isaiah 42 and Isaiah 61, to describe the Chosen People of God.

Last night and this morning, I read the different commentaries on Isaiah—there were four different people to whom Isaiah might have referred in this chapter. Anybody want to tell me who they are? His chosen servants.

One was Jesus, and that's one we're going to talk about primarily. Who else?

A lot of people think he was referring to King Cyrus. And who else?

And to the Israelites themselves, as suffering people who were God's chosen to carry on or support or protect the kingdom of God. That's Jesus, King Cyrus, the Israelites. Who else?...

You and me. These verses were written about us. When Isaiah wrote about the Chosen People of God, do you think that includes us? Yes, it certainly does.

So, let's forget about King Cyrus; we won't completely forget about the Israelites. But this morning, we're going to talk about Isaiah's words as they apply to the Messiah, whom we know as Jesus Christ. And we know a lot more about Jesus than Isaiah could have known or did know, and we are also going to talk about ourselves as being members of God's Chosen People to further his kingdom on earth.

Isaiah's Prophecy Fulfilled

Most of us in this room are Christians. And what does that mean in our relationship with Jesus? We have publicly professed to be followers of Christ—in other words, "little Christians." So we are supposed to take on the characteristics of Jesus. We know this is not possible, for us to be perfect as Jesus was perfect, but we have the same basic tasks to perform, as Christians in a modern-day setting, in our own life environment as did Jesus when he came on earth as the son of God, as God himself, to be the chosen Messiah.

So, you see that Isaiah, in his description here, which we're going to read, it's not all that easy to understand. But the interpretations that we now put upon it will be, primarily, how does it apply to the prophecy of a great man, inspired by God to tell the Israelites about the coming Messiah, to tell us about Jesus Christ, and also to apply it to ourselves?

In addition to the interpretation of scholars that this might have applied to Jesus five hundred years before he was born, how do we know that [the words of Isaiah apply] to Jesus, from the Bible?

His words were fulfilled in the New Testament...

How do we know that?

Luke 4.

In Luke 4. Let's turn to Luke 4.... This is very important. This is not going to refer exclusively back to Isaiah 42, but it will refer back to Isaiah 61. Let's look at Luke 4:18.... This is when Jesus came back to Nazareth and was asked to read the Scripture in his own hometown synagogue, and he picked up the scroll and turned to this particular quote from Isaiah....

[18] 'The Spirit of the Lord is upon me, because he has anointed me to bring good news to the poor. He has sent me to proclaim release to the captives and recovery of sight to the blind, to let the oppressed go free, [19] to proclaim the year of the Lord's favor.'

And he rolled up the scroll...and what he actually said to them, 'Today this scripture has been fulfilled in your hearing.'

You can see that Christ himself identified his own ministry with the ministry predicted by Isaiah. Turn over to Isaiah 61, the first two verses. Does this sound familiar?

[1] The spirit of the Lord God is upon me, because the Lord has anointed me; he has sent me to bring good news to the oppressed, to bind up the brokenhearted, to proclaim liberty to the captives, and release to the prisoners; [2] to proclaim the year of the Lord's favour.

It's an exact quote. So, even though there might be some question among some people that Isaiah is not describing the future life of Christ, Jesus himself, in the first, you might say, sermon that he gave, when he started his active ministry, refers back to Isaiah and said, "This day Isaiah's prophecy has come true at this moment."

What was the reaction of Jesus' contemporaries? What was the reaction of his hometown folks?... They tried to throw him off a cliff and kill him, and he escaped from them and went on, obviously, to fulfill the last three years of his life on earth as the promised Messiah and as the son of God.

Jesus, Realistically

We're going to find here some keys to Christianity. What is the most important day of the year for Christians?

How many of you think Christmas? How many of you think Easter?

Easter is the most important. The birth of Christ is obviously important, but the fact that Christ was crucified, was buried, and was resurrected and lived again, is the essence of Christianity. Paul later said in his writing to the early church, that if Christ did not arise, if he was not resurrected, then all our words about Christianity are hollow. There is no meaning to anything that I say, or that Peter says, or James says. There's no significance to the five hundred people who saw Christ after he was resurrected—the two that went to Emmaus and to the disciples that he came to, and as Paul outlines later on, he enumerated five hundred people that saw Jesus during the forty days he lived after his resurrection, and he said, if our words are not true, there is no such thing as Christianity.

So, what do you get out of Easter? The resurrection is what we like to talk about, but what else? The suffering of Christ.

Sometimes we tend to think about Jesus in a convenient way. We think about Jesus as being very handsome. We think about him as being tall and slender, kind of aesthetic, admired by people, an eloquent speaker, a very convincing speaker. Someone who could control his emotions and knows what's going on in a godlike way. Someone who's very convincing when he gives a remarkable sermon like the Sermon on the Mount. As a matter of fact, all those images are basically false. That's not the way Jesus was.

Let's look just a moment at how Isaiah describes the future Messiah. Let's turn to Isaiah 53. It's quite an intriguing entire chapter, but I'll just read a couple verses—two and three.

2 For he grew up before him like a young plant, and like a root out of dry ground; he had no form or majesty that we should look at him,

nothing in his appearance that we should desire him. [3] He was despised and rejected by others; a man of suffering and acquainted with infirmity; and as one from whom others hide their faces he was despised, and we held him of no account.

That entire chapter describes Jesus' physical appearance and the way he ministered. What was the effectiveness of his preaching? I'd say, basically a failure. At the end of his three years of preaching and demonstration of the perfect life, primarily to his disciples—even when he preached the Sermon on the Mount, he was talking to his disciples. There was a great crowd around him. We understand that he sat on the side of a hill—Rosalynn and I have been there where they claimed the Sermon on the Mount took place—and although there were a number of people there, he was basically talking to his disciples, trying to convince these twelve people, even including Judas, of the facts about his ministry, his life, his character, his meaning. And were they convinced? At times, they were.

The first time Jesus explained to them, in very frank language, which we can understand verbatim, that he was heading toward Jerusalem, and that he would be tried, and he would be executed, and he would be no longer with them, the disciples began to squabble about what? Who is going to be closest to Jesus when his kingdom came. Who was going to be secretary of state, secretary of treasury. Who was going to be chief of staff. Who was going to command, perhaps, the victorious Israeli armies under the Messiah's leadership. That was how much of an impact Christ's words made on them.

Then, when he was arrested and got into trouble, they were fearful and disillusioned, were they not? Although Jesus told them three or four times that his life was going to come to an end, as it did, they still had in the back of their minds a conviction: *This is the Messiah. This is the son of God. He's going to restore the power and independence and freedom of the Israelites. He's going to overthrow the Romans. He's going to transform himself from a humble person that walks around in the dusty roads to someone riding on a white horse with a crown on his head.* They just couldn't get away from that image.

Then, when he was finally arrested and didn't call down legions of angels to defend him, and so forth, they left him. John may have been at the crucifixion—we think he was, but all the rest of them [disciples] were gone, and John didn't take any role in it. Christ did tell John to take care of his mother.

So, even though we think about Jesus in very wonderful ways as far as appearance is concerned, effectiveness of his preaching was concerned, the conviction of his words was concerned, he went through life as a humble what? Servant. And he demonstrated to us the essence of God. Jesus said, "If you've seen me, you've seen the Father."

Our Superiority Complex

What is the essence of God? How do we envision power and majesty? Dominance. But God showed us that God himself is a God of what? Punishment? Love, mercy, a God of forgiveness, a God of gentleness. Isn't it hard for us to envision this—that the Creator of the entire universe, the Big Bang, or however he did it, we don't know, is a God of love and care, and mercy and forgiveness, eager to be reconciled with us individually? There's no way that we could understand this comprehension of God by looking at the Old Testament. It's only with the coming of Christ that we are able to understand the essence, the character, the being, the meaning of God Almighty—God, the Father.

All of us have a struggle, I do, in correlating my image of Jesus with my concept of how God looks on me. I still can't get away from the fact that God is basically a harsh judge and is keeping a checklist of good versus bad. But God is so eager to reach out to us, with not punishment, but forgiveness. Not harshness, but gentleness, mercy, love.

So, our image of Christ is prophesied, or predicted, or given to us very beautifully in Isaiah.... And all the way through, you see a picture of Isaiah describing *What is the characteristic of a servant of God?* Is it someone who thinks they're better than others? Every time the Israelites began to think, *We are Chosen People because of our superiority*, they failed. It was only when they tied themselves to God, in the fulfillment of the various covenants with Abraham, and with Moses, and others, that the Israelites were able to succeed.

Does that teach us a lesson? The Israelites went astray, worshipping golden calves. We go astray, setting our own human standards and saying, "These are God's standards."

Do I want to remember the gentleness, the unattractiveness, the humility, the suffering, the service of Christ as my model? Or do I want to take a more convenient image of a Christian for myself? One, I'd say, of human success, and then we define success in the most convenient way and we tend to elevate ourselves to a superior status as the Israelites did in ancient times. I'm an American. Or maybe, I'm a White American descendant from the early settlers who came here and committed genocide among Native Americans. I'm fairly wealthy—all these things because I'm a little bit superior. God recognizes my superiority, right? So, we bask in the blessings of God, and we don't want to take on the image of Christ, and somehow or another we stretch our mind so that we don't have to.

Look at the actions of Jesus. How much money did he have? None.... His parents, before he was born, didn't even have enough money to buy a lamb for a sacrifice. They had to sacrifice two pigeons, which was the cheapest way to show that they honored God. In fact, your sacrifice was predicated on how much you could actually afford. Some sacrificed an entire ox, a very expensive sacrifice. Others, lambs, goats. The cheapest was two doves and two pigeons, and that's all Mary and Joseph had.

He was descended from royalty, we know, from King David and so forth, but if you read the genealogy of Jesus in Matthew, who else was he descended from?

Rahab.

Rahab, a prostitute. He was descended from a daughter who seduced her own father. It was a very strange thing, by the way, and this is not a part of our lesson, that in the genealogy of Jesus they give four different women, when women, in those days, were pushed aside as servants or even more inferior than servants. But all the way through the life of Christ,...women were exalted and lifted up on an equal basis with men.

This is something again that we have forgotten in our modern-day church. One of the things that divides the Southern Baptists most viciously is whether or not women can be ordained as ministers and can preach the gospel.... I remember, a few years ago, a big church in Oklahoma prohibited Billy Graham's daughter from coming to explain some program that the women were working on because they thought that it wasn't proper for a woman to be in the pulpit instructing men....

The point is, we get away from the gentleness of God, the forgiveness of God, the love of God, the compassion of God, the service of God as personified by Christ in our own lives. We go sideways and begin to figure out different ways for us individually, including me, to be superior to others, and part of our superiority comes from how much we have been blessed by God. But to take on the posture of, or the character of, a suffering servant is not an attractive thing to do.

What did Jesus say about it? "Take up your"—what?—"cross, and follow me." The cross is something we don't want to emphasize, except just as a symbol. Isn't it strange to you that Christianity has adopted a cross as its emblem?

What is a cross? I would say a cross is the same as an electric chair.... It was a place where criminals were executed in the most horribly public and most horribly suffering way. Much worse than an electric chair. Much worse than hanging. Can you imagine any religion taking on an electric chair as its symbol? Or a gallows? Or a hypodermic needle for poison with lethal injections? We take on the emblem of a cross, the same category as other means of execution, as our beloved symbol of the highest commitment of our life.

Why? Why do you think we do this? Why not take an emblem of a cradle?

If Christ hadn't died on the cross, we would have no life. We would have no Christian life. There would be no such thing as a church. If Jesus had been triumphant in the last few days of his life, in the last few hours of his life, if he had proven to the authorities in Jerusalem that he was indeed the Messiah and they had all knelt down to worship him, that would've been a transient thing.

The point that we should remember, and it's not easy to remember, is that we are in the same pattern as Christ, the same image as Christ, have the same responsibilities as Christ.

The Enlightenment of Those Who Are Poor in Spirit

The Jesus that we see in the Bible is one for us to be emulating. Jesus had a life of vigor, and excitement, and courage—of adventure; he tried new things. He was unorthodox. I don't know how many of these adjectives describe you or me. He shocked people just by his own associates...outcast people, Samaritans, Gentiles; a woman caught in the act of adultery whose punishment ordinarily would have been stoning to death; tax collectors who betrayed the Jews—who *were* Jews. They would collect a hundred bucks of taxes, they'd collect twenty-five bucks for themselves—put it in their pocket. And when they got to know Jesus, they admitted it. *I have stolen a lot of money. I'm going to give back four times as much as I stole.* Those were the kinds of people with whom Jesus related.

Lepers, who were looked upon as condemned by God because of their sins. They weren't just sick people; they were people who were being punished by God. "We don't know why," the people would say, "but we know they must have sinned horribly, so we won't associate with these sinful people." Christ embraced the lepers and the prostitutes. He reached out to those who were poor, who were suffering, and all the way through Isaiah, there is an emphasis on suffering servant.

Why do you think suffering? What is there about suffering people that would lead us to believe that they were more attuned to God's message?... What is there about suffering people that we know today that might put them in a category of being more receptive to the message of Christ?

Just take people who live in a country where Christianity is outlawed and where people still retain their faith in Christ. They are in need of something. They're not totally self-reliant. They don't believe that all of their blessings—very few blessings—come from their own worth, their own talents, their own hard work, but they believe that what they have comes from God. They have a little more inclination to trust other people and to need other people. They're reaching out for something.

They are also hoping for a better life in the future, maybe even after death.

There's a significant difference, in my opinion, in a worship service, and I've been to many of them, [between] an African American church [and] most White churches. There's a closeness with God. There's an emotional relationship. There's a feeling of sincerity or genuineness about it.

And as we know, during the civil rights years, it was the church that was the foundation for hope that a better life could come, and there was a tie there, a very good tie—I wouldn't disparage it—between religion on the one hand, you might say, and the state on the other, but the state was on the other side. It was a faith in God that let the African Americans suffer through slavery and through the hundred years after slavery of gross and now embarrassing discrimination. But they never lost hope.

But you can see how someone of this kind who doesn't have enough to eat, who is persecuted, who feels the burden of discrimi nation, would be looking for something that was clean and decent and fair and just and compassionate. Can you understand that? Can we see?

So that's why Christ himself reached out to these kinds of people—to set an example for whom? For us!

But how many of us do follow this example? That's the problem, right? It's not really convenient to associate with this kind of people. We can walk by them and look the other way.

We can walk by folks sleeping on the sidewalk in New York under a plastic sheet, or inside a pasteboard box, or on some newspapers, and we can say, "Well, gee, the government ought to do something about those people," or "They're there on the street because they really prefer to live in the outdoors." I remember President Reagan said this on occasion. There were some people sleeping on a grate near the White House where the warm air came up, there was snow all around, and when he was questioned about it, he said, "Well, I think they really prefer that kind of life."

Well, we look the other way, and we walk on, and we say, "Let the church take care of it." Maybe there are some home missionaries in the area that will take them in. Do we feel an obligation? Maybe for a brief moment. Maybe our conscience kind of twinges for a little bit as we walk by. I'm sure the rabbi and the Pharisee who walked by the beat-up person on the road from Jericho felt that way before the Samaritan came by and picked him up and took him to a nearby hotel, and said, "Take care of this man and I'll pay the bill." Jesus said, "That is a neighbor."

We can very easily go through our entire lives and not quite assimilate either one of the two words that Isaiah emphasized—"suffering" or "servant."

When Jesus was at the Last Supper, and he realized...that all the power of God was on him, and the fulfillment of God's prophecies were his—it was one of the most exalted descriptions of Jesus' assessment of himself as being preeminent—what was the next thing that happened in the Scripture?... He took off his clothes and got a towel and girded himself with a towel and then what? He got down on his knees in front of his disciples and washed their feet. Then what did he say? "Do likewise." How many of us do likewise?

Peter was shocked. It wasn't a common thing to do in those days. Peter said, "Lord, you're not going to wash my feet. No way." And Jesus said, "I wash the feet of those who share my love." Peter said, "Wash my feet." But it was an unorthodox and humiliating thing to do. So, that's another one of those very inconvenient things that we don't do.

Suffering as a Standard for a Successful Life

We very carefully select the elements of Christianity that are most convenient for us, kind of a self-exaltation—I'm talking about me, as well. But the point is, we can't be perfect like Christ. We can't be self-abnegating like Christ. Or self-sacrificial like Christ. But when Isaiah writes these words, he's telling us to take another look, take another thought, reassess your definition of success, of Christianity. How does your life measure up to the standard that Christ set for us? We look at the life of Christ—how parallel is our own life to his? Not very parallel, not in my case. What should we do about it? Try to change.

Try to say, okay, I live in West Palm Beach. I live in Pennsylvania. I live in Ontario, Canada. I live in Plains, Georgia. I have my own circle of responsibilities, my own circle of friends, my own duties to my family, my own career to pursue, my own retirement years to enjoy. That's okay; there's nothing wrong with that. How can I, though, through the remaining weeks or months or years of my life, draw closer to Christ? And the answer to that question has to be individual. I don't know how to answer for you. But what Isaiah is telling us to do is to look at the suffering servant not as a sacrifice, not as an embarrassment, but as a means to exaltation, as a means to success as measured by God, as a means to success as a Christian.

Are there things that you can think about now, or I can think about now, where our lives can be more closely attuned to the ministry of Christ? Will we reach out to those who are suffering, who are imprisoned, not maybe in jail but imprisoned by loneliness, by poverty, by despair, by homelessness? Are there those against whom we have a grudge, or animosity, or hatred, where we might demonstrate Jesus' perfect example of forgiveness? Can we forgive those against whom we have disagreements, who may have actually done something bad to us? Can we raise the standard of our lives a little bit higher and not judge others? How is our life to be judged?

I read a very interesting little story, I don't know if it's true or not, about some, I guess you might say, Southern Baptists. Like I have done in the past, they went into this little village, maybe in Pennsylvania, and they were going up and down the street confronting people, and they were saying, "Brother, are you saved? Brother, are you saved?" You have confronted people like that at the fair or when somebody gets on a soapbox and preaches. And they stopped this, I'll say, Amish farmer and said, "Brother, have you been saved?" The Amish farmer thought for a while, and he said, "Do you have a few moments?" and the visiting missionary was kind of surprised. He said, "Yeah, I guess so." So, the Amish farmer got a piece of paper out of his pocket, and a pencil, and he wrote for a while. He said, "Here are ten people who know me best and I put down their telephone numbers. Go ask them if I've been saved. Ask them if I'm a Christian. I don't want to answer the question myself."

Well, you see, that's the kind of thing all of us should be thinking about. I don't want this to be a negative lesson. But those who know you best, and you know who they are, do they look upon you as an exemplary Christian? As someone who personifies the teachings of Christ? Can we go back for the last year, or two years, or five years, and list some of the things that we've done that were truly sacrificial in nature for the benefit of others, particularly others that we don't even know? I would do anything sacrificial for my grandkids. I wouldn't do quite as much sacrificial for my children. [*Congregation laughs*]

But Christ teaches agape love. Love for the unlovable. Love that's not repaid to us. Love for people who are unattractive, who may be outside of the protective circle that we build around ourselves so we don't have to confront things that are unpleasant.

Jesus broke down that barrier and reached out to people who were different, or in trouble, or lonely, or unattractive, or sinful, or despised, and in the process taught us how to live as Christians. It doesn't have to be big things. We don't have to have great talent to forgive somebody, or to visit some lonely person, or to share our friendship, or our love, or our partnership with people who are a little different from us.

In the process, this is a stretching of our hearts, a stretching of our minds, an expansion of our lives in an exciting and gratifying way. Jesus says this is how we find peace that passeth understanding and joy that we can't even envision.

So, to act in a fumbling way, or a humble way, as Christians is not something that puts us in a box; it's not something that excludes our earthly joy, or pleasure, or self-gratification. It's something that gives us a new dimension of life. It makes our nice houses and our pretty automobiles and our full meals and our freedom and liberty and influence and wealth, equally enjoyable, but not the preeminent things in our lives, and we actually begin to understand what it means to be a suffering servant.

It doesn't mean to be a deprived servant. It means to be a gratified servant of others with a full life, or at least a fuller life, recognizing that we all come short of the glory of God. We can't measure up to the standards of Jesus Christ, but when we don't measure up—that means sinfulness. It means selfishness, which is a sin. It means lying, or gossip, which is a sin. It means hurting others or ignoring others, which is a sin. But through Christ and God forgives us. Partially? Totally.

And even though we have been selfish, we turn to God through Christ and say, "I have been selfish, but I want to be better." Through that act, we are totally redeemed. We are totally reconciled with God. It is as though we had never been selfish. It is as though we had never felt hatred. It is as though we had never been unconcerned.

So, what Christ comes to promise us, to give us, to demonstrate to us is a life of much greater happiness and enjoyment and excitement and challenge and adventure and fulfillment and gratification, and, you might say, success—success as measured by our Savior.

The following week, President Carter continued a series of teachings from the book of Isaiah. He shared this story about the Carters' friends, Jerome and Joanne Etheridge, as an example of shadowing our lives in the humble ministry of Jesus, as prophesied in Isaiah hundreds of years before Jesus' life on earth.

In 1976, two remarkable things happened in Plains inside one little Baptist church. One family was chosen to go to the White House—I won't tell you which one [*congregation laughs*]—and the other family volunteered to be missionaries in Africa; I would say that's the greatest of the two.

Jerome and Joanne Etheridge. Jerome Etheridge was an agronomist in the experiment station on the edge of Plains; he was not a preacher—had no religious training. He and his wife volunteered, had to learn French, and went to Togo in West Africa.

Their job as new missionaries was to teach the children in the village how to read and write. The only requirement was that the children had to listen to one presentation of the plan of salvation. This was a village of Muslims. They witnessed for seven years and had very little success in converting people from Islam to Christianity, although they taught a lot of kids how to read and write.

Then...they were assigned to a remote area called East Mono.... and when Jerome and Joanne got there, they decided to look more closely at the ministry of Jesus, not just sit on a chair and teach people how to read; not just to have a religious service and preach on Sunday; not just to knock on people's doors and tell them the plan of salvation—I'm not knocking any of this. They said, "Let's try to decide what are the greatest needs of the people in this area, and we'll meet their needs as Jesus did with blind people and hungry people and lepers, and let the Holy Spirit determine the results of our ministry."

Jerome immediately implemented better farming practices because he was an agronomist. That was his profession, and in some cases, he increased the production of corn ten times greater than it had been.

He also realized that the villages didn't have any water. In a rainy spell, they would fill up a mud hole; we would call it a pond, and sometimes the hole was deep enough, and enough water ran into it to last during the dry season. In one village, he told us the women had to walk sixteen miles a day to get water—eight miles to a water hole and eight miles back toting water. Half the women went every day, and the other half stayed back and took care of the children and did the chores around the village.

Jerome got some help from North Carolina Baptists they raised money and paid for a well-drilling outfit on the back of a diesel truck, and Jerome went to every village within sixty miles—it took him eight years— and he drilled 160 wells. And all over that whole area of East Mono there is granite—sometimes on the surface, sometimes sixty feet down; every well, he had to go through granite. In 130 of the wells, he found water. Every village now has water, a well, and a pump.

Even though they increased the production of sorghum and millet and so forth, he knew they needed more protein. So, he got a bulldozer and began to dig ponds. He dug nineteen ponds, placed strategically around the area, deep enough so that they would hold water all during the dry season, and he filled them up with tilapia, which is a very fast-growing fish. Now, the villagers go with nets, and they catch tilapia so they will have a protein source.

In the meantime, Joanne was holding schools on the Bible, and on healthcare, and on immunization of children, and on better ways to prepare meals.

She would take the sick people to the hospital, which is a long way off. They had an old beat-up van, and she would let them pay half the cost of the gas, and they would pay the other half, and haul the people to the hospital and back. And she constructed a pharmacy and the government had promised if she would build a building and a place for the pharmacist to live, we will supply the drugs. So, she did that.

The worst problem that the East Mono people had was that four months of the year they couldn't leave East Mono because there was a river called the Mono River that was a torrent during the rainy season. It was impossible. There was only one dugout canoe that was used in an emergency that could go across the river during the rainy season.

Jerome went back to his North Carolina Baptist friends and he got the money. A few of them went over as volunteers, and this one missionary and volunteers built a bridge across the Mono River. When Rosalynn and I were there, we were amazed—this bridge is 230 feet long, a concrete structure that spans this enormous river.

What was the result of this? When Jerome and Joanne went to this area, in the whole East Mono region, which is 2,500 square miles, there were two tiny Catholic groups and five very small Muslim groups; these people were adamant, and they resisted any sort of evangelism. As he built a bridge and dug the wells, he did it in the name of Christ. And when Rosalynn and I visited the Etheridges, there were eighty-one new churches and five thousand new Christians.... Well, this is what one Christian has done. They've been there twenty years now; they're going to stay four more years.

It makes me feel very inadequate, but it's an inspiration to me to see what can be done by a Christian, not all that talented—Jerome has a hard time making a speech—but who emulates the teachings of our Savior. It shows us what we can do, ourselves, just by visiting someone who's lonely, or demonstrating in some tangible way, *I am a Christian.*

✑

This lesson, showing us the interrelationship between the ancient New Testament times and modern-day times, between the promised Messiah, Jesus Christ our Savior, and me individually, and you individually, is a very sobering and, perhaps, inspirational lesson. I hope it will change our lives, including my own.

September 20, 1998

When All Is Said and Done

Maranatha Baptist Church
Plains, Georgia

Lesson Scripture

Ecclesiastes 3:1–22 (NRSVA)

1 For everything there is a season, and a time for every matter under
heaven:
2 a time to be born, and a time to die;
a time to plant, and a time to pluck up what is planted;
3 a time to kill, and a time to heal;
a time to break down, and a time to build up;
4 a time to weep, and a time to laugh;
a time to mourn, and a time to dance;
5 a time to throw away stones, and a time to gather stones together;
a time to embrace, and a time to refrain from embracing;
6 a time to seek, and a time to lose;
a time to keep, and a time to throw away;
7 a time to tear, and a time to sew;
a time to keep silence, and a time to speak;
8 a time to love, and a time to hate;
a time for war, and a time for peace.

9 What gain have the workers from their toil? 10 I have seen the
business that God has given to everyone to be busy with. 11 He has
made everything suitable for its time; moreover he has put a sense of
past and future into their minds, yet they cannot find out what God
has done from the beginning to the end. 12 I know that there is nothing
better for them than to be happy and enjoy themselves as long as they
live; 13 moreover, it is God's gift that all should eat and drink and take
pleasure in all their toil. 14 I know that whatever God does endures forever; nothing can be added to it, nor anything taken from it; God has
done this, so that all should stand in awe before him. 15 That which is,
already has been; that which is to be, already is; and God seeks out
what has gone by.

16 Moreover I saw under the sun that in the place of justice, wickedness was there, and in the place of righteousness, wickedness was there as well. 17 I said in my heart, God will judge the righteous and the wicked, for he has appointed a time for every matter, and for every work. 18 I said in my heart with regard to human beings that God is testing them to show that they are but animals. 19 For the fate of humans and the fate of animals is the same; as one dies, so dies the other. They all have the same breath, and humans have no advantage over the animals; for all is vanity. 20 All go to one place; all are from the dust, and all turn to dust again. 21 Who knows whether the human spirit goes upward and the spirit of animals goes downward to the earth? 22 So I saw that there is nothing better than that all should enjoy their work, for that is their lot; who can bring them to see what will be after them?

Ecclesiastes 11:4–6 (NRSV)

4 Whoever observes the wind will not sow;
and whoever regards the clouds will not reap.

5 Just as you do not know how the breath comes to the bones in the mother's womb, so you do not know the work of God, who makes everything.

6 In the morning sow your seed, and at evening do not let your hands be idle; for you do not know which will prosper, this or that, or whether both alike will be good.

What visitors can tell me what the Wisdom Books are?

Proverbs.

Ecclesiastes.

Song of Solomon.

Job.

Very wise. Very good. I told you this was a high-quality group. [*Congregation laughs*]...

This Sunday we are going to talk about Ecclesiastes. What do you know about Ecclesiastes?

Apparently, it was written by Solomon.

Well, I think all the biblical scholars claim that it's not written by Solomon. The author claims in the first couple of verses, and so forth, that it is Solomon, but the language used and the historical knowledge in it place it at about 300 B.C., which is five hundred years after Solomon. But in the Hebrew tradition, any acts or thoughts of wisdom were pretty frequently attributed to Solomon, but it's doubtful that it was written by Solomon.

It was written by a person who, depending on the translation of the Bible that you read, is called the Preacher, or the Teacher, and he has a name that he calls himself, Qohelet....

Ecclesiastes's approach to God...it's very impersonal, very reverential—approaching God as distant. All-powerful, but unapproachable. Ecclesiastes never refers to God as "You." He refers to God in the third person, as "Elohim," or "the Creator," a distant, impersonal God.

Ecclesiastes had some very interesting things to say. Do you remember any phrase Ecclesiastes used?

A time for everything.

What else? There was a special word he liked to use.

I might point out that although I always search for some relationship between the Old Testament text and the New Testament, I think it's almost impossible to find any correlation between Ecclesiastes and the New Testament message of Christ except that we ought to revere God and accept our plight on earth. That's basically it.

What Ecclesiastes points out, primarily, is that God created the universe, that he set universal physical laws that are unchangeable, that death is a great leveler, not only between persons, but what else? Between people and animals. He drew no distinction at all between the transient nature of life on earth, and death, bringing it into the temporary existence of both humans and animals.

What else did he say about time? He said, we should enjoy it. You know what "carpe diem" means? Enjoy the pleasures of the moment and don't worry about the future. That was Ecclesiastes's basic lesson.

But in the process of giving us this message, which is quite discouraging and has no concept of life after death, or ultimate reward, or even reward for doing good—that's very rarely mentioned, if at all, in Ecclesiastes— Ecclesiastes tried to analyze the fact that we have certain circumstances in life to face, and how should we face them....

The Vastness of God

Let's read now, Ecclesiastes, the first chapter, the second verse.

> 2 Vanity of vanities, says the Teacher, vanity of vanities! All is vanity.

What do you think vanity means? It doesn't mean vain, as we use vanity these days.... So, what do you think it does mean?

Fleeting.

Empty.

Meaningless.

Futile.

Those are very good synonyms, but they are not the ones that I prefer. I think the best interpretation about what it possibly means is "incomprehensible." If you insert this word "incomprehensible"—or "you just can't understand it"— into the verses, it comes out fairly reasonably.

I don't believe that Ecclesiastes is saying everything is insignificant, or nothing, or worthless, or futile, I think he means that we just can't understand it. It's beyond the concept of human thought, human analysis, human logic. Even the nature of God, the creation of the universe, is beyond the comprehension of human thought. Even the most advanced scientists who deal in astronomical matters or subatomic matters can't understand it.

There have been a lot of articles in the last few months, in some of the most noted scientific magazines, about how increasingly the number of scientists who believe in God Almighty or in a Creator is growing. More and more, as they approach the truth about universal matters, they have come to the conclusion, sometimes reluctantly, that there must have been a superior power or superior intellect in some fashion. And exactly how to describe God is something that none of us can do.

When I was a child, I thought about God as being an old man with a long white beard that was sitting in Heaven with a notebook, and he was watching me and had two pages in his notebook. On one side were the good things I did. On the other side were the bad things I did, and I tried to conceal from God the bad things I did. It was a kind of judgmental God.

Then, afterwards, obviously, as I became more and more familiar with the Christian faith, I learned other things about God. What are some of those things? What's the most significant thing? What did Jesus say about God? When his disciples said, "Show me God. Explain to us God," what did Jesus say? "If you've seen me, you've seen God. You've seen the Father."

Also in the Bible, we know God is what? One word. Love. Judgment, punishment, severity, insensitivity? No. God is love. God is full of grace, forgiveness, love for me, and when I do wrong things, God—all-wise, with omniscience, with all-knowledge—knows what I did.

God is also all-powerful, but there's a limit to God's use of his power. I won't even say, "his"; we don't know what sex [God is].

Daily Guidance

God gives human beings, from the very beginning, a very precious but troubling gift. What is that? Free will, the ability to make our own choices, to accept or reject basic premises that are given to us to guide our lives.

And these premises come not only from the Bible text. Where else do they come from? They come from our parents' teachings. Unfortunately, sometimes from our parents' examples.

They come from our education. My character has been shaped substantially by my life at the US Naval Academy, where the highest possible crime was lying. No matter what else you did, you could possibly get away with it. But if you ever lied about anything, you were out. If you stepped on the grass in front of Bancroft Hall, it was ten demerits; you were supposed to stay on the sidewalk. If you stepped on the grass, and an upperclassman saw you step on the grass and asked you about it, and you said, "I didn't step on the grass," you were out of the navy in disgrace for lying.

Those kinds of things about which we learn through teaching and from our own experience shape our lives. God's given us the right to make our own decisions about those things. God has given us the authority, not just to be a puppet or a robot controlled by strings from heaven, but to decide how to treat other human beings. To be kind or gentle, or harsh and punitive, oppressive of the weak or give assistance to the weak, to accept Christ as our Savior or not. Those decisions put a tremendous, heavy responsibility on us.

All those things we know now about the concept of God—Ecclesiastes didn't know these things. Ecclesiastes, Job, Solomon, even, had no concept of Christ, so far as we know, and the gentleness, the sharing, the humility, the forgiveness, the compassion—the love that epitomized or personified God was not a concept that was existent or known in the time of the Books of Wisdom.

The Books of Wisdom, then, were written not for theological purposes, but for what purpose? To give us guidance in our daily lives. How [then] should we relate to each other?

An Obsession with Time

Let's turn now to Ecclesiastes 3, where most of our lesson is going to come from. And I'm going to read the first eight verses because these are perhaps the most well-known verses from Ecclesiastes.

> 1 For everything there is a season, and a time for every matter under heaven:
> 2 a time to be born, and a time to die;
> a time to plant, and a time to pluck up what is planted;
> 3 a time to kill, and a time to heal;
> a time to break down, and a time to build up;
> 4 a time to weep, and a time to laugh;
> a time to mourn, and a time to dance;
> 5 a time to throw away stones, and a time to gather stones together;
> a time to embrace, and a time to refrain from embracing;
> 6 a time to seek, and a time to lose;
> a time to keep, and a time to throw away;
> 7 a time to tear, and a time to sew;
> a time to keep silence, and a time to speak;
> 8 a time to love, and a time to hate;
> a time for war, and a time for peace.

This emphasis on time has become increasingly pertinent to modern day life. As Rosalynn would testify enthusiastically, I'm obsessed with time and being on time and keeping time. In fact, if you look at my watch, it would rarely be five seconds off, which...shows some unpleasant idiosyncrasy—for somebody to want his watch to be exactly on time. But I have lived that way. I was taught that maybe in the navy.

My daddy was even worse than I was. My daddy lived two hours ahead of time. If we had to get a train, for instance, to go from Americus to Atlanta and the train left at eight o'clock, we would leave home at six o'clock, and we would be there an hour and a half before the train got there to make sure that we were not late. I guess I inherited some things genetically, and other things I got from my navy time.

We have a lot of proverbs about time. Can you think of any of them?

There's not enough of it.

Time heals all wounds.

How about a stitch? A stitch in time does what?

Saves nine.

Can you think of any others? Time waits for—

No one.

Time is, what?

Money.

Time is on what? Time is on our side sometimes. But you see that our life and the little secular wisdom that didn't come out of the Bible, a lot of it from Benjamin Franklin and others, and from our ancestors, have come down about time. We are infatuated with time.

In fact, when Rosalynn and I got married, on our wedding day—Rosalynn and I have some dispute about this; this is not the only thing, by the way [*congregation laughs*]—I had been in the navy for three years. I graduated from Annapolis, and I had to do some training duty on an aircraft carrier and in a long-range patrol plane out of Jacksonville and in a blimp out of Glynco [Naval Air Station], Georgia, and I came home [and] we got married.

We didn't honor the thing that brides and grooms shouldn't see each other ahead of the wedding. So, we were at her mother's house, and we got in my car—I was watching the time. We drove in front of the church, I would say, ten seconds before three o'clock—we were supposed to be married at three—and they were playing "Here Comes the Bride" for the second time. So, we got there, dashed down the aisle and we got married successfully, and it's lasted fifty-two years. After that, though, I couldn't get away from my preoccupation with time.

For years, Rosalynn and I had the worst arguments, and they were very serious arguments, about punctuality. When we got ready to go to church, or to a movie, or to anything, I began to look at my watch about five minutes ahead of time, and if I thought Rosalynn was going to be late, which she claims she never was, and we won't get into that this morning because she's here, we had a very unpleasant relationship.

What about five minutes, Rosalynn?

It was more than five.

Whatever, Rosalynn. [*Congregation laughs*]—I was trying to be very cautious—no matter what I say about this, Rosalynn disputes it. But anyway, it was a constant matter of aggravation. Quite often, we'd get in the car to drive to church, or to drive to a movie, or drive to a party, or to drive to anywhere, and we would be angry with each other because of that argument about punctuality.

So, one day, about ten years ago, I woke up in the morning and went in my study to work on one of my books. I turned on my computer and it said, August the 18th, and I said, "Oh no." It was Rosalynn's birthday, and I had forgotten it. As a matter of fact, it was Sunday morning, and the stores were all closed, so I said to myself, *What can I do?*

So, I finally wrote out a note to Rosalynn and put it in a gift envelope, and I said, "Never again in my life will I make an unpleasant comment about punctuality." I signed it and gave it to her, and I've been pretty religious in eliminating that part of arguments between me and Rosalynn, which leaves plenty of room for other kinds of arguments. [*Congregation laughs*]

But the point is time infatuates us. Human beings these days live on a schedule, and one of the nicest things about going to our mountain cabin or going on vacation is that I take my watch off and put it in a drawer and I try not to even look at it anymore. So, time presses on us.

This is one of the things that Ecclesiastes is emphasizing—there is a time for us to make a judgment about what we should do. There is a time to love. There is a time to embrace. There is a time to pile up stones. There is a time to plant. There is a time to harvest. There is a time for different matters in our lives, and the judgment that we make, Ecclesiastes is insinuating, is up to us. And we should make a wise judgment....

Our Finest Moments

Let's read on down now the next few verses, from 9–15.

9 What gain have the workers from their toil? 10 I have seen the
business that God has given to everyone to be busy with. 11 He has
made everything suitable for its time; moreover, he has put a sense of past and future into their minds, yet they cannot find out what God
has done from the beginning to the end. 12 I know that there is nothing
better for them than to be happy and enjoy themselves as long as they live;

And that is the ultimate goal throughout the book of Ecclesiastes—to be happy and enjoy themselves as long as they live.

13 moreover, it is God's gift that all should eat and drink and take
pleasure in all their toil. 14 I know that whatever God does endures forever; nothing can be added to it, nor anything taken from it; God has
done this, so that all should stand in awe before him. 15 That which is,
already has been; that which is to be, already is; and God seeks out what has gone by.

Here, Ecclesiastes is giving us some thought. I would say the main impact that it has on me is to remove the tension from a person's life. Why worry about things that you cannot control? Set your own standards. Enjoy your life. Find out, though, how to enjoy life.

One way to enjoy life, obviously, is to do as Christ commanded. To have a sense of self-respect, a sense of worthiness, a sense of utility, a sense of purpose in life.

Ecclesiastes could find no purpose in life except to have a good time. Christians also want to have a good time; we want to enjoy life. In fact, Christ promised what? Peace that passes understanding—Joy. Christ promised us the ultimate in enjoyment and personal peace through, however, the finest things in life. A commitment to justice, to peace for others, as well as for ourselves, to humility, to service, to compassion, to love, to forgiveness, those are the kinds of things that Christ said will give us happiness and joy and peace in our own lives. To do the right things, as they relate to other people, primarily. That was Christ's admonition.

So, Ecclesiastes is not in contravention of the New Testament teachings when he says, enjoy life. Enjoy your work. Have a good time.

What are the good times? What are the successes in life?... When you look back from the perspective of seventy-four years old, which I will soon be, or ninety-four years old, or fifty years old—when you look back on life, what are the finest moments of existence?

When you give.

Okay, when you give. Let's be frank with each other now, not just idealistic, not just what other folks want us to say. What are the finest moments? I would say the simplest things in life.

There are times, for instance, between me and my littlest grandchildren, that when I consider them, bring me a warm feeling in my heart. More, even, than when I was inaugurated president.

That was a great day for me. It wasn't as great for some other people. My mother, for instance, had a way of bringing people down from their own self-constructed, beneficial cloud.

I was inaugurated president of the United States of America, and we walked down Pennsylvania Avenue, which some of you may remember. We sat in a reviewing stand. When we got through reviewing the parades, it was cold and everything, we started walking toward the

White House—my mother and I, and Rosalynn, and our children, and my press secretary, Jody Powell, and we were surrounded by news reporters, TV cameras. All of them wanted to get the first crack at the First Family, and Jody Powell said, "Nobody talks to the news reporters." And my mother, typically, said, "Jody, you can go to hell. I'll speak to whom I please." [*Congregation laughs*]

So, the news reporters then turned to Mama, and they said, "Miss Lillian, aren't you proud of your son?," and I was just waiting for Mama to say something nice. And Mama said, "Which one?" [*Congregation laughs*]

Well, I would say as we go through life together, the simplest little things that happen to us in relationship to people who love us and whom we love, or whom we forgive, who have been alienated from us, there are times of reconciliation, there are times of sharing, a time of quiet contemplation with someone that's close to us—those will probably be the finest moments that we can recollect in the last hours of our life. Those are the things that really count.

And, in effect, that's what Ecclesiastes is saying. Not to be rich. I would guess when we are lying on our death bed, we're not going to be thinking about if we have $146,523.48 in the bank, right? We are going to be thinking about the things that have made our lives warm and personal and livable and enjoyable and peaceful and gratifying.

Living Life as an Adventure

I happen to be a farmer. In fact, I was out in the peanut fields yesterday, and I picked out some peanuts that I am going to boil when I get home. Farming is part of my life, and I grew up in a farm family. In fact, my family has lived in this country for 350 years, or so; we've all been farmers.

I don't have a child who's a farmer, unfortunately, or maybe fortunately for them, but a farmer is taught to observe the weather. To know when to plant, or when you might have a drought where your seeds dry up and don't sprout, and so forth. I remember my father used to walk up and down, outside in the midnight, looking at the clouds to see if it was going to rain or not.

Let's read the fourth verse. So, listen to what Ecclesiastes says.

[4] Whoever observes the wind will not sow;
and whoever regards the clouds will not reap.

Isn't that strange? See, that's just contrary to what I said, isn't it? And down in the sixth verse:

> [6] In the morning sow your seed, and at evening do not let your hands be idle; for you do not know which will prosper, this or that, or whether both alike will be good.

What do you think he means by whoever observes the clouds and the wind will not either sow or reap? I would say, timidity. Some people forego the good, waiting for the perfect, and a lot of people, not excluding me, are worried about taking a chance.

Suppose I try this, and it doesn't work. Everybody is going to see that I failed. Why don't I just be cautious? Why should I reach out and do anything that's adventurous? Why should I take a chance on coming in contact with people that I don't even understand—who I know are different from me and may not even speak the same language as me, certainly don't have the same color skin as I do? Why should I get out of my self-constructed enclosure that protects me from surprises or unwanted obligations, you might say? I'm too old to be adventurous. All I want to do is rest on my laurels, to be secure in my older age, not be embarrassed, not be called upon to do something that might take away or reduce my bank account or take any of my own time. So, we forego the opportunity for excitement and adventure and challenge and unpredictability.

That's what Ecclesiastes is talking about. What does he say? He says, "Take a chance, for goodness' sake. Reach out and experiment. Stretch your heart. Stretch your mind. Learn more about God's world. Learn more about God's people." That's the way he says you can have a gratifying life.

I think it's a very good lesson for us to learn. As Christians, most of us, including me, get in a rut. Okay, I'm a good Christian. I go to church pretty regularly. I give a little bit of what I earn to the church. I pray for our foreign missionaries. I don't get caught violating the Ten Commandments. I take care of my own family. I don't violate the laws of my nation or my state. Therefore, I'm a good Christian....

What I described is self-gratification. It is convincing ourselves that we're okay—that we have met the standards of Jesus Christ adequately.

What Ecclesiastes is saying, I'm interpreting it for Christianity, is to move away from that to see if we can't emulate Christ or copy Christ in his words and actions a little more fervently. If we're timid about failing, so be it. If we try something and fail, okay. If we try something that succeeds, that's great.

Will Christ forgive us if we try something and fail, if we do it in his name? Of course. Will it add a new dimension to our lives? Yes. It doesn't have to be to strangers, or to people who speak a different language, or to homeless people lying on the street. It could be to our own wife, our own husband, or to our own estranged children, perhaps, or to a brother or sister that we don't feel very close to, or that we don't quite understand.

Can we utilize the teachings of Christ to take the initiative to break down that barrier between us and another person that we ought to love? That's a good question. Can we forgive someone who has harmed us in some way? Those are good questions.

And that's what Ecclesiastes is saying in the eleventh chapter and fourth verse. Take a chance for Christ.

That's what Ecclesiastes is talking about. What does he say? He says, "Take a chance for goodness' sake. Reach out and experiment. Stretch your heart. Stretch your mind. Learn more about God's world. Learn more about God's people." That's the way he says you [illegible] a gratifying life.

I think it's a very good lesson for us to learn, as Christians. Most of us, including me, get in a rut. "Okay, I'm a good Christian. I go to church, went regularly. I give a little bit of what I earn to the church [illegible] I don't [illegible] violating the Ten Commandments. I take care of my own family. I don't violate the laws of [illegible]. Therefore, I'm a good Christian."

What [illegible] is [illegible] It is convincing ourselves [illegible] quietly.

[illegible] Ecclesiastes is [illegible] to move away from it [illegible] we can [illegible] Christ in his words and actions a little more [illegible] failing [illegible] try something and fail [illegible]. If we try something [illegible]

[illegible]

Can we apply the teachings of Christ to [illegible] down [illegible] that we ought to love? That's a good question. Can we forgive someone who has harmed us in some way? Those are good questions.

And that's what Ecclesiastes is saying in the eleventh chapter and fourth verse: Take a chance for Christ.

The 2000s

There was a saviour
Rarer than radium
Commoner than water, crueller than truth;
Children kept from the sun
Assembled at his tongue
To hear the golden note turn in a groove,
Prisoners of wishes locked their eyes
In the jails and studies of his keyless smiles.

The voice of children says
From a lost wilderness
There was calm to be done in his safe unrest,
When hindering man hurt
Man, animal, or bird
We hid our fears in that murdering breath,
Silence, silence to do, when earth grew loud,
In lairs and asylums of the tremendous shout.

— Dylan Thomas
from "There Was a Saviour"

January 14, 2001. Amid his ever-expanding work advocating for human rights around the globe with the Carter Center, building affordable homes with Habitat for Humanity as a part of the annual Carter Work Project alongside Rosalynn, and authoring numerous books, Jimmy Carter always prioritized teaching Sunday School at Maranatha Baptist Church.

Courtesy *Arkansas Democrat-Gazette*

December 9, 2007. Jimmy Carter greets visitors before teaching a Sunday School lesson entitled "The Call of Humility."

Courtesy Jen Bates

December 9, 2007. Before he began teaching on Sunday, Jimmy Carter asked class members where they had traveled from to attend. Many people called out states from around the country, and others called out countries from around the world.

Courtesy Jen Bates

As the word spread about Jimmy Carter's Sunday School class, thousands of visitors from diverse backgrounds and varied religious affiliations journeyed to Plains for the opportunity to hear the former leader of the Free World teach a lesson from the Scriptures.
Courtesy Andrew Greer; photograph by Grant Blankenship

Anwar Sadat packed his bags and stacked his luggage on the porch of his cabin in a sign of abandoned protest. Or perhaps it was a weary surrender. The Egyptian president was eleven days deep into peace negotiations with Israel's prime minister, Menachim Begin, a man he generally regarded with antipathy. For Begin, the feeling was mutual. But so were both leaders' high regard for President Carter, a dramatic enough respect to confer the two men with the courage to accept Carter's invitation to talk lasting Middle East peace within the calming environment of the secluded presidential retreat at Camp David in Maryland. If ever there was a party who could shepherd the contentious pair into amicable territory, it was Jimmy Carter.

But bad blood boiled and enmity over past offenses stalled any true compromise. Sadat was arranging his journey back home. The Camp David peace talks were, in effect, stalemated.

Long before he found himself formulating foreign policies as leader of the free world, Carter had been entranced by the Middle East. In the summer of 1973, Jimmy, along with Rosalynn, then governor and first lady of the state of Georgia, visited Israel for the first time. The Carters were in awe.

The couple, both confessing Christians, shuffled between historic sites and sacred places, tracing the footsteps of he whom they called Savior, Jesus of Nazareth, and witnessing firsthand the motherland of the Scriptures they had been taught from and studied their entire lives. The same Scriptures the Carters opened up together every night. In fact, when their separate travels wedged miles between them, the committed couple would read from the same passage in the Bible as a way to inspire deeper connection with one another as well as receive directives from God. The pair even sometimes read from a Spanish translation to further cultivate their foreign language skills.

The pilgrimage spurred an unflagging passion and almost fanatical obsession in Carter for the birthplace of his religion. Compelled by his devout religious faith, Carter began a pursuit for peace in the Middle

East that would persist until the day he died. As Carter would later confess, "I was infatuated with the Holy Land."

In September of 1978, President Carter positioned himself in the middle of mediations between Israel and Egypt in what would become a history-making thirteen-day peace summit. The first three days of discussions with Begin and Sadat were a brawl, generating nonstop heated debates and a near-hopeless impasse, necessitating a separation and consigning the two hotheads of state to their respective cabins. Carter's shuttle diplomacy went into overdrive as he moved between Begin's and Sadat's quarters—negotiating changes with Begin, hand-delivering those to Sadat, relaying Sadat's revisions back to Begin, and returning yet again for more edits in a relentless loop of detail driven diplomacy.

The negotiations could not hold up beneath the weight of Begin's single-minded truculence and Sadat's deepening skepticism of Israel. On day eleven, without an agreement, and with Sadat threatening to throw in the towel, Carter had no other choice but to return to Washington and admit defeat.

Before withdrawing, President Carter's personal executive secretary, Susan Clough, reminded him that Begin had requested he sign a photograph of the three leaders for the prime minister's eight grandchildren. In a stroke of intuitive genius, Clough had procured the names of each of the grandchildren; Carter personalized the pictures with an inscription for each child. As Begin looked through the short stack of photos, reading aloud the names of each of his grandchildren, he transfigured from a pugnacious prime minister to a tenderhearted grandfather. Begin began to cry. As this rare display of emotion unfolded, Carter softly shared, "I wanted to be able to say, 'This is when your grandfather and I brought peace to the Middle East.'"

A few days later, on September 17, 1978, a day that lives on in the chronicles of peacemaking, Egyptian President Anwar Sadat, Israeli Prime Minister Menachim Begin, and United States President Jimmy Carter signed the Camp David Accords. The unlikely trio clasped hands, and with beaming smiles, embraced in a declaration of hope for the future of Middle East peace, and peace around the world. Following the ceremony, Begin remarked, "The Camp David conference should be renamed. It was the Jimmy Carter conference."

Later that year, the Nobel Peace Prize was jointly awarded to Anwar Sadat and Menachim Begin "for their contribution to the two frame agreements on peace in the Middle East." Nearly twenty-five years later, in 2002, Jimmy Carter was awarded the same prestigious prize—encompassing an even wider scope of his compassionate humanitarian work—"for his decades of untiring effort to find peaceful solutions to international conflicts, to advance democracy and human rights, and to promote economic and social development."

Four years later, in 2006, Carter raised headlines again, but this time for the controversial title of his book, *Palestine: Peace Not Apartheid*. The provocative manuscript detailed a two-state solution to the raging Israeli-Palestinian border schism, with Carter writing, "Israel's continued control and colonization of Palestinian land have been the primary obstacles to a comprehensive peace agreement in the Holy Land," reprimanding the people of the Promised Land for their belligerent, unilateral expansion into Palestinian territory. Carter's detail on this approach registered little to no surprise for those who faithfully followed his Middle East peace playbook. But as he toured the country to drum up support for the book, the man who had consistently interceded on behalf of oppressed peoples around the world weathered incredible criticism from Jewish leaders, fellow Democrats, and even his own Carter Center compadres. Fourteen members of the Carter Center's advisory board resigned in protest and lambasted the book's content as "unbecoming of a former president," accusing Carter of having "abandoned your historic role of broker in favor of becoming an advocate for one side." Given that Carter was better known for his quiet servitude than for wielding power—he made a habit of bending down low to lift others high for the good of humanity, rarely to any advantage of his own—the claims struck a nerve and rang untrue.

Peace is tricky. It's layered. It is not simple. The pursuit of peace is riddled with failure, a lot of hard tries and dead ends. Jimmy Carter seemed to never fear failing. His faith simply demanded that he try.

"We will not learn how to live together in peace by killing each other's children," Carter stated in a speech delivered after he was minted as a Nobel laureate during the peace prize ceremonies in Oslo, Norway. "The bond of our common humanity is stronger than the divisiveness of our fears and prejudices. God gives us the capacity for choice. We can choose to alleviate suffering. We can choose to work together for peace. We can make these changes—and we must."

The gospel of peace, according to a lifelong peacemaker like Jimmy Carter, mandates that the men and women who govern and lead consider the price of pursuing conflict before pawning young men and women off to war. Carter's take on Christianity demands an equality of mind and spirit—a reaching out to people who we may disagree with, who we do not easily understand, who may be difficult to love, who may be difficult to live with, and yet we must learn to love and live in peace with them anyway. It's counterintuitive, this gospel that instructs us to love our enemies and pray for those who persecute us. Still, in these following few lessons, Jimmy Carter asks us to grapple with our prejudices, confess our preconceived ideas, develop our minds, and increase our hearts by examining and following the precepts of Jesus, the Prince of Peace.

Blessed are the peacemakers,
for they shall be called children of God.
(Matthew 5:9)

February 17, 2002

Reaching Out to People of Different Cultures

Maranatha Baptist Church
Plains, Georgia

Lesson Scripture

Jonah 1 (NRSV)

1 Now the word of the LORD came to Jonah son of Amittai, saying, 2 'Go at once to Nineveh, that great city, and cry out against it; for their wickedness has come up before me.' 3 But Jonah set out to flee to Tarshish from the presence of the LORD. He went down to Joppa and found a ship going to Tarshish; so he paid his fare and went on board, to go with them to Tarshish, away from the presence of the LORD.

4 But the LORD hurled a great wind upon the sea, and such a mighty storm came upon the sea that the ship threatened to break up. 5 Then the mariners were afraid, and each cried to his god. They threw the cargo that was in the ship into the sea, to lighten it for them. Jonah, meanwhile, had gone down into the hold of the ship and had lain down, and was fast asleep. 6 The captain came and said to him, 'What are you doing sound asleep? Get up, call on your god! Perhaps the god will spare us a thought so that we do not perish.'

7 The sailors said to one another, 'Come, let us cast lots, so that we may know on whose account this calamity has come upon us.' So they cast lots, and the lot fell on Jonah. 8 Then they said to him, 'Tell us why this calamity has come upon us. What is your occupation? Where do you come from? What is your country? And of what people are you?' 9 'I am a Hebrew,' he replied. 'I worship the LORD, the God of heaven, who made the sea and the dry land.' 10 Then the men were even more afraid, and said to him, 'What is this that you have done!' For the men knew that he was fleeing from the presence of the LORD, because he had told them so.

11 Then they said to him, 'What shall we do to you, that the sea may quieten down for us?' For the sea was growing more and more tempestuous. 12 He said to them, 'Pick me up and throw me into the sea; then the sea will quiet down for you; for I know it is because of me that this great storm has come upon you.' 13 Nevertheless, the men rowed hard to bring the ship back to land, but they could not, for the

sea grew more and more stormy against them. [14] Then they cried out to the LORD, 'Please, O LORD, we pray, do not let us perish on account of this man's life. Do not make us guilty of innocent blood; for you, O LORD, have done as it pleased you.' [15] So they picked Jonah up and threw him into the sea; and the sea ceased from its raging. [16] Then the men feared the LORD even more, and they offered a sacrifice to the LORD and made vows.

[17] But the LORD provided a large fish to swallow up Jonah; and Jonah was in the belly of the fish three days and three nights.

Jonah is one of the briefest books in the Bible—about 1,300 words or so. What is peculiar about Jonah?

Let's get that out of the way. [*Congregation laughs*] Okay, what was it? Everybody knows.

Swallowed by a fish.

Okay, he was followed by a fish. What else is there about Jonah?

He was a Hebrew.

Tried to run away from God.

We'll get to that in a minute.

But some people have said that the book of Jonah is the most Christ-like book in the Old Testament. Why do you think that could possibly be true? You may or may not agree; I'm not sure I do.

God is forgiving people.

This is one of the most remarkable demonstrations of God's forgiveness, not only of Jonah, but also of whom?

Nineveh.

Of the people of Nineveh.

Nineveh was a great city of that time. It was in Assyria. And Jonah lived in the eighth century B.C. He was from the Northern Kingdom, Israel. He was a rich kid. The evidence is that he moved easily, even in the royal palace—his family must've been quite influential. He was what you might call an archconservative. He was jingoist, in that he thought that anybody not related directly to Israel was wrong, and inferior, and even subhuman. He was very prejudiced against foreigners. But he was tapped by God to perform a very important task.

So, Jonah comes to us in this lesson as a very interesting and intriguing person. And this lesson overall is going to be related to God's grace.

And while we go through Jonah this morning. I hope that you will try, if possible, to put yourselves in the role of Jonah, which is not a pleasant thing. But when we study these episodes in the Bible, we learn, repeatedly, about people who make mistakes. Since none of us can live long enough to make all the mistakes, we have to learn from others who make mistakes that we might not make so that we can correct our own lives and not repeat the mistakes that we have described, for instance, in the Bible.

But for the Grace of God, Go I

Who are some of the people that are very famous that you love in the Bible who made serious mistakes?

Peter.

Yeah, Peter's a very good one. Who else?

King David.

Abraham.

Abraham lied about his wife. He said she wasn't even married to him, that she was his sister. Who else?

Paul.

How about Paul? Paul denied Christ and persecuted the Christians.

How about James, John? Remember them? They went to Jesus and said, "Put us above everybody else when you get to be in your kingdom. We want to be your secretary of state. Or your secretary of defense. Or secretary of treasury. We want to be right next to you."

So, you can go down a list of people in the Bible who are heroic in the totality of their lives, but who, in their individual actions made serious mistakes. And the intriguing parts of the Bible are how did God accommodate these violations of his basic premises and laws and precepts and standards and moral values and even covenants?

What does the Bible say about all of us, as far as mistakes? All have sinned and come short of the glory of God, and the wages of sin is?

Death.

Eternal death. So, all of us are basically in the same category in relation to God, as was Jonah, as was Moses, as was Abraham, as was Peter, Paul, John, James, David, and we shouldn't go into any lesson in the Bible with the feeling that I am superior in my relationship with God to those about whom I am reading or studying. So, as we go into this lesson about Jonah, instead of saying, I'm above him—I'm glad I didn't make that kind of mistake, we should say, how am I related to Jonah in my relationship with God? and what can I learn from this lesson that would prevent the ultimate consequence, which is death, but where I can mirror God's relationship with Jonah after he made his mistake?

...Ninevah, by the way, was a large city. It was established by Nimrod, according to the Old Testament, the great-grandson of Noah. It was inhabited by Gentiles. It was known to be an enemy of Israel.

At this particular time, Jeroboam II was the King of Israel, and he was a very benevolent and a very wise king, so, there was a good relationship between Israel and the surrounding countries. Israel was not conquered. No Israelites were in captivity. Israel was not endangered by a powerful military force that wanted to overwhelm Israel. So, it was a pretty secure country and prosperous country in the time of Jonah. And I'm sure Jonah took the position then that since Israel was prosperous, it was particularly blessed, and therefore, the people of Israel were in good shape with God and also superior to the countries around them because of their great blessings. Just like we Americans are—we are particularly blessed, so therefore we must be particularly worthy of blessings.

The Bible says, in a couple of places, how large Nineveh is. It's described as having walls a hundred feet high and taking three days to either walk across or to go around the perimeter of Nineveh. I thought about that—do we have very many people here from Texas? Just a few.

This Texan had a cousin in north Georgia, and he came to visit his cousin, and the cousin was very proud because he had worked all his life up in north Georgia and he had bought some property up in the mountains. So, the first morning his cousin from Texas was there, they went out on the front porch and the Georgian says, "Just look at all the property that I have accumulated. If you look up the top of that mountain, mine goes about halfway up. And that valley, all that belongs to me," and so forth.

The Texan interrupted him. He said, "Look, that's nothing." He said, "If you go to my ranch I can get in my pickup truck in the morning and I can ride westward 'til ten o'clock, and then I turn southward, I can ride 'til noon, and then I turn back eastward, I can ride two more hours and it takes me two or three more hours just to get back home. What do you think of that?"

And the Georgian said, "Yes sir." He said, "I used to have a pickup like that myself."

[*Congregation laughs*]

The Call of God and Jonah

Well, Jonah is looking with fear and consternation and condemnation and animosity and hatred, you might say, at the people of Nineveh. Because, although they are not threatening Israel at this point, they are non-Jews and they have the potential, which we saw realized later on with the conquest of the Hebrews, as one that would threaten Israel, and he was a very jingoistic or patriotic person.

Let's read now the first two verses of the first chapter of Jonah.

[1] Now the word of the LORD came to Jonah the son of Amittai, saying, [2] 'Go at once to Nineveh, that great city, and cry out against it; for their wickedness has come up before me.'

Why do you think Jonah felt as he did? There are a lot of reasons. I've already outlined a few of them. What are some of them?

That's the way he was raised.

Nineveh was a bad bunch of folks. They were fearsome people, potentially...and he saw this as a very powerful group. The message that God wanted him to take to Nineveh was a very unpleasant message, and Jonah was a lowly, not very well-known prophet. So, he could see himself having to go into this strange enemy territory and preach their condemnation from a God that the people in Nineveh didn't even worship. "My God says that you're going to be condemned because of your sinfulness." That's a very difficult message to preach even to home folks, much less folks up there.

The second thing is—he really didn't have anything to gain. If God condemned Nineveh and destroyed it, which, by the way, did happen a hundred years later when Nahum was the prophet, then Jonah would get the blame for it. But suppose Jonah went up there and preached a message of condemnation and then Nineveh was not destroyed, he would be looked on as a false prophet. So, he didn't have anything to gain.

Most of us know what he did. Let's see what he did. Start with the third and fourth verse.

[3] But Jonah set out to flee to Tarshish from the presence of the Lord.

Tarshish is generally believed to be in the southern tip of Spain, not too far from Gibraltar. But symbolically, Tarshish was the end of the world. That was at the far end of the Mediterranean Sea, and there was very little, if any, exploration of territory beyond that. So, instead of going in one direction that God told him to go, he very quickly booked passage on a ship going as far in the other direction as he possibly could, trying to escape, the Bible says, from God.

And the fourth verse.

4 But the LORD hurled a great wind upon the sea, and such a mighty storm came upon the sea that the ship threatened to break up.

The sailors on the ship thought that this was an extraordinary storm. It wasn't just a storm that would normally come with the weather. There was something special about this storm. So, they began to cast about in their own minds, "What is the cause of this catastrophe falling upon us?" The Bible says they started throwing cargo over the side to lighten the ship—to reduce its prospects of being sunk. Then they saw that didn't happen, and they thought, "Something must be wrong." So, they began to pray to their own gods and the storm just got worse and worse.

Finally, they said to themselves, "What could be causing this condemnation of our ship with this strange storm?" They threw lots, like dice, and the lots fell on Jonah. So, they searched about and they found Jonah. Where was he?

Asleep.

He was asleep down below.... When they woke him up, they questioned him, and he said that he was a Hebrew from Israel and they began to wander about this strange person. And he finally confessed that he thought that this terrible storm was probably his own fault...that he had tried to escape from his God.

Then the Bible says these sailors began to pray to Jonah's God and to ask Jonah to pray as well. Jonah didn't do it, and the storm continued. Finally, they asked Jonah, "What can we do?" and what did Jonah say?

Throw me overboard.

"Throw me overboard," he said.

So, rather than repent and pray and be reconciled with God, Jonah decided to do what? To commit suicide. He was obviously in anguish. Having separated himself from God, Jonah decided to commit suicide rather than seek reconciliation with God.

Let's turn now to verse eleven.

11 Then they said to him, 'What shall we do to you, that the sea may quieten down for us?' For the sea was growing more and more tempestuous.
12 He said to them, 'Pick me up and throw me into the sea; then the sea will quieten down for you; for I know it is because of me that this great storm has come upon you.' 13 Nevertheless,...

What did the sailors do? They didn't do it. They were reluctant to kill or to murder someone who worshipped the Hebrew god.

...the men rowed hard to bring the ship back to land, but they could not, for the sea grew more and more stormy against them. And then they cried out to the LORD,...

They are praying to whose god? They are praying to the Hebrew God. To God Almighty. To Jonah's God.

...'Please, O LORD, we pray, do not let us perish on account of this man's life. Do not make us guilty of innocent blood; for you, O LORD, have done as it pleased you.' 15 So they picked Jonah up and threw him into the sea; and the sea ceased from its raging. 16 Then the men feared the Lord even more, and they offered a sacrifice to the Lord and made vows.
17 But the LORD provided a large fish to swallow up Jonah; and Jonah was in the belly of the fish three days and three nights.

And then Jonah had a transformation in his attitude. That next group of verses...is a beautiful poem, very reminiscent of Psalm 139:7–10, which says, "No matter where I go, you are there."

Jonah 2 1:9 (NRSV)

'I called to the Lord out of my distress,
and he answered me;
out of the belly of Sheol I cried,
and you heard my voice.
3 You cast me into the deep,
into the heart of the seas,
and the flood surrounded me;
all your waves and your billows
passed over me.
4 Then I said, "I am driven away
from your sight;
how shall I look again
upon your holy temple?"
5 The waters closed in over me;
the deep surrounded me;
weeds were wrapped around my head
6 at the roots of the mountains.
I went down to the land
whose bars closed upon me for ever;
yet you brought up my life from the Pit,
O LORD my God.
7 As my life was ebbing away,
I remembered the LORD;
and my prayer came to you,
into your holy temple.
8 Those who worship vain idols

forsake their true loyalty.
[9] But I with the voice of thanksgiving
will sacrifice to you;
what I have vowed I will pay.
Deliverance belongs to the LORD!'

It's interesting to note that a repentant Jonah, praying to God, became quite confident—you noticed?—of his deliverance. He had faith in God's grace. That if he turned away from his sinful ways and acknowledged the power and omnipotence and omnipresence of God, that God would indeed forgive him and let him be of service again.

Christ's Example in Our Life

What do we get out of this lesson, so far? I asked you earlier to think about what relationship Jonah might have to us? What lesson do you see?

Sometimes we are afraid of the unknown, and therefore, we, out of our own fear to do what God's will is, we choose not to do it. And sometimes God lets us sink to the very lowest in order for us to really appreciate what his plans are for us.

Sometimes we fear the unknown and we refuse to accept the will of God, even though we know what it is. We try to escape from God. We turn from God. We might even become alienated from God and blame God for our troubles, forgetting that God's desire is for forgiveness, and reconciliation, and a new harmonious working relationship with us.

No matter who we are, no matter what our status in life might be—well-known, influential, wealthy, perhaps famous, that doesn't matter. Each person has a relationship, or a potential covenant with God.

And God calls to us, either through the Scriptures, or through our own personal experiences, through our relationship with Jesus Christ, through our temptations, through our encounters with other human beings, and God is telling us in every one of these individual—you might say minute or relatively insignificant experiences, "I want you to act" how? As Christ acts. You have professed to Me through a personal covenant that you are a little Christ. You have claimed to be a what? "A Christian, which is a little Christ."

And in that contract, or promise, or pledge, or covenant, you have pledged, when you accepted Christ as Savior, that you would emulate, or copy, or pattern your lives after the life of Christ. That you would relate to the poor, as did Jesus Christ. That you would reach out to the forlorn and the helpless and the suffering, as did whom? Jesus Christ.

You have promised to do that, and that is God's commandment to us—to emulate or copy the words and actions of Jesus Christ.

That is a fearsome prospect for many of us, maybe for all of us. Just as fearsome, perhaps, in our own circle of influence, as was Jonah's command to go to Nineveh, because it is not easy to cross the chasm that separates us from those in need. It's a natural human trait to encapsulate ourselves in a cocoon that encompasses people just like us. People whom we love, with whom we can relate easily, who maybe even love us, who speak the same language, who have the same color skin, who go to the same church, who live in the same neighborhood, and to exclude others who might be poor, suffering, isolated, fearful, inarticulate, forgotten, ignored, in need.

We could spend our entire life living in an egocentric cocoon. A cocoon of self-satisfaction, afraid to reach out because we might encounter an unanticipated circumstance which could involve a request that we share with a person whom we would rather exclude from our lives. And that's a very difficult decision to make.

The Decision Is Ours

These people that I'm describing who are in need, I'm not talking about in Burkina Faso, or Nigeria, or Haiti, I'm talking about in our own neighborhood, and the choice we make is to accept the will of God or to reject it. And the rejection is not a public rejection. The rejection of God's will for us is a very private thing, for which we would not be condemned by others, but between us and Jesus Christ, there is a deliberate separation.

I decide in my life that I will live a self-centered existence. I will not reach out and share my wealth, my time, my friendship, my love with people who are different, or unattractive, or in need, who might put a burden on me. [But] our covenant with God through Christ, that I will do what Christ did. He reached out to the lepers, and to the Jews who collected taxes from their own people for the Romans, and to those who were very sinful—committed adultery, and to the absolutely despised, like the Samaritans.

And we go through life with an element of prejudice and arrogance, always, though, with the opportunity to be reconciled with God, as was Jonah in the belly of a fish because he prayed sincerely to God for forgiveness, and he resubmitted himself, reattached himself, to the Almighty Creator of the universe.

Sometimes, when we are somewhat guilty, or somewhat fearful, or somewhat in sorrow, or somewhat disappointed that we didn't reach our maximum objectives in life, we forget that there is an Almighty God who knows everything, who is everywhere, and who is all-powerful, who is waiting for our prayer of submission, and our prayer of repentance, and our prayer of commitment and dedication. And then we can reattach ourselves, as a partner in life, to the Creator of the entire universe. Who is filled, not with condemnation, but with love and grace and compassion and friendship and forgiveness.

But too many times, all of us, including me, go through a period of our lives, or maybe for a long period of our lives, and are not sure that our lives are compatible with that of Christ. Thinking that it might be too difficult to make the kinds of innovative efforts to reach out and do things in the name of Christ.

Well, I think the book of Jonah, even the first half of it, is a very good lesson for all of us.

As Jonah found, and as the sailors on the ship found, we cannot escape from the presence of God. God is with us. God knows what we're doing, and no failure of our own, no mistake of our own is final. There is always that invitation from God, through Christ, "Come and place yourself in my bosom. Come and clasp the hand of Jesus Christ and be reconciled and forgiven."

But it requires, as in the case of Jonah, that we acknowledge our need. That we eliminate some of our superior, self-satisfied attitude, and say, "I am a sinner in the eyes of God, and what I deserve is death, but through my Savior, Jesus Christ, I am given total forgiveness, as though I had never sinned." As Christ takes upon himself on the cross the punishment for our sin. God loved us so much that he gave us his only son, that through our Savior, Jesus Christ, we can be saved and have eternal life, beginning now.

I don't think it's a coincidence that Christ was in the tomb three days and Jonah was in the belly of the fish three days. Maybe that's a prediction, at least symbolically, of things to come. The fact that Jonah was so totally alienated from God because of his own decision, and then became so completely reconciled with God because of his own decision, sends us a very clear signal about what we can do with our own lives. Do you agree with that?

February 24, 2002

An Inclusive Gospel

Maranatha Baptist Church
Plains, Georgia

Lesson Scripture

Jonah 3 (NRSV)

1 The word of the LORD came to Jonah a second time, saying, 2 'Get up, go to Nineveh, that great city, and proclaim to it the message that I tell you.' 3 So Jonah set out and went to Nineveh, according to the word of the LORD. Now Nineveh was an exceedingly large city, a three days' walk across. 4 Jonah began to go into the city, going a day's walk. And he cried out, 'Forty days more, and Nineveh shall be overthrown!' 5 And the people of Nineveh believed God; they proclaimed a fast, and everyone, great and small, put on sackcloth.

6 When the news reached the king of Nineveh, he rose from his throne, removed his robe, covered himself with sackcloth, and sat in ashes. 7 Then he had a proclamation made in Nineveh: 'By the decree of the king and his nobles: No human being or animal, no herd or flock, shall taste anything. They shall not feed, nor shall they drink water. 8 Human beings and animals shall be covered with sackcloth, and they shall cry mightily to God. All shall turn from their evil ways and from the violence that is in their hands. 9 Who knows? God may relent and change his mind; he may turn from his fierce anger, so that we do not perish.'

10 When God saw what they did, how they turned from their evil ways, God changed his mind about the calamity that he had said he would bring upon them; and he did not do it.

How many of you feel that every day you are confronted with different cultures? We really are. Quite often we can learn a lot from people who are quite different from us....

There is a disparity of cultures around us, and sometimes we are not aware of how different people are because we tend to enclose ourselves in a homogenous environment. Do you agree with that? And this is a natural human trait. I'm guilty of it, too. I'm more at ease when

I'm with people just like me—that like the same songs, and listen to the same newscasts, and watch the same sports events, and have the same color skin, and go to the same kind of church. That's a natural human trait.

But, that is really, in a way, contradictory to what the Bible teaches us we should do....

The Israelites felt that they were the exclusive, blessed people of God, and they enclosed themselves in a sometimes self-satisfactory and sinful environment and alienated God and were punished accordingly, and sometimes they benefitted from the covenant with Abraham and others. Of course, in the New Testament, Paul explained that the children of Abraham were all those who shared his what? Faith! Not his bloodlines—his faith. And he pointed out that Abraham was blessed by God before he was circumcised, not afterwards. So, in the early church, Paul had to explain that God's grace, God's mercy, extended to many people.

What do you think is the difference between those two things–grace and mercy? What does God's mercy mean?

His love for us.

Well, it's a little bit different. When you are merciful on someone, what have you done?

Forgiven them.

They have done something wrong, and you have mercy, and you forgive. Mercy is when God doesn't give us something we deserve, and grace would be, what?

When he gives us what we don't deserve.

Exactly. There's a subtle difference, but it's an important difference.

Whether God doesn't give us the punishment we deserve and gives us a blessing that we don't deserve. They are two different things, very closely related. God's mercy on the one hand. God's grace on the other.

It's easy for us to accept the power of God, is it not, because we look upon God as the creator of the universe, all-powerful. It's easy for us to think about God as omniscient. What does omniscient mean?

All-knowing.

God has all-knowledge, perfect judgment. Those two things are easy to see and hear and comprehend. But God's gentleness, God's compassion, God's grace and mercy—which we've just described—is difficult for people to accept and that's really the essence of Jonah's story...and it's different from the writings of all the other prophets.

In what way? What is the difference between Jonah and all the rest of them?

All the other stories of the prophets, Isaiah and so forth, we extract from them the message of what the prophets were saying. In Jonah, the story is just about the prophet himself...

The message from God is that love endures forever. One psalm that you might want to read or remember in your mind is Psalm 136. In this psalm, there are twenty-six verses, and each one of them describes some strange thing that happened that relates to God, and at the bottom of each verse it says, "God's love endures forever." So, twenty-six different times, those exact words: "His love endures forever."

Devotional Scripture

Psalm 136

1 O give thanks to the LORD, for he is good,
for his steadfast love endures forever.
2 O give thanks to the God of gods,
for his steadfast love endures forever.
3 O give thanks to the Lord of lords,
for his steadfast love endures forever;
4 who alone does great wonders,
for his steadfast love endures forever;
5 who by understanding made the heavens,
for his steadfast love endures forever;
6 who spread out the earth on the waters,
for his steadfast love endures forever;
7 who made the great lights,
for his steadfast love endures forever;
8 the sun to rule over the day,
for his steadfast love endures forever;
9 the moon and stars to rule over the night,
for his steadfast love endures forever;
10 who struck Egypt through their firstborn,
for his steadfast love endures forever;
11 and brought Israel out from among them,
for his steadfast love endures forever;
12 with a strong hand and an outstretched arm,
for his steadfast love endures forever;
13 who divided the Red Sea in two,
for his steadfast love endures forever;
14 and made Israel pass through the midst of it,
for his steadfast love endures forever;
15 but overthrew Pharaoh and his army in the Red Sea,
for his steadfast love endures forever;

16 who led his people through the wilderness,
for his steadfast love endures forever;
17 who struck down great kings,
for his steadfast love endures forever;
18 and killed famous kings,
for his steadfast love endures forever;
19 Sihon, king of the Amorites,
for his steadfast love endures forever;
20 and Og, king of Bashan,
for his steadfast love endures forever;
21 and gave their land as a heritage,
for his steadfast love endures forever;
22 a heritage to his servant Israel,
for his steadfast love endures forever.
23 It is he who remembered us in our low estate,
for his steadfast love endures forever;
24 and rescued us from our foes,
for his steadfast love endures forever;
25 who gives food to all flesh,
for his steadfast love endures forever.
26 O give thanks to the God of heaven,
for his steadfast love endures forever.

God's Forgiveness Is for Everyone

Now we've come down to the third chapter of Jonah, and I'll read the first four verses.

> 1 The word of the LORD came to Jonah a second time...

He gave Jonah another chance, which God does to all of us, if we deserve it.

...saying, [2] 'Get up, go to Nineveh, that great city, and proclaim to it the message that I tell you.' [3] So, Jonah set out and went to Nineveh, according to the word of the LORD. Now Nineveh was an exceedingly large city, a three days' walk across. [4] Jonah began to go into the city, going a day's walk. And he cried out

This is a summary, obviously.

'Forty days more, and Nineveh shall be overthrown!'

Jonah did this with a great deal of enthusiasm. Why?

Because they were Syrians.

They were Syrians and he liked the message, did he not? What was the message? Forty days and Nineveh will be overthrown. This was a very happy thing for Jonah. He couldn't wait for it to happen. There's no record at all, and even the commentaries that I read last night and this morning say that never did Jonah mention forgiveness or repentance or anything like that, he was just declaring the destruction of Nineveh.

He had gotten deliverance himself, for which he had expressed, beautifully, his thanks, but now he had no desire for Nineveh to have a second chance like he had.

He preached an unlikely message to an unlikely people with certainly an unlikely attitude for God's prophet.

Let's read the fifth verse now.

[5] And the people of Nineveh believed God; they proclaimed a fast, and everyone, great and small, put on sackcloth.

The next few verses describe how the king himself put on sackcloth.

So, as far as we know, they didn't repent and put on sackcloth and admit their guilt with any promise of forgiveness. But they recognized the presence of the omnipotent, omniscient God Almighty. So, the presence of what we know as the Holy Spirit was obviously among the people of Nineveh, and on their own, not to get eternal life, not to get God's forgiveness, they knew that they had done wrong—we don't know their exact sins—and they put on sackcloth, and ashes, and submerged themselves in a spirit of contrition and repentance.

Let's read down to the tenth verse.

10 When God saw what they did, how they turned from their evil ways, God changed his mind about the calamity that he had said he would bring upon them; and he did not do it.

Here are people with no promise of forgiveness, no promise of reward, hardly knowing who God was, as far as we know, unanimously, because of their own volition and the orders of the king, asking God for forgiveness. Let's pause there just for a minute to compare ourselves with the people of Nineveh.

We Christians know all about God, as much as we can comprehend with our human minds. We Christians know that Jesus Christ was the son of God. We Christians know that God loved us so much that he sent his only son to take the punishment that we deserve for our own sins on himself, on the cross, and gave his life in anguish, screaming out, "My God! My God! Why have you forsaken me?," as he took upon himself my sins and your sins.

Why? Because God loved us so much, John 3:16 says. And we're promised forgiveness, compassion, love, and eternal life.

Now compare the way we feel about our own sinfulness, our own determination to do better, to live a worthy life, to please God, which is often lackadaisical, if it exists at all, with the determination and sincerity of the people of Nineveh. In each one of the Old Testament not only books, but individual episodes or stories or events, God has let us have this Holy Word so that we could not just know with casual interest about this interesting guy called Jonah, but to derive from the story of Jonah facts, and truths, and guidance that would affect us.

It's quite often very difficult for me, and I presume you, to put ourselves in the role of the people who make mistakes. But almost all of the biblical heroes made serious mistakes...and sometimes it's our tendency to look upon them as kind of different from us. But the Bible wants us to use these vivid stories, some of them humorous, some of them very sad and troubling, and say, "What can I do to make sure that my sinfulness"—which is recognized by God, all have sinned and come short of the glory of God—that my sinfulness "is forgiven"? Because of my abject admission of the sins, and my repentance before God, and my knowledge, which will be fulfilled, that God will forgive me.

Even this character that ran away from God, in a somewhat humorous but tragic way, was given a second chance, almost immediately, when he repented after he was cast upon the shore and gave a prayer of acknowledgment of God's grace. So, let's put ourselves in the role of Jonah for a few minutes.

A Different Kind of Judgment

By the way, God's judgment fell on Ninevah, did it not? What does God's judgment mean? We ordinarily think of God's judgment as punitive. God's judgment fell on Nineveh, did it not? And God's judgment was what?

Forgiveness.

Forgiveness.

As our pastor says, "God always answers prayer. Sometimes the answer is 'Yes.' Sometimes the answer is 'No.' Sometimes the answer is 'You gotta be kidding.'" [*Congregation laughs*]

If we pray a selfish prayer, a prayer that would exalt ourselves at the expense of others. If we pray for blessings without acknowledgement of our need for repentance and forgiveness. If we pray that navy will beat army next fall, God's going to say, "You gotta be kidding. I got just as many prayers on the army side." [*Congregation laughs*] Well, anyway, we tend to pray without thought, and if we are willing to accept responsibility for the outcome and pray that even the things that we request from God are compatible with the will of Christ, then the answer that God gives us will be "Yes."

Let's read now Jonah 4:1–5.

> 1 But this was very displeasing to Jonah...

This is God's forgiveness.

> ...and he became angry. 2 He prayed to the LORD again and said, 'O Lord! Is not this what I said while I was still in my own country? That is why I fled to Tarshish at the beginning; for I knew that you are a gracious God and merciful, slow to anger, and abounding in steadfast love, and ready to relent from punishing. 3 And now, O LORD, please take my life from me, for it is better for me to die than to live.' 4 And the Lord said, 'Is it right for you to be angry?'

Jonah is furious because of several reasons. One is that he had said that God was going to destroy Nineveh, and it made him look as though he had given the wrong statement. Also, he was furious that God had shown special favor to Gentiles, who might, on occasion, and—we know later—became enemies of Israel. And, as he said, he was furious to realize, very reluctantly, that God was a God of all people. Instead of being a punitive God, which pleased Jonah very much, God was also a God of love and compassion and grace and forgiveness and mercy.

This is a characteristic of God that we cherish for ourselves, but we are sometimes reluctant to share God and God's blessings with others because of jealousy. Because we tend to feel that we are more worthy, and we don't quite want there to be an absolutely even ground in front of the cross.

Surely, we are superior in God's eyes in some ways. Otherwise, why would we be so blessed in America? Why would we be so rich and powerful and secure? And maybe those people in Africa, or other places, that are suffering so much, maybe they are just not as worthy in God's eyes. We tend to feel that way, even if we know it's wrong.

So, what did Jonah do?

5 Then Jonah went out of the city and sat down east of the city, and made a booth for himself there. He sat under it in the shade, waiting to see what would become of the city.

He still had hopes that Nineveh would be destroyed, and he wanted to see this glorious event from a safe place. It was hot, so God created a bush, or a vine, to give Jonah some shade, and Jonah was very grateful and very much loved that bush, which he saw as miraculous, having come up overnight. Then God sent what else? A worm. And the worm attacked the bush, and the bush died. Then God made it especially hot and Jonah was sitting exposed to the sunshine....

10 Then the LORD said, 'You are concerned about the bush, for
which you did not labor and which you did not grow; it came into
being in a night and perished in a night. 11 And should I not be con-
cerned about Nineveh, that great city, in which there are more than a hundred and twenty thousand persons who do not know their right hand from their left'...

That means about God.

'and also many animals?'

That's the end of the book—kind of an abrupt ending, is it not? But the story is one that lingers in one's mind.

Most people just think about Jonah and the fish, that's it. But here was a man who tried to encapsulate God—he tried to put God in a box that Jonah created and put limits on God, and God's mercy, and God's love, and God's concern about all humanity. It was so grievous to him that he would rather die than face it.

A Compassionate Life

It's a good lesson for us to remember and to ask ourselves, do we practice, in any way, an exclusionary life?

I would guess that almost everyone in this group, if honest, would have to say, yes, I do practice an exclusionary life. As I said earlier in this lesson, it's a human trait to exclude people who are, first of all, different. Who might be unattractive. Who might be needy. And who might have harmed us in some way and whom we might consider inferior or even, on occasion, subhuman—not worthy of God's blessing.

We all have a tendency in that direction, and the essence of the ministry of Christ was exactly the opposite from it. If you go down the list of all the vivid impressions that we have of Jesus' words and actions, they encompass those very same kinds of people, do they not?

He reached out to the AIDS victims of that age, who had what?

Leprosy.

And in those days, in Jesus' time, all the people felt that these lepers were sick because they had committed such terrible sins that this was God's way to punish them. They didn't know what the sins were. The only thing they knew was, "You are a leper, therefore you are a sinner and God is punishing you. I wish I knew what you did, but you deserve it, obviously."

And they were not only excluded from society because their disease was contagious, but they were also excluded from society because they were subhuman. And Christ deliberately reached out to the lepers and ministered to them, on more than one occasion—one time to ten lepers. He told them, "You are forgiven. Your leprosy will be cleansed.

Go bathe. Tell the priest. Show the priest that your sores are healed." And one of them came back. Who was that? A Samaritan came back—one out of ten—and Jesus said, "Where are the rest of them?"

Another time, someone asked Jesus, "Who is my neighbor?" and who did Jesus say was our neighbor? He said the Samaritan exemplified what a neighbor was.

The Samaritans were so despised in that era, much more despicable than anyone in our society. There are about six hundred Samaritans left. Rosalynn and I have been there. We were there just before Menachim Begin built a Jewish settlement on top of the Holy Hill of the Samaritans. And they are so "filthy" that the shadow of a Samaritan falling on a Jew's feet meant that that person couldn't go to the temple to worship until a cleansing ceremony was performed. But Christ embraced the Samaritans.

Another time, he went to the well in Samaria, and a woman came there who was not only a Samaritan, but, you might say, a prostitute. She had had five husbands. Christ embraced her, and she became a provocative witness for Christ to the people among her society.

The Jews that betrayed their own people and collected taxes for the Romans collected more than they should—Jesus embraced them and went to their homes and had supper with them, which was an imprimatur of legitimacy and equality that was startling in those days.

A woman found in the act of adultery that was being stoned, according to the law, came to Christ. And he expressed God's forgiveness for her and told the attackers, "Let him who is without sin cast the first stone." Then he told the woman, "Go and sin no more."

I could spend a whole hour delineating for you the different episodes and parables that Christ used to teach us—how should I relate to other human beings? And where does Jesus concentrate his attention? It's on the people who are different. Who, quite often, too often, are excluded from our hearts, and our minds, and the sharing of our own Christian faith.

This is the lesson of Jonah eight hundred years, more or less, before Christ was born.

God Within Us

Let's turn now to Ephesians 3:20, a verse that I think is pertinent to this lesson. You may or may not agree. This is what Paul wrote to the Ephesians.

> 20 Now to him who by the power at work within us is able to accomplish abundantly far more than all we can ask or imagine....

That is the same God that Jonah was dealing with, that the people of Nineveh were dealing with. What is the essence of that verse? Where is the potential power for God to exhibit his domain on earth? What does it say? Two words. Within us!

That's kind of a surprising thing, but it's also a sobering thing, to say that God's power is there—he created everything, he knows everything. But in order to implement God's will on earth to further the realization of God's kingdom, God's power has to be utilized or demonstrated where? Within me and within you.

That's the lesson that we should remember this morning. Not the fish. Not the pagan sailors. Not even the people of Nineveh. Not even Jonah and the bush and the worm, although it's dramatic. The essence of it is that God's power, in the case of Nineveh, was exhibited through his presence and through some reluctant words of Jonah, and Jonah was not a good man in God's eyes. But we who know Christ, who know God's mercy and love and care and forgiveness and compassion, with a promise of eternal life, have a much greater responsibility or opportunity to expand our hearts, and expand our minds, and encompass others, and to emulate, or copy, the example that Christ set for us. That's our responsibility.

We can leave here and go the rest of our lives—two days, two years, twenty years, the rest of our lives—and never fulfill the essence of our being as Christians, which means what? "Little Christ." Are we accurate when we say, "I am a little Christ?"

December 9, 2007

The Call of God

Maranatha Baptist Church
Plains, Georgia

Lesson Scripture

Luke 1:26–38 (NRSV)

[26] In the sixth month the angel Gabriel was sent by God to a town in Galilee called Nazareth, [27] to a virgin engaged to a man whose name was Joseph, of the house of David. The virgin's name was Mary. [28] And he came to her and said, 'Greetings, favored one! The Lord is with you.' [29] But she was much perplexed by his words and pondered what sort of greeting this might be. [30] The angel said to her, 'Do not be afraid, Mary, for you have found favor with God. [31] And now, you will conceive in your womb and bear a son, and you will name him Jesus. [32] He will be great, and will be called the Son of the Most High, and the Lord God will give to him the throne of his ancestor David. [33] He will reign over the house of Jacob forever, and of his kingdom there will be no end.' [34] Mary said to the angel, 'How can this be, since I am a virgin?' [35] The angel said to her, 'The Holy Spirit will come upon you, and the power of the Most High will overshadow you; therefore the child to be born will be holy; he will be called Son of God. [36] And now, your relative Elizabeth in her old age has also conceived a son; and this is the sixth month for her who was said to be barren. [37] For nothing will be impossible with God.' [38] Then Mary said, 'Here am I, the servant of the Lord; let it be with me according to your word.' Then the angel departed from her.

Who was John the Baptist's mother?

Elizabeth.

And what was his father's name?

Zechariah.

What was Zechariah's profession?

A priest.

He was a very respected, older priest. And what was their problem in their family?

No children.

No children at a very advanced age, and so Zechariah thought they would never have children. What happened to him? Who came to see him?

Gabriel.

Where was he?

In the temple.

He was in the temple and Gabriel came to Zechariah and told Zechariah that Elizabeth would have a child although she was quite advanced in age. What was Zechariah's response?

He laughed.

He said, "Ah! It's not possible," and so Gabriel punished Zechariah because he had doubts. What was the punishment?

No speech.

He said, "You'll be stricken dumb because you doubted," and so, when Zechariah came out of the temple, he mumbled and made signs and so forth, but he couldn't speak, and he finally let people know that some miracle had happened.

That was in the temple in Jerusalem, the center of religion for those days, and Zechariah was a very high priest. That particular month he was the one that went into the Holy of Holies, and he was anointed by God to be blessed with the birth of John the Baptist. That's the way Luke begins his story of the life of Jesus Christ.

Luke was what kind of person? What do we know about Luke?

He was a Gentile.

A Gentile what?

A physician.

He was a medical doctor and a close friend of Saint Paul. Did Luke ever meet Jesus personally?

No.

No, he didn't.

He got his information from talking to Paul and Peter and all the apostles who traveled with Christ, but Luke became an expert on the life of Christ and wrote it in a highly personal way. He was the only Gentile among those who wrote the Gospels. What else did Luke write?

The book of Acts.

The book of Acts tells the best stories of the forming of the early Christian church. So, Luke was a very important figure and wrote in a kind of an emotional way about the birth of John, and then Christ.

Let's follow the same story. It's not going to be in the center of religion of the Jews. It's not going to be in a big city. It's not going to be with a highly respected priest. We're going to move to a different place, and it'll be in a little remote village in the northern part of the Holy Land in Nazareth with a young, fairly unschooled, uneducated peasant girl who most scholars now say was about thirteen years old. And she was betrothed to whom?

Joseph.

And Joseph had what kind of profession?

A carpenter.

He was a carpenter. We've got a very bright group this morning. [*Congregation laughs*] What was Mary's credentials, as far as her family background was concerned?

We don't know. The Bible doesn't say anything about Mary's background except that she was related in some way to Elizabeth—she was a cousin of Elizabeth. But her husband-to-be, her betrothed, Joseph, was a descendant of King David. So, you might say he had royal blood in him, although he was not directly related to Jesus Christ. But he inherited the proximity through family ties to King David, and David's home base was where?

Jerusalem.

Not quite.

Bethlehem.

Bethlehem! All right, how do we know that? Because they went to pay their taxes and to be registered, in effect, as citizens of Rome in David's home village of Bethlehem.

The Last Shall Be First

Let's turn now to the book of Luke, the first chapter, and we'll pick up on the twenty-sixth verse.

26 In the sixth month...

The sixth month of Elizabeth's pregnancy. You see how important Luke considers the birth of John the Baptist to be because he times the revelation of this miraculous event concerning Mary to how pregnant Elizabeth was. That was how he dated this revelation to Mary.

26 In the sixth month the angel Gabriel was sent by God to a town in Galilee...

A little insignificant town.

...called Nazareth, 27 to a virgin engaged to a man whose name was Joseph, of the house of David. The virgin's name was Mary.

The word "Mary" is translated, "the exalted one." By the way, let's stop there just for a moment. Why was Mary exalted? It wasn't because she was a high priestess. It wasn't because she came from a royal family. She was exalted by what? Through God's grace.

Because God chose her to receive a special blessing, endowed on her, not because of her stature, not even because of her family background, but because of God's love and compassion for her, and he picked her out, I'm sure, because she was a pure and holy person. That's important for us to remember because all the way through the New Testament, Mary was not all that important, but she was humble, she was patient, she was a very dedicated person to serving God, as we'll see in just a moment. Not through her own credentials, but through God's grace.

She was betrothed, or engaged, to a man whose name was Joseph. What does that mean in modern times?

Engagement.

Engagement, but it was a lot more than that. Back in those days, a betrothal, or an engagement, was binding on the husband and wife. Once they became betrothed, arranged almost exclusively by their parents, that was a binding commitment, and they could not break that commitment except through the same procedures as a divorce. It was just as though they were married. Although they hadn't had sex with each other, they hadn't slept with each other, but they were dedicated officially, in effect, to each other.

That was a time, too, when women had no real stature in the community, as is the case now in a lot of nations in the world. In some countries in Africa, where Rosalynn and I go quite often, the women have no rights; they can't testify in court. We have a special law program now in the nation of Liberia, and our Carter Center people are working in the interior of Liberia, where women cannot inherit property, and where rape is not even a crime. Women are completely subservient to their husbands, or to the males there, or to their fathers.

That was the way Mary was. She didn't have any choice in who she married. It was arranged by her father and by Joseph's parents, and she was subservient to her husband-to-be and to her father. This is a precursor, you might say, kind of a preview of what the life of Christ is going to be.... How does Mary compare to the kind of people whom Jesus is going to serve?

Humble.

Humble. Kind of outcast, without any power or authority. Needing to be supported by God's grace. And we know all the way through Jesus' ministry he reached out to the disadvantaged, to the people without authority or power, to what the people in Nepal call the "marginalized" groups—the ones that have been kept on the margin of life. So, that's what Mary epitomized or personified in this early time.

Same Angel, Different Responses

Let's read on down through the twenty-ninth verse.

[28] And he came to her and said, 'Greetings, favored one! The Lord is with you.' [29] But she was much perplexed by his words and pondered what sort of greeting this might be.

You see, he hadn't really said anything to her so far except "Greetings, favoured one! The Lord is with you," but I'm sure the appearance of an angel was a startling thing for her. By the way, although she was not an educated woman, she naturally had known, had absorbed the fact, that the prophets, the prophet Samuel, in particular, and later Isaiah, had predicted what?

A virgin would conceive.

I'm not sure they talked about the virgin then. Well, maybe Isaiah did—you might be right.

The Messiah was coming.

A Messiah was going to be coming. And here, Mary and Joseph and Elizabeth and all of them were living under a Roman dictator. They didn't have any authority over their own affairs. All of the Holy Land was occupied by Rome and the Romans were very wise administrators in that they let the local people, no matter who they were—it just happened that the Jews were one group—they let them run their own local affairs. They could repair the potholes in the roads, and they could educate their own children, and collect garbage, and they could worship the way they wanted to. The Roman Emperor didn't care how they worshipped; he didn't care anything about worship anyway. But they had been promised by the prophets down through the ages that a Messiah was going to come and bring liberation and would be endorsed by God. They knew that there were covenants, or promises by God, beginning with Abraham, actually even before that with Noah, and then with Moses later on, when Moses liberated the Israelites from

Egypt, and then later David was promised by God that his descendants would inherit the throne forever.

Let's read on. This is getting more and more exciting to me....

[30] The angel said to her, 'Do not be afraid, Mary, for you have found favour with God.'

And now comes a very startling message from Gabriel.

[31] 'And now, you will conceive in your womb and bear a son, and you will name him Jesus.'

By the way, Jesus is a name that is really similar to Joshua. If you look through the Old Testament, it starts out with Joshua, and later it changes to Jeshua, and then later it changes to Jesus. So, it's the same basic word.

[32] 'He will be great, and will be called the Son of the Most High,
and the Lord God will give to him the throne of his ancestor David. [33]
He will reign over the house of Jacob forever, and of his kingdom there will be no end.'

This is about as high an accolade, as great a promise, as could be made concerning any human being. He will reign over the world and his reign will be how long?

Forever.

Forever. He will be the son of God, and he will inherit all of the promises that were made by God to the forebearers of the Jewish people—to Abraham, to Isaac, to Jacob, and to Moses, and also to David.

This is a mind-boggling promise that Gabriel has sprung on this little girl, and she was then filled with consternation. The first time, she just was wondering what was going on, and now what's going to be her reaction? Let's read the thirty-fourth verse.

[34] Mary said to the angel, 'How can this be, since I am a virgin?'

Mary is doing the same thing that Zechariah did; she's questioning Gabriel's message from God. When Zechariah said, "How can this be, because my wife is already too old to have children," he was stricken dumb all the way through Elizabeth's pregnancy. He couldn't speak again until after John the Baptist was born. Here, Mary, though, said, "How can this be since I am a virgin? I've never slept with a man. How can I possibly have a child?" What was her punishment? No punishment. Why, do you think?

He's not going to choose her and then punish her.

Well, he chose Zechariah and punished him.

Women are special. [*Congregation laughs*]

He was empowering her.

That's right. He was giving her power. Also, she was young and innocent, and that was a natural, inevitable question.

But, as you know, when Abraham and Sarah didn't have any children, it was well known by Mary, and by Joseph, and everybody else what happened with them—when Abraham was one hundred years old, and his wife Sarah was about eighty-nine years old. So, Mary knew that in the past, old people had had children, and she may have known, too, about Elizabeth. She may have heard, since Elizabeth was her cousin—here's this old lady, my cousin, is going to have a baby. So, she was already familiar with that kind of miraculous power of God to let old people have babies after their normal time of pregnancy. But for a virgin to have a baby, that was unprecedented even in biblical terms.

So, I think it was a natural question....

She was just inquiring, not through disbelief—there is no indication that she didn't believe it, is there? She said, "You've told me I'm going to have a baby. I never had sex with any man. How can it be?" She didn't say, "I'm not going to do it." She didn't say, "You are wrong." So, she was not punished.

It's an interesting comparison between her and Zechariah.

Fully Divine, Fully Human

...This was a time when most of the Jewish people had pretty much given up on the fulfillment of the prophecy that a Messiah was going to come. Year after year after year had gone by; it had been about 450 years since the last book in the Old Testament was written, and nobody had heard anything about a Messiah, and the Romans were still dominating the Holy Land. So, most people thought this was a fairy tale. They kind of lost faith, and here, all of a sudden, Gabriel is saying, "You, little girl, are the one that's going to have the promised Messiah." It was a mind-boggling sort of revelation....

35 The angel said to her, 'The Holy Spirit will come upon you, and
the power of the Most High will overshadow you; therefore the child
to be born will be holy; he will be called Son of God.

And Gabriel continued,

36 And now, your relative Elizabeth in her old age has also conceived a son; and this is the sixth month for her who was said to be
barren. 37 For nothing will be impossible with God.'

And here comes Mary's response under this extraordinary circumstance.

38 Here am I, the servant of the Lord; let it be with me according
to your word.' Then the angel departed from her.

You can see what a dramatic story this is with this innocent young woman.

There's quite a bit of difference in the attitude of the Roman Catholic Church and the Protestant church to Mary. In fact, over a period of centuries, the top biblical scholars or theologians have differed about the birth of Christ. The first couple of centuries after Jesus' death, it was pretty well considered that Christ was not human—that Christ was divine only. It wasn't until the fourth century...Saint Augustine began to say that he couldn't understand how Christ could be born of a woman and still not have original sin—that Jesus Christ had to be without sin. So, Saint Augustine promulgated the idea that it was because of the virgin birth and that Christ in his birth had not inherited the original sin that God imposed on Adam. So, we know that Christ lived a sinless life, not born in sin but born of a virgin.

Then, it was not until the Reformation that came along in the fourteenth or fifteenth century that there was a general presumption among all Christians that Christ was both divine and human. So, it's a difficult thing for us to accept—that Christ was God, and the Son of God, and, at the same time, human.

This is a difficult but a beautiful concept to have in that if Christ was only divine, it would be much more difficult for me, at least, to relate to the human activities of Jesus. But we know that Christ came on earth pure and the Son of God but lived as a human being. He was dirty and sweaty and dusty and tired and tempted and he was weak, on occasion. He was in despair, on occasion. He felt that God abandoned him, on occasion. He prayed to God, bleeding, sweating almost drops of blood, that God would take his burden off him and not make him go through the ordeal of the crucifixion. Hanging on the cross, Jesus cried out what?

My God, my God, why have you forsaken me?

There was a time in Christ's final moments when he felt separated from God. Why was that? Because Christ became what? Sinful. In what way was Christ sinful?

He took others' sins upon himself.

He took my sins on his shoulders and all of yours. Everyone who believes in Christ, we know our burdens, our sinfulness is transferred to Jesus. Lies and cheating, even murder, rape, adultery, child abuse—became the guilt of Jesus Christ who was pure. He took upon himself the sins of every human being who believes in Christ. We can put our sins on Christ.

Sometimes it's a difficult thing to appreciate. Because it's kind of an impersonal relationship. We don't feel guilty enough because we put our sins on Christ. We feel that, okay, I'll go through today and I'll gossip about people, I'll cheat a little bit, I won't take care of the poor people around me, and so forth, and then this evening, I'll pray, and all of my sins will be forgiven, and I'll start all over again.

I had a realization awhile back when Amy came along as a little baby, *what if all my sins were on Amy*? Or pick out your favorite grandchild. Suppose all of your sins would be afflictions on the person that you love the most. It would be a difficult thing for us to tell a lie during the day's time because there would be a realization that the punishment for this lie is going to be on this little grandchild of mine. Well, we ought to feel the same way about Christ.

It's not a matter of a blank check for us to continue in our sinful ways just because we know we're going to be forgiven through the love of Christ, through the grace of God. It should be an impediment, a blockage, a prohibition, an offense that keeps us from committing further sins and placing more sins on Jesus Christ....

Properly Esteeming Mary

Ten years ago, there was a tremendous crusade—I'm not criticizing the Catholics—in the Catholic Church that was mounted by people who wanted Mary to have equal status with Christ. There was a *Time* magazine devoted almost entirely to this. They wanted to make Mary a co-redeemer. That the belief in Mary could equal the same belief in Christ to give us eternal life. And the pope, it said, was getting a hundred thousand letters a day from Catholics around the world who wanted to elevate Mary to the same status as Christ.

When Rosalynn and I were in Spain a few months ago, we traveled to some of the ancient cathedrals that were built during those times. Sometimes, we'd go into a cathedral and there would be, maybe, twenty statues of Mary and no statues of Christ. Eventually, the Catholic Church decided not to elevate Mary to the status of a co-redeemer with Jesus. In fact, the Gospel writers pay very little attention to Mary.

What other times do we know about Mary's being mentioned in the Bible after the birth of Christ?

Cana.

At the wedding in Cana, she was there and asked Jesus to make some wine. When else?

At the crucifixion.

That's in John only, not in the other three Gospels. Mary is at the foot of the cross, and Jesus asked John to take care of Mary as her son. And the other time, Jesus' mother and brothers showed up outside of a house where Jesus was having a prayer meeting, or something like that. And what did Jesus say?

Who is my mother?

They said, "Your mother and brothers are here to see you." He said, "Shucks. Who is my mother and brother? My mother and brother are these folks in here that are searching for the truth from God." He discounted Mary.

Well, nobody wants to discount Mary, but the fact is that we worship Jesus Christ as Savior, and we're saved by the grace of God through our faith in Jesus Christ, not through our faith in Mary. And, of course, other religions have special prophets through whom sometimes one can pray.

The Call of God

What do we get out of this lesson today? How do we relate ourselves to Mary?

I always try, sometimes unsuccessfully, it may be unsuccessful this morning, to take the message in the Bible, no matter what it is, whether it's from the Old Testament or the New Testament, and say, "How does that apply to us?" This is a very interesting and dramatic event, for this young girl to be visited by an angel and told you're going to have a baby without having sex and your baby's going to be the redeemer of the world and his kingdom's going to live forever. That's a wonderful story, but how does it relate to us?

God reached out to Mary, not because of her high status but through his grace. It shows that God can touch even the most humble person and exalt that person to perform great things. Mary accepted God's calling, really, without question.

How many of us are called by God?

We all are.

All of us. You don't have to be a pastor. You don't have to be a missionary. You don't have to be a special person in God's kingdom to be called by God.

How are we called by God?

To be a servant.

How does God call us to be a servant?

Through his work on this earth.

But how do we get the message?

Through the Spirit.

Through faith.

Through the Spirit. Through the Holy Bible. Through God's message to us. All of us who are now Christians have taken a solemn oath before God to attach our lives permanently to the life of Christ. To live according to the standards of Christ. To try to emulate or copy the life of Christ. To believe in Christ as our Savior and as our guide, as our example in life.

One good thing about the New Testament is it tells all of the difficulties that Jesus had and how he related to other people. Just like we have to relate to other people every day of our lives. He related to some good friends who supported him. He related to some that betrayed him. He related to some that were below him in social status, particularly the Samaritans. They were in the bottom of the social order.

So, Christ set an example for us for peace. That's a harsh word in America today. Not all Americans exalt peace. A lot of Americans exalt what? War. Preemptive war. We support unnecessary war. We worship the Prince of Peace, but we endorse and support unnecessary wars.

Humility, instead of pride. Service, instead of withdrawing into our own cocoon where we just live with our own friends and family and people just like us. Forgiveness of those who might hurt us in some way. Compassion for those who are different from us. Love for those that don't love us back.

Those are the kind of pure things that Christ represented, and we know about them, right? That's a calling of God to us. Live like Christ lived, and when we become Christians, we pledge ourselves to do so.

So, I think, that's a similarity to Mary. She did the best she could with what she had. She accepted the grace of God, the beneficence of God, the gift of God, the love of God, and made the most of it. And she tried to live her own life in accordance with God's will.

That's the lesson we get today. I think it's a beautiful lesson....

August 24, 2008

An Admonition for Humility

Maranatha Baptist Church
Plains, Georgia

Lesson Scripture

James 4:1–12 (NRSV)

[1] Those conflicts and disputes among you, where do they come from? Do they not come from your cravings that are at war within you? [2] You want something and do not have it; so you commit murder. And you covet something and cannot obtain it; so you engage in disputes and conflicts. You do not have, because you do not ask. [3] You ask and do not receive, because you ask wrongly, in order to spend what you get on your pleasures. [4] Adulterers! Do you not know that friendship with the world is enmity with God? Therefore whoever wishes to be a friend of the world becomes an enemy of God. [5] Or do you suppose that it is for nothing that the Scripture says, 'God yearns jealously for the spirit that he has made to dwell in us'? [6] But he gives all the more grace; therefore it says,

'God opposes the proud,
but gives grace to the humble.'

[7] Submit yourselves therefore to God. Resist the devil, and he will flee from you. [8] Draw near to God, and he will draw near to you. Cleanse your hands, you sinners, and purify your hearts, you double-minded. [9] Lament and mourn and weep. Let your laughter be turned into mourning and your joy into dejection. [10] Humble yourselves before the Lord, and he will exalt you. [11] Do not speak evil against one another, brothers and sisters. Whoever speaks evil against another or judges another, speaks evil against the law and judges the law; but if you judge the law, you are not a doer of the law but a judge. [12] There is one lawgiver and judge who is able to save and to destroy. So who, then, are you to judge your neighbor?

James is a unique book in the Bible. It's one of my favorites and always has been, at least for the last thirty years. What is special about the book of James?

It is written by the brother of our Lord.

There's been a lot of controversy over the centuries as exactly who was James because he doesn't identify himself in the book, but the general consensus is James, "the Just," who was the half-brother of our Lord. What do we know about James, who was born of Mary?

He was a prominent lay leader in the Jerusalem church.

I wouldn't say lay leader. He was *the* leader of the central Christian church during the early years of Christianity. He was the head of the Christians who were in Jerusalem, and Peter, and Paul, and all the apostles who had gone out to spread the gospel throughout the Mediterranean Sea area looked upon James as their spiritual leader in those days.

A Matter of Faith

Peter and Paul sometimes got into intense arguments with each other, and when they did, in order to resolve the arguments and not let it fester and divide the church even further, they would come back to Jerusalem and let James preside. They would debate, and some of their debates are in the book of Acts, and so forth, and then they would decide what was the premise on which the Christian church permanently would be based.

One of those arguments was whether you had to be a Jew first, before you could be a Christian. Peter, basically, was saying, that's true. That you couldn't become a Christian unless you accepted the Jewish faith first, and were circumcised, then you could become a Christian. Paul took great issue with that; they had intense debates about it, even some ugly words, as a matter of fact. Finally, they went back and debated in Jerusalem and decided that you do not have to be a Jew, first, to become a Christian.

This carried over into the questions that arose all the way over into Turkey, and Greece, and even to Italy, using modern-day geography. Because a lot of Christians there, particularly those that had been familiar with the synagogues, that were spreading the Jewish faith—and very positively, I'm not knocking that—they wanted to know, how can we fit into the great promise or commitment or covenant that God made with Abraham?

They were familiar with the Jewish text. They were familiar with the Old Testament. And they said, "The Old Testament says that Abraham got a special dispensation from God that his descendants would be the Chosen People, and now, in effect, Paul, you're asking us to become Christians. We are not descendants. We're not Jewish. So how do we qualify?" Do you remember what Paul said?

"The special covenant that God had with Abraham that your descendants will inherit the earth is not based on race at all." It's based on what?

Faith.

Faith. The fact that Abraham had faith in God, unshakable faith, was the measuring rod by which God said that you can have special dispensation as a chosen people.

So, Paul said, "Any of you who share Abraham's faith in God, through Jesus Christ, are just as much part of the descendants as if you were born a Jew." That was a big argument. Or dichotomy. ("Dichotomy" is a fancy word for an argument or a debate about two theologies or two philosophies or two groups of opinion.)

So, that was the basis for this book.

Obviously, James was a Jew, as was Jesus. He didn't travel around much. So far as we know, James had always had his base of operation, his base of awareness, and his circle of constant friends, his responsibilities, inside Jerusalem or very close to Jerusalem.

So, that was the background for James.

A Question of Legitimacy

There were many devout and very important Christians down through the ages who never did fully accept the book of James, the most notable of which was Martin Luther. And sometimes, many of the early Catholic leaders—they questioned whether the book of James should be in the Holy Scriptures or not. Does anybody know why? It's important as we study James. Rosalynn? [*Congregation laughs*]

Because if your faith is true, then you will do good works.

Because James, in effect, equated works with faith. We know that we're saved by the grace of God, through faith in Jesus Christ, not through good works. But in the Jewish faith, good works was the measuring stick by which you were judged by God to be acceptable. And your holiness.

Remember, the Pharisees would even tithe one-tenth of the mint that they grew in the garden, and they would brag about how good they were, and how perfect they were, and how many of the six hundred-and-something rules in the Jewish faith they obeyed. How meticulous they were washing their hands before they did certain things. How many steps they could take on the Sabbath—those kinds of things.

Jesus said that was not important—whether you measured up by keeping the rules. Faith was important. James said, though, that, "without works, faith is," what?

Dead.

Dead. So, he wasn't elevating works above faith. He was saying that the measurement of your faith in Jesus Christ is how you live. It's what you say. It's what you do.

But Martin Luther had very castigating, or ugly things, to say about the book of James. He didn't think it was a legitimate part of the New Testament. So, there was a lot of controversy about it.

The Gift of Hardship

I mentioned earlier that James has always been one of my most, I'd say, important books. And it was really because of my sister Ruth. When I was governor, and when I campaigned for president for a whole year, Ruth was still more famous than I was.

Ruth Carter Stapleton was a famous evangelist. She was an evangelist all over the world and she did wonderful work. She wrote five books, and she would make speeches to thousands of people in different parts of the nation and the world. And Ruth always treasured the second, third, and fourth verses of the first chapter of James.

Let's turn to that just for a moment. Although it's not in today's lesson, it's always something that I have remembered and maybe you would like to review. James says,

> [2] My brothers and sisters, whenever you face trials of any kind, consider it nothing but joy....

Which is a startling thing to say

> [3] because you know that the testing of your faith produces endurance; [4] and let endurance have its full effect, so that you may be mature and complete, lacking in nothing.

Ruth ministered to people who were in trouble. This would include those that had marital difficulties, or drug addicts, or hopeless alcoholics. She always tried to emphasize to them, in the depths of their despair, when they had lost confidence in themselves and in their ability to fight against sinfulness, or bad habits, or whatever that was destroying their health or their lives, that having difficulties was a foundation of joy. Because it was the difficulties that induced you to have endurance and to cast away your dependence on yourself. And to put your faith in Jesus Christ and to form a partnership with God, through Christ, and "you and God together," Ruth would say, "can overcome your difficulties." [A difficulty] strengthens, not weakens, your faith in Christ.

You can see it was a very important basic consideration for Ruth, and she had many different approaches to that same fact.

In fact, she ministered to me one time. I lost the governor's race in 1966 to a racist, Lester Maddox, and I was completely disillusioned with myself, with God, with politics, and everything else. Ruth was living in Fayetteville, North Carolina, and she came down to witness to me. We went off by ourselves, and Ruth took her Bible with her, and she read those three verses to me. She said, "Jimmy, you've suffered a defeat. You've lost confidence in yourself, and in your ability, and in the judgment of Georgia people. You should look upon this as a way to strengthen yourself and to strengthen your faith in Christ. Turn to Christ." So, it was from that advice that I decided to do some missionary work.

Turning Toward God and Others

I would go regularly to different places in the United States as part of the Southern Baptist Convention Pioneer Mission Program. I would go to areas that needed to hear about Christ and the plan of salvation, and I would witness to people, and it changed my religious life.

We went to Lock Haven, Pennsylvania, and some Christians in State College, Pennsylvania, which is where Penn State University is, had a watch line....And they had called everybody in the phone book in Lock Haven, and they'd found a hundred families who said on the telephone that they did not belong to any church. So, I was assigned to go and spend as long as it took to visit all one hundred families.

Luckily for me, I had a partner with me who was also a peanut farmer from [near] Dallas, Texas. His name was Milo Pennington, and he was uneducated—he had never finished high school. I was a college graduate, and I could read the Bible fluently and all that, but Milo Pennington would just kind of fumble through the plan of salvation.

And as we would go knock on these people's homes who didn't have any elements of Christianity in the home and go in and start to try to present to them what we call the "Plan of Salvation," it was a very difficult task for us. We would kneel down in the street in front of the house and pray before we knocked on every door, and eventually, we were kind of impervious to any sort of consequences. We didn't worry about what was going to happen, because, Milo Pennington explained to me, it's not how we talk, it's not what we do, it's not how we look, it's the presence of the Holy Spirit. So, we would go in and talk to these people and we had incredible results.

By the end of the week, when we got through with our hundred families—we went to all of them—we had forty-eight people that accepted Christ. Not because of me, I didn't do anything but read the Bible, but Milo Pennington, in his fumbling way—I thought he was completely incompetent [*congregation laughs*]—would explain the plan of salvation, and with the presence of the Holy Spirit shaping the outcome of his words, the people accepted Christ.... His words, although uneducated, and not eloquent at all—he would just kind of fumble through—with the presence of the Holy spirit, were pervasive.

Another year, I went to Springfield, Massachusetts, with a Cuban pastor from Brooklyn whose name was Eloy Cruz, and we were charged that year with giving the plan of salvation to Hispanics only, in Spanish. I learned my Spanish in the navy, and it was a completely different vocabulary. [*Congregation laughs*] So all that Reverend Cruz would let me do—he had a tiny little church in Brooklyn we visited later on, about fifty members, but he would let me read the Bible and he would explain to those people what the verses meant. Again, we had remarkable success.

At the end of the week, I asked Reverend Cruz, "What is the secret of your presentation?" We often cried, wept with joy and Christian communion. It broke down all barriers between us and people mostly from the Caribbean. He said, "You only have to have two feelings in your heart. One is a love for God, and the other one is a genuine love for the person that happens to be in front of you at any particular time." I've never wanted to forget about that.

That's a very difficult thing. The person in front of you at any particular time may be somebody that's competitive with you in a job, or it may be somebody you just see in passing on an elevator in a high rise building or sitting next to you on a bus or in an airplane, or something of that kind. And to attune your heart to actually love that person, that may be just a chance encounter, when they're not attractive at all, is kind of stretching the normal dimensions or size of a person's heart. Do you agree with that?

It's a very wonderful thing to say—just his words, "the person in front of you at any particular time."

When I was inaugurated as president [and] when I got the Nobel Peace Prize, I quoted our local teacher here, Miss Julia Coleman. Miss Julia used to say to us young men and women in the high school right down the street here that we "had to accommodate changing times, but cling to unchanging principles." That statement itself, just one sentence long, could encompass a person's entire philosophy. We do have to accommodate changing times with cellphones and airplanes and computers and automobiles and things of that kind, and changing circumstances about our awareness of the outside world, but cling to unchanging principles. And, of course, for Christians, those unchanging principles are the teachings of Jesus Christ.

Living Witnesses

James has the ability, all the way through his book, sometimes in a very aggravating way, sometimes in a negative, kind of condemnatory way, to be harsh in equating claims of faith and claims of holiness and claims of being religious with what you actually do and what you actually say. He makes us face up to the facts about ourselves. So, sometimes, James is not very pleasant to read.... You see, the essence of James is a tough, very critical analysis of early Christians.

By the way, everybody to whom James was writing was already a Christian. He was not an evangelist in this particular book, going out trying to get people to be Christians. He was talking to people that were already Christians, primarily those that had a Jewish background. And about the time James wrote this book, the early Christian church was under duress. It was under pressure because it was just beginning to bubble up as significant.

As long as the early Christian church was just a few scattered radicals of weirdos along the few villages along the shoreline, then nobody paid any attention to it. But when it got to be a little bit popular, it was a threat to two entities. It was a threat to the Jewish faith, because there was almost always a synagogue nearby that saw some of their members becoming Christians, and it was also becoming a threat to the Roman Empire, because this was the only vocal group in those early days that challenged the divinity of whom?

Caesar.

Of Caesar. You'll note in earlier writings, particularly Paul, he always warned you to revere, I think, maybe too much, political leaders. He said, "Pay homage to political leaders. Abide by the laws. Don't criticize them." But at the same time, Paul would say, as Christ said, that the ultimate authority on earth was not Caesar, which was a very bad thing to say in those days. So, in that time, pressures began to arise, and criticisms, and threats, sometimes to the very life of the early Christians, and these were the Christians to whom James was writing.

James wanted to strengthen the early Christians. How could he strengthen them? By strengthening their faith. By making sure that the people who saw the Christians—you're not going to like this—could assess the life of the Christian and know, without being told, "That is a Christian. I can tell that's a Christian by the life they lead."

A sermon that was taught over at First Baptist Church when I was a young man [was] "If You Were Arrested for Being a Christian, Would There Be Enough Evidence to Convict You?" I always thought I could probably talk my way out of it. They can't really prove I'm a

Christian. I did go to church, and I did teach Sunday school, and so forth, but they can't really prove I'm a Christian. I was just trying to build up my business. Get some more votes when I ran for office.

That's a very disturbing thing for each one of us to have to assess in our own lives—if you were arrested for being a Christian, would there be enough evidence to convict you?

Wordly Affairs

One day this week, I was invited to go over to the Plains Methodist church to speak to a group of church leaders, bishops, and others from the Catholic church, and also from the Anglican church, the Episcopal church, the Presbyterian church, and Primary Methodist Church. And they wanted me to talk about the interrelationship or conflicts between religious beliefs and daily life, particularly political life, and that's exactly what the lesson's about today.

Obviously, there should be no incompatibility between our deep beliefs in Jesus Christ and the way we live every day. There shouldn't be. And there shouldn't be any distinction drawn between the application of our religious faith and our duties in public life, either a corporation, or a job that you have, or the educational system, or a lawyer, or president of the United States, or governor, or whatever.

I've only had one incompatibility with which I had to struggle, and that was the question of abortion because when I was sworn in as president, I took an oath before God to obey the laws of the United States and to interpret and to make sure that I protected them. And the laws of the United States are those as interpreted by the Supreme Court, and one of the interpretations of the Supreme Court is *Roe v. Wade*, which legalizes abortions up through the first trimester. I have never believed that Jesus Christ would approve abortions, but I had to accommodate that law. And it was a difficult struggle for me, and I would say this in my press conferences, and so forth. So, I did everything I could to analyze how I could possibly reduce abortions in the United States.

The United States had a pretty high abortion rate, about twenty per thousand births. Other countries that have no laws about abortion have much fewer abortions. In Scandinavia, Norway, Sweden, Denmark, they have about seven per thousand, about a third as many as the United States. Whereas in some countries, like in Latin America, that are heavily Catholic, it's absolutely illegal to have an abortion. They have about fifty per a thousand. What is the difference?

Well, I'm not getting sidetracked on abortion, but—I guess I am for a moment [*congregation laughs*]—the difference is, whenever a woman knows that she can have her child, and that she and the child will be cared for with enough food to eat, and good health care, and so forth, and if she knows that there is an adequate adoption procedure in her community, then she will have the baby. And that's the difference between Norway and the United States. In Norway, every woman knows that when her baby is born, whether she planned for it or not, that she and the child will have total care as the child evolves. And if she doesn't want to keep the child, then there are laws that would permit adoptions that are not embarrassing. So, these are the kind of things you get into as you go through the differences between them.

We have to get involved in worldly affairs. Rosalynn and I have been to places like the northern part of Ethiopia where holy people will go into a little cave in the side of a rock...and they live in that cave. And people who share their faith will come and give them enough food to survive on every day. They never come out. They never sin. But that's not the mandate of Christians. Why not? Why is it directly contrary to the teachings of Christ? (I'm not criticizing the holy people.) What's the Great Commission?

Go.

Go! Go into the entire world and preach the gospel and let them know about your faith. So, we are mandated by Jesus himself, and by the example set by the early apostles who went all over the Roman

Empire to spread the gospel, to do the same and to interrelate to people and not to isolate ourselves. But we always have that chance, that inevitable opportunity, to absorb too much of the world in order to accommodate and to make ourselves feel more comfortable. You might say that instead of having a link with the outside world, it becomes a sponge relationship. We absorb so much of the world in order to accommodate and to exalt our own ambitions that we become indistinguishable as Christians from the rest of the world that are not Christians.

That's a very harsh thing that James is saying here. James also says that most of the divisions that come within churches arise because of this same characteristic.

Facing Our Prejudices

Let's turn now to James 4:1–3.

[1] Those conflicts and disputes among you, where do they come from? Do they not come from your cravings that are at war within you?
[2] You want something and do not have it; so you commit murder. And you covet something and cannot obtain it; so you engage in disputes and conflicts. You do not have, because you do not ask. [3] You ask and do not receive, because you ask wrongly, in order to spend what you get on your pleasures.

One of the things that James mentions in other places is, something that causes divisions in the church is a desire of individual people to be dominant, to be superior, even within the church. There's a struggle in almost every denomination, including the Catholics and Baptists and Methodists and the Anglicans and Episcopalians, all over the world, because some members of the hierarchy say, "I'm the one that can interpret the Scriptures, and anyone who disagrees with me is wrong. Since I'm close to God, anybody who disagrees with me is ungodly. Since I'm interpreting the Scriptures correctly and you disagree, you're also inferior to me."

It's a matter of ascendancy, or superiority. Just the opposite of Jesus' admonition for humility. And a natural inclination of everybody is to show that I'm better than other people. If I'm a man, I'm better than women. That's one of the biggest arguments in the Christian church today, all over the world, is whether women have an equal place in the eyes of Christ.

We went through a hundred years in the South of, I'm White, therefore I'm better than what?

Blacks.

Blacks. And the church believed it. All the denominations believed it. I never knew of anybody in any church, or any lawyers in the American Bar Association, that came out and said, "This is wrong." And you could have distinguished people come to our church, take the Scriptures, and say, "Look, here it is. Slaves be loyal to your masters and don't dispute them." It referred in the Old Testament to Ham, who was dark-skinned, who was inferior to the lighter-skinned people, and so forth. It was not even questioned.

The first question I ever knew about it was Harry Truman. In 1948, he was my commander in chief; I was a submarine officer. And he, just by the stroke of a pen one day, said racial discrimination in all the military services is over. Period. That was it. Nobody could dispute him. The Congress had nothing to say about it. It was a long time afterwards before Rosa Parks sat in the front seat of a Montgomery bus or before Martin Luther King Jr. became famous. But that's the way we believed, and it was a very sincere belief based on the Holy Scriptures.

So, we tend to think that whatever I am is inherently better, and when we want to argue about something, we pick some particular descriptive verse that doesn't apply to me and say, "This is so important."

The most important thing right now on a global basis is gays. If you are homosexual, you are now completely condemned and the worst sinner on earth, and you're not even amenable to coming into the Christian faith. That's being questioned, but it's difficult.

I noticed on the front page of *USA Today* this past week, they asked Christians, "What is the greatest sin?" Did anybody read that? Among Christians, what do you think Christians believe to be the greatest sin? Adultery. What is adultery?

Breaking a promise.

Breaking a promise. Breaking a holy commitment. Being disloyal to an entity or faith to which you have pledged your loyalty. Most of us would say it's infidelity in marriage. But let's read the next verse—the fourth verse.

> 4 Adulterers!...

He's not talking about marital infidelity, is he?

> ...Do you not know that friendship with the world is enmity with God?

James is reminding them, and us, that when we form an adulterous relationship with the outside world, we are being disloyal or adulterous in our relationship with God.

> ...Therefore whoever wishes to be a friend of the world becomes an enemy of God.

Jesus said, "You can't have two masters." You remember that? In the Sermon on the Mount. 5 Or do you suppose that it is for nothing that the scripture says..."God yearns jealously for the spirit that he has made to dwell in us"?

With your permission, I'm going to skip over that verse, because you can look at eight or ten different translations of the Bible and there's no two of them that are alike. But, in effect, it says, if you read the Scriptures, you might surmise that God is jealous of our faithfulness.

And the sixth verse.

> [6] But he gives all the more grace; therefore it says,
> 'God opposes the proud,
> but gives grace to the humble.'

Here James is coming back to the essence of humility. Let's read on down, seven through twelve.

> [7] Submit yourselves therefore to God. Resist the devil, and he will
> flee from you. [8] Draw near to God, and he will draw near to you.
> Cleanse your hands, you sinners, and purify your hearts, you double-
> minded. [9] Lament and mourn and weep. Let your laughter be turned
> into mourning and your joy into dejection. [10] Humble yourselves be-
> fore the Lord, and he will exalt you.
>
> [11] Do not speak evil against one another, brothers and sisters.
> Whoever speaks evil against another or judges another, speaks evil
> against the law and judges the law; but if you judge the law, you are
> not a doer of the law but a judge. [12] There is one lawgiver and judge
> who is able to save and to destroy. So who, then, are you to judge your
> neighbor?

There's a whole group of admonitions there that James puts one on top of the other. Submit yourself. Come near to God. Wash yourself. Purify yourself. Grieve, mourn, and wail. What does he mean by grieve, mourn, and wail?

It means, as we look into our own hearts and minds and courageously inventory our sinfulness, we should grieve, and mourn, and wail. That's one of the most difficult things to do if we want to comply with James's admonition.

How many of us can be so distressed with our own sinfulness that we actually weep, or mourn, or wail? We don't want to do that because we have a tendency, which is almost insurmountable, to ignore our own sinfulness. Or to say some phrase like, "Forgive me my sins." We don't want to face them. We don't want to analyze what they are. Just, in general, "Father, whatever sins I have, please forgive it." Let's don't talk about it. Let's don't change it.

You see, James really puts the pressure on. He says that slander of others is a direct violation of the law—that we're not only hurting the ones we're talking to ugly, we're not only hurting the ones we're talking about, we're hurting ourselves. And this is not only a sin against a human being, but it's a violation or challenge to the ultimate law. What is the ultimate law which James is talking about?

Do unto others as you would have them do unto you. Christ says, "Love others as you love yourself." And if we slander another person, just kind of slyly gossiping about somebody else that tears down their reputation in the minds of the people [we're] talking to, and ultimately it hurts those people, then we're not only slightly sinful against a certain person, but we're being directly in confrontation or violation of the most important single law that Christ gave us in dealing with other human beings.

God said there are two laws: Love God and love your—

Neighbor.

—your neighbor. You see, what James is doing here...he's talking to us. And it's not an easy thing.

Becoming One with Jesus Christ

James doesn't leave any room for doubt or for ambiguity. There's no way to beat around the bush here and say, "Well, maybe he's not talking to me." Because if you read the book of James and listen to what he says, he's talking to you and he's talking to me. And he's saying that all of us have a choice to make, and that we have the power given to us as human beings, by God, to make the choices.

We are not automatons. We're not robots. We're not puppets. God gives each one of us, in effect, autonomy. We can accept or reject faith in Christ. We can accept or reject compliance with the biblical laws…in the individual decisions we make, as we relate to other people, or relate to ourselves, or submit or not submit to God. We're the ones that make those decisions.

And what James is saying to us is, become so intimate with God, through prayer, through contemplation, through self-analysis, through courageous looks at ourselves, that we form a binding commitment that's almost like breathing with Jesus Christ. So, we're not an outsider that penetrates the Christian faith every now and then, when it's convenient or when there's a crisis in our life. But we live within that womb, within that environment that includes Jesus Christ, and this gives us protection against those temptations that James points out.

It gives us protection against sorrows and disappointments and disillusionment and failure because we form a binding partnership with God, through Christ. A partnership with an entity who knows everything and who has all-power. And with that foundation of assurance that we are on God's side, and accept the invitation from God to understand his desires through the study of Jesus Christ, and through our faith in Jesus Christ, we are strong.

We'll all sin. James said, "Everybody sins." He emphasized that. All of us sin and come short of the glory of God. So, what do we do about it?

We submit ourselves to God. We form an intimate, permanent, minute-by-minute relationship with Jesus Christ. So, every time we do anything that relates to another person, it's as though Christ was there holding our hand.

That's a big undertaking, but that's what's expected in our covenant with Christ.

The 2010s

Grief thief of time crawls off,
The moon-drawn grave, with the seafaring years,
The knave of pain steals off
The sea-halved faith that blew time to his knees,
The old forget the cries,
Lean time on tide and times the wind stood rough,
Call back the castaways
Riding the sea light on a sunken path,
The old forget the grief,
Hack of the cough, the hanging albatross,
Cast back the bone of youth
And salt-eyed stumble bedward where she lies
Who tossed the high tide in a time of stories
And timelessly lies loving with the thief.

— Dylan Thomas
from "Grief Thief of Time"

December 16, 2018. Jimmy Carter enters the sanctuary at Maranatha Baptist Church to teach Sunday School. Carter taught thousands of lessons from the Bible during his lifetime.

Courtesy Jill Stuckey

August 16, 2015. Carter reaches to embrace his brother Billy's family following an emotional Sunday service at Maranatha Baptist Church. This was the first time many people had seen Carter since he shared that he had been diagnosed with cancer.

Courtesy *The Atlanta Journal-Constitution*; photographs by Ben Gray

August 23, 2015. After sharing his cancer diagnosis with the world during a press conference held at the Carter Center, ninety-year-old Jimmy Carter was back at Maranatha Baptist Church teaching Sunday School. Record numbers of people lined up at the church before daybreak hoping to secure a seat in the sanctuary, forcing hundreds to watch the lesson remotely at the nearby Plains High School.

Courtesy Grant Blankenship

June 2016. Jimmy and Rosalynn Carter introduce themselves to Macy Shoulta, the infant daughter of Maranatha Baptist Church's then-pastor Jeremy Shoulta and his wife Valarie (pictured far right) in the church office before Carter joined visitors awaiting his arrival in the sanctuary.

Courtesy Jill Stuckey

October 2017. A group of Mercer University and Wesleyan College students gather with the Carters after a Sunday morning service at Maranatha Baptist Church. Chris Fuller (pictured top left), leader of the Baptist Collegiate Ministries at both campuses at the time, often brought his students, including many international students, to hear Jimmy Carter teach. For some of the students this was their first time attending a church of any kind.

Courtesy Chris Fuller

July 12, 2015. In the lesson Jimmy Carter taught at Maranatha Baptist Church on this day (included in the following section), he shared a story about speaking at the Church of the Exceptional in Macon, Georgia, a church comprised of congregants with intellectual disabilities. Here, Jimmy Carter is pictured with members of the congregation, Rosalynn, and Ruth Stafford Peale, founder of *Guideposts* magazine and wife of Norman Vincent Peale (seated immediately to his right), July 1974.

Courtesy *Guideposts*

Jesus' own proverb "the spirit is willing, but the flesh is weak" took on a more literal meaning for Jimmy Carter in the decade that began with 2010. With indications of agedness natural for a person transitioning from eighty-something to ninety-something, Carter pared back on his international travels, handed over the reins of The Carter Center to his oldest grandson, Jason, and spent more time and energy involved in the affairs of Plains and in teaching Sunday school at Maranatha. The connected two lessons, taught at Maranatha by President Carter delve into lament and help to cultivate a response to the inevitability of suffering in our lives—topics fit to be taught by a man who, in his tenth decade of living, continued to live a very full life.

❧

The only time Jimmy Carter was late to teach Sunday school was on the morning his grandson died.

President and Mrs. Carter had been awakened the night before by a phone call communicating the distressing news that Jeremy, their twenty-eight-year-old grandson, had been rushed to the hospital after his heart had stopped beating while at home the evening before. Inside the cover of midnight, Secret Service detail hurried the Carters one hundred miles north from Plains to Peachtree City, to tend to their family in what would be Jeremy's final hours of life. The dedicated security and authorized vehicles reflected the status of a former president and first lady, but at this dark hour, and under these tragic circumstances, Jimmy and Rosalynn were not world leaders, they were simply worried sick grandparents.

In Plains, it was a typical Sunday morning in December. The quiet air was perforated by foggy plumes distinctive of the brisk and damp mornings that preface winter solstice in the South. Downtown, as the locals refer to the single row of historic, two-storied storefronts that line the south side of the railroad track, had been prepped in anticipation of Christmas, charmingly outlined with amber lights and decked out by a large artificial tree topped off with a classic star. Just up the road at Maranatha Baptist Church a few hundred out-of-towners emerged from their cars, bleary-eyed from napping overnight in the Maranatha Baptist Church's parking lot to make certain they would obtain a coveted spot inside the bucolic A-frame that famously hosted Sunday school with Jimmy Carter.

Even amid the intensely personal and tragic events that had taken place within the last several hours of Jimmy Carter's life, he was still mindful of his commitment to teach Sunday school, and the pews of people that would be eagerly awaiting him for the occasion. So, Carter phoned his niece, Kim Fuller, a fellow Plains-for-lifer, to share the unsettling news about Jeremy and to request that she begin teaching the morning lesson until he arrived. An English literature teacher at an area high school, Kim and her "Uncle Jimmy" were bonded together not just by blood relationship, but as voracious readers and researchers with a deep passion for teaching from the Bible and an abiding affection for their hometown of Plains. On "non-Jimmy" Sundays when Carter was not scheduled to teach, Kim led the lesson for the few dozen folks who comprised the church's local membership, including her uncle Jimmy and aunt Rosalynn.

Earlier that year, Carter, at the age of 90, had been diagnosed with cancer. After a suspicious tumor was removed from his liver, his doctors discovered melanoma had spread to his brain. During a news conference held at his beloved Carter Center in Atlanta, the elderly statesman shared with the public the details of his diagnosis, fielded questions from the press, and recounted his initial response when they confirmed he did, indeed, have cancer: "I've had a wonderful life, I've had thousands of friends, and I've had an exciting, and adventurous, and gratifying existence, so I was surprisingly at ease. Much more so than my wife was," Carter grinned, a perpetual hope emanating from the twinkle in his crystal-clear blue eyes. "But now, I feel it's in the hands of God, whom I worship, and I'll be prepared for anything that comes." Immediately following the press gathering, Carter began a prescribed regimen of radiation that his doctors complemented with a drug administered intravenously to help boost his immune system.

After the news spread, Sunday school attendance at Maranatha soared. People from all over the globe pilgrimaged to Plains to check off a long put-off bucket list item: hearing a president from the history books share about his faith in a supreme being from the Good Book. A few months later, on December 6, Carter prepared a lesson from Luke 1 featuring the Magnificat, Mary's hymn of praise to God for extending his favor to her in choosing her to deliver the Messiah, the one who would rescue her, the Israelites, and the world, from their sins. In the passage, often titled "Mary's Song," Mary articulates her worship, expressing, "My soul magnifies the Lord, and my spirit rejoices in God my Savior...the Mighty One has done great things for me." Just before teaching the lesson, Carter gave his own praise account to the packed class—his cancer was gone. His life had been spared.

Two weeks later, his grandson, Jeremy, would draw his last breath of life.

The order of life seemed all wrong. Jeremy, not yet thirty years old, was unexpectedly dead. His grandfather, Jimmy, a nonagenarian with brain cancer, was unexpectedly alive.

About a half hour into the lesson, Kim caught sight of her uncle out of the corner of her eye. In his usual Sunday school fashion, Carter strode into the sanctuary from the side door nearest the organ and smiled at the crowd gathered. He kissed Kim on the cheek, and they embraced—that knowingness that connects family members after something unexplainable has occurred. You could see it in his face. Sadness.

"Sorry I'm late," he began, "It's the first time I've ever been late getting to Sunday school." The crowd did not demand an apology of

Carter that morning. Rather, they carefully welcomed him in, as if to offer a sacred space for the grieving grandfather and his pain, and, if even for just a few moments, shoulder some of the weight of the hurt with him.

You see, for this hour in time, Carter was not a commander in chief, responsible for the security of a nation. Nor an international peacemaker, pursuing conflict resolution among the world's most war-torn nations. This morning, he was not a handy home builder, constructing houses for families needing an affordable roof over their heads. He wasn't a warrior against disease; he could not problem solve the illness that afflicted his grandson, nor the ache that now afflicted him, and Rosalynn, and his family. He was simply a human being in the midst of a hard ache of the heart.

"Jeremy was a special person, a wonderful young man who we loved very much," Carter said, memorializing his grandson for the class that morning. "He was full of life, and from the time he was a little boy, he was a special child to us. A little different than his brothers." Then, he proceeded to summarize the objectives of the morning lesson from his perspective, shaped by the tragedy from the night before. "We should be filled with a sense of joy and thanksgiving," Carter stated before challenging the class, and himself, with a difficult question. "What is there in my life that I have received from God for which I'm thankful, and which should bring me joy, even in the face of sorrow like I have today?"

> But where shall wisdom be found?
> And where is the place of understanding?
> Mortals do not know the way to it,
> and it is not found in the land of the living. (Job 28:12–13)

Death is no discriminator of persons. Not even presidents. For those of us left among this land of the living, grief finds us all.

June 22, 2014

Prayers of Lament

Maranatha Baptist Church
Plains, Georgia

This month we're studying about—who knows what?

Prayer.

And it's a subject of discussion here in Maranatha, and in many other churches like ours.... We've already had three lessons, this is the fourth one this morning. We have one more lesson next Sunday.

I want to ask you, how many of you resort to prayer? I presume that most of you, at some time in your life, whether you're deeply religious or not, have resorted to prayer, to talking to God. What is the reason, or necessity, or benefit from prayer?

Sharing.

Relationship.

Peace.

Help.

Honoring God.

Confession.

Assurance.

Being thankful.

So, you've pretty well covered the subjects of this month's teachings. We'll review the first three just briefly and then I'll get to the fourth one. But the first one is praising God—that was our first lesson.

Why does God need praise?

He's the creator of everything.

He's the creator of everything, but that doesn't tell me why he needs praise.

He doesn't need praise, but we need to praise him.

God does not need praise, so why do we praise God? The Bible tells us to praise God, so why does God tell us to praise him?

To remind us that he is the creator.

So, when we give praise to God, what are we doing? We are forming a relationship with our creator, a partner that knows everything and can do anything. And when we praise God, we are actually repeating an affirmation or a declaration of that partnership. Can you think of a similar occasion, in our own human lives, when we do that?

Marriage.

Marriage! When you stand at an altar, or before a justice of the peace, or whatever, and you look at the person who is your choice in life—a husband or wife with whom, at that moment, you're in love—you want to affirm that for the rest of your life, you will be loyal. And you expect loyalty from your partner. So, it's a solemn declaration of a permanent relationship between you and someone who is precious to you. Does that sound pretty similar?

That's what praise is. And that's why we need to praise God. It's to make sure that we reaffirm in our own minds, *I am re-declaring my allegiance to you, God, because I know I can count on you to take care of me as well.*

And that's the same relationship I had with Rosalynn when we were married, and still have after almost sixty-eight years. We have pledged our loyalty to one another, our fidelity to one another, until death do us part. So, for our eternal life we are forming a permanent, binding, solemn, happy, grateful commitment to God Almighty.

What a reassurance that is to us! If you were starting a new business and you wanted to have a partner, wouldn't it be nice to have a partner that knows everything and can do anything? That's what we have; we have a partner that created us, gave us life, and will care for us.

Praying as Gratitude

Our next lesson was about thanksgiving. Thanks to God. Gratitude. What does that imply? What do we get from thanking God, and so forth? What's the difference between praise and thanksgiving, or gratitude?

Humility.

When we say a prayer of praise, or that's part of our prayer, it acknowledges who God is. And gratitude, or thanksgiving, is what?

What God does. So, you see the relationship, but it's interrelated. Two conditions—they're not separate.

We praise God. We have confidence in God. And we thank God for what he does for us.

Praying as Confession

Someone down here mentioned confession—which is not a very pleasant word. But why is confession important?

To clear the page.

To start over.

To cleanse the soul.

Confession is also important in a relationship between two human beings. If we make a mistake or violate our pledges or promises to someone that we love, it's better to confess and to clear the page, or to start over again with a new commitment. And God knows that all of us are sinful—all have sinned and come short of the glory of God.

Is confession a negative thing?

No.

It's really a gift. Why would you consider confession a gift from God?

It allows you to start over.

It allows us to start over. God has promised us that if we confess what we have done wrong and pledge ourselves to correct our mistake, or to do better in the future, or not to repeat our sinfulness, then what?

He'll forgive you.

Then we are forgiven. Partially forgiven?

No.

Totally forgiven, as though we had never sinned. And God can't abide sin...because God demands perfection. So how do we get around that very serious problem?

We ask for forgiveness a lot. [*Congregation laughs*]

Yeah, I hope we do. But it's not easy to ask for forgiveness because a human being has a natural inclination not to admit that I've been mistaken, not to admit that I need forgiveness. So, it's a matter of humility. We are forgiven because God sent his son, Jesus Christ, to accept the punishment for our sin, and that's one of the most remarkable gifts that can be imagined. Jesus Christ, who was perfect, who never sinned, accepts the punishment for our sins. We are saved by the grace of God through our faith in Jesus Christ. If we have faith in Jesus Christ, then we can turn over our sins through confession to God, and the punishment is leveled on our Savior Jesus Christ, who was perfect.

That's the essence of Christianity. That's the essence of our faith. We have to be convinced that if I do confess my sins, and I turn to Jesus Christ in faith, then my sins will be forgiven, and I will be reconciled with God or made okay with God.

So those are the first three lessons that we discussed, in quite a lot more detail. Let's turn now to the fourth lesson, and to the fourth aspect of prayer.

Lament in the Psalms

All during this month we've been using the psalms to illustrate through biblical teaching what the lesson has been, and most of the psalms were written by or about David–not all of them, but some of them. It indicates in most of our Bibles that this is a song about David or by David, and so forth. So, we kind of relate back to David.

And this morning we're going to be studying Psalm 31. And the subject of our lesson this morning is a difficult word. It is called lament. What does the word lament mean?

Regret.

And lament has more of a meaning than just "I'm sorry." Lament can also mean what else?

Sorrow.

Complaint.

A complaint, an unanswered question, a doubt. And also sorrow or despair. I give up because I've been so terribly aggrieved, and I can't overcome the problems that I face. So, you see, lament has a lot of different meanings to it.

Some of the scholars say that if you take all of the psalms and put them together, most of them—not a majority, but a plurality—they're songs of lament. And the one we're going to study this morning is kind of a complex series of these particular feelings that David had.

And what do we know about David before we read the Scripture?

He was a terrible sinner.

He was a terrible sinner! Yeah, he was.

He was a man after God's own heart.

But he was a man after God's own heart. That's the two basic things.

A man of God.

Yes, he was a man of God. David committed terrible sins—adultery and murder—but David was contrite, he confessed his sins, he asked God to forgive him, he expressed his trust in God, and God forgave David completely and gave David a blessing of a covenant that affects everyone here who's a Christian. What was that covenant? That a descendant of David would be what?

A king.

A king for how long?

Forever.

A king of the earth forever, and that is Jesus Christ. So, Jesus Christ was a direct descendant of David, and that covenant, or promise, that God made to David despite his sinfulness, but because of his faith, because of his confession of his sin and his repentance, has been a blessing for all of us.... Let's turn now to the thirty-first psalm.

Lesson Scripture

1 In you, O LORD, I seek refuge;
do not let me ever be put to shame;
in your righteousness deliver me.
2 Incline your ear to me;
rescue me speedily.
Be a rock of refuge for me,
a strong fortress to save me.
...
9 Be gracious to me, O LORD, for I am in distress;
my eye wastes away from grief,
my soul and body also.
10 For my life is spent with sorrow,
and my years with sighing;
my strength fails because of my misery,
and my bones waste away.
11 I am the scorn of all my adversaries,
a horror to my neighbors,
an object of dread to my acquaintances;
those who see me in the street flee from me.
12 I have passed out of mind like one who is dead;
I have become like a broken vessel.
13 For I hear the whispering of many—
terror all around!—
as they scheme together against me,
as they plot to take my life.
14 But I trust in you, O LORD;
I say, 'You are my God.'
15 My times are in your hand;
deliver me from the hand of my enemies and persecutors.
16 Let your face shine upon your servant;
save me in your steadfast love....
...

19 O how abundant is your goodness
that you have laid up for those who fear you,
and accomplished for those who take refuge in you,
in the sight of everyone!
20 In the shelter of your presence you hide them
from human plots;
you hold them safe under your shelter
from contentious tongues.
21 Blessed be the LORD,
for he has wondrously shown his steadfast love [to] me
when I was beset as a city under siege.
22 I had said in my alarm,
'I am driven far from your sight.'
But you heard my supplications
when I cried out to you for help.
23 Love the LORD, all you his saints.
The LORD preserves the faithful,
but abundantly repays the one who acts haughtily.
24 Be strong, and let your heart take courage,
all you who wait for the LORD.

You can see here the diversity of feelings that David was expressing. It seems like a kind of conglomerate of conflicting ideas and thoughts.

At first, David says, "God, you're my rock. I know I can depend on you." Then, he goes through a litany of all the things that are wrong with him—he's in a depression, his eyes can't see anything, he's scorned on the street, and so forth.... Then he goes on, "I trust you to save me," "bless me Lord, with your faithful love," "let my heart take courage," and then he closes by saying, "My future is in your hands." So, this is a wonderful example of the diversity of feelings that we have when we pray to God.

What would you say are most of your prayers? Praise? Thanksgiving? Confession? Or the one we just discussed? What do you think?

Probably praise and asking for things.

Well, I think asking for things is what we're talking about today, don't you? Because David was expressing his thoughts about a terrible situation he was in—this maybe is in one of his times of regret about what he had done. But he's also in a difficult situation with his enemies. And at some point in his life he was weak and felt that he didn't have any power or influence and that nobody would even meet him on the street; they would cross the street so they wouldn't have to meet him. He's in bad shape. This is the kind of prayer that most of us, I think, repeat to God in the most fervent way.

When we are doubtful about the presence of God, when we have a potential sorrow in our hands, if someone that we love is ill and we are afraid they might pass away, or if we have had a failure or an embarrassment. It might be healthy to review, for each one of you, a time in your life when you've had the most difficult challenge of believing in God, and what you did with it. I've been through that stage.

A Turning Point

I was in the navy for a long time; I was in the submarine force. I resigned from the navy and came home. I worked hard around Plains. I built up a good business; I was a farmer, and I sold products to my people. I was head of the Lions Club, and I helped with different projects on a statewide basis with better seed, and so forth. Eventually, I was on the school board, and I was the chairman of the school board. I was on the hospital authority, I took care of the hospital in Americus, and things like that—I had a lot of jobs. I was on the jury, and I was chairman of the grand jury. So, I worked myself up from a former military officer to a fairly prominent person in the community. I was really hardworking at it, and my wife was side by side with me.

Then I ran for the Georgia State Senate to protect the public school system. Because the Democratic candidate—there were not any Republicans in Georgia, then, who admitted it [*congregation laughs*], all the public officials were Democrats—would hold up a finger and say, "No, not one," which meant if a single Black child went in a White school, he would close down the public school system. And I decided to run for the state senate to save the public school system; that was my idealistic and naive commitment. So, I was elected to the state senate, and I served two terms, and then I ran for governor.

My number one opponent was the number one segregationist in Georgia. His name was Lester Maddox. And I felt and I misled myself into thinking that I was kind of ordained by God to be governor of Georgia. I worked hard; my wife worked hard. There was hardly a factory-shift line in Georgia that we weren't there when the people came to work early in the morning. We handed out pamphlets, we shook hands and I was defeated. Nobody got a majority in the general election, and the Georgia Constitution said the legislature could choose a governor. So, they chose Lester Maddox to be governor. And I was disillusioned with the people of Georgia and with God. I basically renounced God because I felt that I was somehow betrayed.

I had a sister in North Carolina named Ruth Carter Stapleton who, at that time, was a very famous evangelist. She wrote five books, and she gave speeches, sometimes to tens of thousands of people, and so forth. Ruth heard about my despair, and she came down to Plains from Fayetteville, North Carolina, and we had some private conversations. Ruth convinced me that troubles and setbacks in life could be the basis for renewed hope and expectation and successes and a vital existence. She quoted mostly from the book of James to show me that God intended for us to be disappointed on occasion and that that was a means by which we could have our faith renewed and our strength increased. She asked me if I had ever done anything for God. Which was kind of an embarrassing question. But I wasn't embarrassed because I had been a deacon in the Baptist church here, and I had been out to witness to people in their homes and got some of them to join the church, and that sort of thing. But just after that, the Southern Baptist Convention put out a call for private missionaries—for lay people to go on missionary trips. And I volunteered to go because of Ruth's advice.

So, I went to Pennsylvania...to Massachusetts. I later went to Atlanta. And so, I had a kind of rebirth of my life. I decided to run for governor again, and I happened to be successful then. But that was a turning point in my life, very similar to what David apparently is experiencing here.

And I'm sure you have had some times in your life when you had a grievous disappointment, or an unexpected loss of a loved one, or your expectations were not realized, or you had doubts about your relationship with God. And that's what this particular kind of prayer is designed to correct. It's a call from God for us to really level with God, and to express our doubts, and express our frustrations, and express our sorrows, and our alienation, and our despair, and our regrets in an unadorned way. In other words, to let our hair down in our conversation with or our prayer to God.

A Truthful Church

I don't believe God ever meant to create a Christian church that was filled with happiness. Christians are not always happy. We have the same unhappy times in our life as other people, but God created a church to be filled with truthfulness, which is a startling thought for me. We're not supposed to always be happy, but we are supposed to always be truthful—truthful not just with each other, but also truthful with God.

We're supposed to be absolutely frank and unadorned and honest when we pray to God. If we have doubts about God's character, say it. "God, I'm doubtful about this. I need to understand the truth." And God has given us the ability, if we have the courage, to be reconciled with our Creator by putting ourselves on an equal basis with God, at least in our prayer.

David, in Psalm 31, has expressed a whole wide range or gamut of feelings about God. He knows that God is a rock on which his life can be built. He then goes through a litany of doubts about God and failures of himself, and so forth.

David was a powerful man in his day. I was the president of the most powerful nation on earth. Some people claim that the president is the most powerful person on earth; maybe I was the most powerful person on earth, I don't know. But I had times of needing God to give me guidance on what I should do. And I would say that my four years in the White House was a time when I prayed most fervently, and maybe even more truthfully to God, because I was faced with great challenges.

The most constant challenge was that I had thirty thousand nuclear weapons at my disposal. On one submarine, I had nuclear weapons that could destroy every city in Russia of a hundred thousand people or more, and Brezhnev had the same thing on his side. Just one doubtful day in the life of Leonard Brezhnev in Russia might have caused him to launch one of his nuclear missiles at the United States, and I had to decide how to respond. So, I prayed to God, not only to give me guidance, but to give Brezhnev guidance [*congregation laughs*], and to make sure that I didn't do something inadvertently or accidentally that would cause him to think that he was under such danger from the United States, and so forth. But I prayed a lot. I think that's the lesson for today for all of us whether we're in a position of power or influence or not.

So, the word lament has multiple meanings, and what God intends for us to do, when we are in a stage of doubt or fear or sorrow or uncertainty or failure is to turn to him in our own prayer and then to act in a proper fashion afterwards. How should we act?

Christlike.

We should try to emulate the perfect life of our Savior, Jesus Christ. That is a relatively simple answer to a very complicated question.

When we get in a stage in our life when we are lamenting to God, or expressing a doubt to God, or reaching out to God for help, the answer is sometimes uncertain through prayer, but we always have a permeating, unchanging direction from God. Whenever you are in sorrow, or doubt, or fear, or uncertainty, or when you've made a mistake, just act like Jesus Christ, who was the epitome—or highest—representation in human form of peace and justice, of humility and service, forgiveness, compassion and love.

It's not an unhappy relationship, is it? It's the avenue to peace and joy and acceptance of our Creator through our faith in his son, Jesus Christ.

July 12, 2015

Seeking Wisdom Through Suffering

Maranatha Baptist Church
Plains, Georgia

Lesson Scripture

Job 28:1–4, 12–13, 23–28 (NRSV)

1 "Surely there is a mine for silver,
and a place for gold to be refined.
2 Iron is taken out of the earth,
and copper is smelted from ore.
3 Miners put an end to darkness,
and search out to the farthest bound
the ore in gloom and deep darkness.
4 They open shafts in a valley away from human habitation;
they are forgotten by travellers,
they sway suspended, remote from people
. . .
12 "But where shall wisdom be found?
And where is the place of understanding?
13 Mortals do not know the way to it,
and it is not found in the land of the living.
. . .
23 "God understands the way to it,
and he knows its place.
24 For he looks to the ends of the earth,
and sees everything under the heavens.
25 When he gave to the wind its weight,
and apportioned out the waters by measure;
26 when he made a decree for the rain,
and a way for the thunderbolt;
27 then he saw it and declared it;
he established it, and searched it out.
28 And he said to humankind,
'Truly, the fear of the Lord, that is wisdom;
and to depart from evil is understanding'."

We're going to have a good time this morning studying one of the most difficult Bible lessons I think that I've ever taught. It's very complicated. Alfred Lloyd Tennyson, a great poet that we all studied in high school, said it's the greatest poem ever written.

Who knows what the Books of Wisdom are?

Proverbs.

Ecclesiastes.

Psalms.

And Song of Songs, and the one we're going to study this morning.

Job.

Job! Those five.

Job is a very difficult book to study and also, I think, to teach. It's easier to read than it is to teach. Last Saturday, when I got ready to teach my first lesson in Job, I read the whole book through, and then I read a couple of other books that relate to a basic question that has been asked down through the history of human beings about relationships with God. What is that question? Why does God do what?

Why does God let bad things happen to good people?

Why does God let bad things happen to good people? And vice versa, why does God let good things, seems like, happen to bad people? That's a very difficult question addressed off and on, in the book of Job.

Job, the Person

Job is a very challenging book. Who knows anything about Job?

I know that he had to suffer great hardship, but through perseverance and faith in God, he was able to be more blessed in the end, even though he suffered greatly.

He suffered great hardship, but in the end, he was blessed. What do we know about him personally?

Apparently, he was an international businessman.

He was an international businessman and a very successful trader. [*President Carter calls on a young girl with her hand raised.*] Yes, darling, what do you want to tell me?

He had about two thousand sheep.

That's true! He did. He had about two thousand sheep and he had about a thousand camels. How many sons did he have? How many boys did he have?

Ten?

Well, that's pretty close. I think he had seven. How many girls did he have? How many daughters?

Three.

Three—very good. Don't you want to teach the class? [*Congregation laughs*] What country was he from?

Ur.

Ur—that's in the East somewhere, in what would presently be the Arab countries, and he was not from Israel, like many other characters in the Bible.

So, Job was from the East. He was a very rich man, a trader. He was blessed with a wonderful family, a good wife and children, all of whom were very compatible. In fact, the Bible says that when the boys had a party, they always invited their sisters in to participate in all the enjoyable things of life, which wasn't really the custom back in those days. So, Job was really blessed.

And then there was a meeting of some kind in heaven. In a way, God was proud of Job, how good a man he was. The devil was there—Satan—and Satan said, "No wonder Job is good. He has everything; why wouldn't he be good? He's got a whole bunch of children, he's got a nice-looking wife, he's got money and land and sheep and goats and camels and so forth. Everything that has happened to Job has been a blessing, so why wouldn't he be grateful for it? Why wouldn't he be loyal to you?"

"But," he said, "what would happen if Job didn't have all those good things?"

A Legalistic Gospel

That was a very good question in those days. We don't know if the people around Job knew about Moses, but Moses taught, maybe later than Job lived, as a matter of fact, that God had a particular way of dealing with people. What was that?

It's a reward system.

It's a reward system. If you are good, God will bless you; if you're bad, God will make you have a difficult life. Moses taught that, and that was a general philosophy or relationship with God down through the ages, all the way to the time of Christ.

And as we know, that's what the Pharisees and the Sadducees and the teachers of the Law believed. Because they were very powerful and healthy, I presume they were healthy, they were at least financially healthy, and they were endowed by the Romans with the rights to run, you might say, what we would call now the Holy Land.

The Romans were conquerors, but the Romans were very wise administrators, and [they did not] interfere with the local customs. They didn't tell the Jews how to worship. They didn't tell the Jews how to clean up the streets, or how to run their elementary schools, or how to collect garbage. They let the local people run their own affairs, provided they would pay their taxes and keep the peace. That's all the Romans said, "You keep the peace, you pay the taxes, and you run your own affairs the way you want to."

So, they had the Sanhedrin there the religious leaders in Jerusalem who ran the Holy Land as, you might say, surrogates, or representatives, of the Romans, and they were very well off. They had everything they wanted, something like Job, and they assumed because they had everything that what? That they were good! And God was blessing them because they were so good. They had a rule and regulation for everything. I think there were over six hundred rules spelled out in the Old Testament and Deuteronomy and Leviticus and so forth, and they had a lot more of that in the Jewish holy books and writings. So, they went out of their way to prove how good they were.

When they would pray to God, they would do it with a lot of people listening, and they would do holy things in a very ostentatious way. They would wash their hands very carefully before they ate every meal, and they were very careful what they did on the Sabbath day.

When I wrote my first book after I left the White House, I had a very devout and very wonderful Orthodox Jew who was my editor, and she was one of the best editors I've ever had. She would come down to Plains sometimes to help me with my first book—it took me all year to write it—and she would stay in a motel in Americus. But I couldn't call her on the telephone on Sunday because she was not permitted to pick up a telephone and answer it on a Sunday. And she could not open a doorknob on Sunday. If she felt she was going to leave, she would ask somebody else to open the door for her, or she would leave the door unlocked—she was permitted to push the door, but she could only take twenty-five steps, or something like that, on Sunday. So, I knew that she was just out of circulation on Sunday. And I admired her because she was so devout and because she honored the religion that was important to her.

But, you see, that's why there was still that general premise that if you do good, God will bless you; if you do bad, God will curse you and afflict you with all kinds of problems. And Jesus took that as a direct confrontation, or contradiction, to the teachings of God. Jesus said that good and bad falls on everyone, and instead of concentrating on the cause of suffering, Jesus concentrated on the response to suffering. And that was a profound change. So profound that the holy leaders of Jesus' day decided to kill Jesus because he was upsetting the standard procedure of relating between human beings, and also relating between a human being and God, that they had already taught and which they were demonstrating so vividly with their own lives.

Learning to Respond

But remember this: Jesus didn't talk about the cause of suffering—that God punishes bad people, not good people—but how do you respond to suffering? And that question, under Jesus' teaching, related to two kinds of people. One, a person who was suffering. How do you react when you, yourself, have a terrible failure, or an embarrassment, or a sorrow, or a challenge that you can't meet? How do you respond to that? And also how do you respond to suffering among other people?

One of the basic premises of Jesus' life was to demonstrate, to us, and to all Christians, and to the people of his day, as well, that we should reach out and elevate in importance, in our own minds, people around us that we know are in need and share whatever we have. We know that God gives everybody an adequate amount of intelligence, and prestige, and influence to be reconciled with God. It doesn't matter what our IQ is, it doesn't matter whether we have a PhD, or haven't ever been to college, or even finished high school; it doesn't matter if we have money or no money in the bank, it doesn't matter if we live in a nice house or have no automobiles or anything else, it's how we relate to God that makes the difference between whether we are a good person or not in the eyes of God.

It's how we react not only to ourselves, but also to people around us. Jesus demonstrated that the outcast people and the inarticulate people—they couldn't speak for themselves—and the blind people and the leprous people, whom a lot of people considered were sick and crippled and blind. Why? Because they were bad: either they or their ancestors had done something wrong and God was punishing them with a physical affliction just because that was the way he looked upon human beings. And Jesus said that is not the case at all.

But, you see, this was a tremendous revolution in the interpretation of the relationship between God and human beings.

Long before the New Testament was written, long before maybe most of the Old Testament was written, we don't really know, the book of Job was written...and the first couple chapters just spell out what

I've already described to you—that Job was a rich man, and so forth, and God let the devil punish Job and take away his riches and his children and his good life—do everything he could except to hurt Job physically, at first. Later, God let the devil actually afflict Job physically by creating boils, or sores, it says, from the top of his head to the soles of his feet. Eventually, Job went and took off his outer clothes and covered himself with ashes and sat on a pile of ashes and stayed there as his reaction to the troubles that had come upon him.

Although it's ancient, and it deals with Job, and we don't even know who he is—we don't know who wrote the book of Job, we don't know when he lived or exactly where he lived, except it was in the East, but we're going to find out how this question of Job's suffering applies to us.

Job was convinced that God had betrayed him because Job felt that he had been a good person. He had been loyal to God, and he knew inside of him that he had not been bad enough to deserve the afflictions and the sufferings that he had.

Job had three so-called friends who came to be with him, and for seven days they sat around in the same bed of ashes sympathizing with Job, to some degree, but every one of them believed what? That he was really sinful! That he had been a sinful person all his life and he had been concealing his sins from his friends. And, finally, God caught up with him and was punishing him because he was so sinful.

They went back and forth from the third chapter in Job through the thirty-first chapter in Job, with three rounds of debates between a friend, and then Job, and then a friend, and then Job, and then a friend, and then Job. Job kept on maintaining, "I have not been a sinful person," and they said, "Well, you're lying. You must have been a sinful person because look at you. Everything bad that could happen has happened to you. So, you must have been much more sinful than the average person. Because you're suffering more than the average person." ...

Job has maintained his allegiance to God, his reverence for God, but he lost his trust in God, his confidence in God. He doesn't understand how God could have betrayed him when he didn't deserve it.

Have you ever felt that way? You suffered and you couldn't understand why God made you suffer. Maybe you lost a very close friend or member of your family who was too young to die. Or maybe you had good ambitions to carve out a career in life that would've been beneficial to yourself and to other people. Or maybe you tried something that was notable and it failed. All kinds of things that you could think of that happened to you or someone that you love that was maybe not deserved—that's what's happened to Job....

Defining Success

This is called the wisdom chapter of the book of Job—the twenty-eighth chapter. Let me read a few verses from it just to give you an explanation. Remember, these are the words of Job. He's first talking about the source of wealth.

1 'Surely there is a mine for silver,
and a place for gold to be refined.
2 Iron is taken out of the earth,
and copper is smelted from ore.
3 Miners put an end to darkness,
and search out to the farthest bound
the ore in gloom and deep darkness.
4 They open shafts in a valley away from human habitation;
they are forgotten by travelers,
they sway suspended, remote from people.

He goes on to say that people who have, I'd say, intelligence have figured out a way to go deep in the earth and extract things that are very valuable to other people and to themselves—gold and silver and iron and copper. And they have shown a great deal of incisiveness, and a great deal of ambition, and a great deal of dedication, and a great deal of intelligence.

Let's read another few verses. I'm going to read the twelfth and thirteenth.

> 12 'But where shall wisdom be found?
> And where is the place of understanding?
> 13 Mortals,
> that is, human beings,
> do not know the way to it,
> and it is not found in the land of the living.
>
> 23 'God understands the way to it,
> and he knows its place.
> 24 For he looks to the ends of the earth,
> and sees everything under the heavens.
> 25 When he gave to the wind its weight,
> and apportioned out the waters by measure;
> 26 when he made a decree for the rain,
> and a way for the thunderbolt;
> 27 then he saw it and declared it;
> talking about wisdom.
> he established it, and searched it out.
> 28 And he said to humankind,
> "Truly, the fear of the Lord, that is wisdom;
> and to depart from evil is understanding."

You might say that wisdom and understanding are synonyms. They have the same basic meaning, but that last verse is what we want to remember.

"And he said to humankind"—that is, God said to all human beings, including us—"The fear of the Lord, that is wisdom; and to depart from evil is understanding."

How many of us tend to think that searching out things of value, or making things of value and our getting ahold of them, is a way to happiness—is a way to success? Most of us do, don't we? We think that when we can get something that's valuable, and get more and more, maybe more than our neighbors, that is success. Maybe in the eyes of God, we think.

If we are given life by God, which all of us have been given, and we're given an element of intelligence, and an element of freedom, which all of us have, then to use that freedom and that intelligence and life to gain advantages for ourselves, if we do that successfully, and I'll say legally, for a change, [*congregation laughs*] then that is a measurement of success.

And if we stop maybe by ourselves, and take a piece of paper, and write down—if you weren't in church—"What is success?," we would say, get a good education, go to a good college, get a degree, get advanced degrees. Carve out for ourselves an honorable and challenging and exciting and interesting career, and plan for that career, then undertake it—and we know we'll be in competition with other schoolteachers, we'll be in competition with other lawyers, we'll be in competition with other farmers, businesspeople—and we excel, we do well, and we are able to move into a nice home, and a nice part of town, and we have two or three automobiles for ourselves and our members of our family, and we have money in the bank, and we have some provisions for our old age, and maybe even have enough assets to share them with our children and grandchildren to send them to good schools, and if we have a reputation—that I'd say is a good reputation—that's it! That's all we need. That is the essence of many people's definition of success, in the eyes of God, even.

There was one perfect life on earth, and whose is that?

Jesus.

How many of those things did Jesus have?

None of them.

His friends all abandoned him. He didn't have a place to sleep, no money, no donkey to ride on, much less automobiles. He was disgraced toward the end of his life. He was executed as a criminal. But Jesus was perfect in the eyes of his Father, God, and if we want to be perfect in the eyes of God, or as near perfect as possible, how many of those worldly things do we need?

Success Redefined

I would say the number one word to describe Jesus' ministry is "love." I often think about a child who has a problem with down syndrome. Have you ever seen a more perfect example of modesty and love than that? I would say they would be almost perfect in the eyes of God.

I was riding the other day, and I went by a village where Norman Vincent Peale's church was; I went by the church. And I knew Norman Vincent Peale when he was very famous.

I was governor and Norman Vincent Peale called me on the phone one day, and I was really excited. I had admired this great Christian man and philosopher for quite a bit. He said, "I want to come to Georgia," and I said, "That's great!" He said, "I have a program where I choose the outstanding church—the most exceptional church in America. And this year it's going to be in Macon, Georgia." I said, "I hope you can come, and you'd certainly be welcome in Georgia." He said, "I want you to be on the program with me. I'd like for you to make a speech before I make mine," and I said, "Oh, me," because he was probably the greatest speaker that I knew about, and I hated to be in front of him. [*Congregation laughs*]

There were about 7,500 people in the new civic center in Macon, Georgia, and he gave the church award to the Church of the Exceptional. And what it comprised was about thirty-five [intellectually disabled] people, and they had a very vibrant Christian life.

I made my speech; nobody remembers what I said. He made his speech; I don't think anybody remembers what he said. And then they had a program where the church members got in a big aisle in the middle and came down. They had chosen one woman, about thirty-five years old, to light the big candle. She had a taper and she came up and she tried to light the candle. Her hands were shaking, and she couldn't make the flame hit the wick. Everybody in the audience, including me and Norman Vincent Peale, were really nervous.

The pastor came forward and said, "Let me hold your arm," and she pushed him away. "No." She tried again and the candle lit. And so did her face light up. I would say her face lit the whole auditorium. She was so proud. And I would guess that everybody there, almost forty years later, still remembers what she did.

That's what success is in life, and that's what Job is trying to insert into this beautiful poem about him and his friends and his devastating blows and his struggle to understand the essence of God's teaching.

So, the lesson for us is, go ahead, be successful, study, get degrees, start a career, be a good teacher, a good lawyer, a good farmer, or a good businessperson, but don't put that as the number one goal in life. Because as far as the measurement by God of me and you, as a human being, that's not important—how much money we have, and so forth.

We can make money in our legal career or as a farmer, and we can use it the way Jesus did—to help other people. We can meet difficulties and sorrows and failures and not worry about what caused it, but how do we react to it? If we see failures or disappointments or needs among others, we should do as Jesus did, and that is, put that person as a top priority in my life.

You see, it sets a whole new kind of a vision, in the words of this ancient person that we don't know much about, in the eyes and minds of every one of us. What should we put as the top priority?

Hope for the Future

What do we do when we fail? Or when we have a terrible loss?

When I was much younger, everybody in my family died with pancreatic cancer. My daddy died with pancreatic cancer; he was in his fifties. My only brother died with pancreatic cancer; he was fifty-one. My youngest sister died with pancreatic cancer; she was in her fifties. For a while, the Carter family, my family, was the only one in the world, that they knew, where four people had died with pancreatic cancer. I didn't feel it was fair of God to take all my family. But I now see more clearly that I was not being punished, but that I had to know how to respond to, or react to, my disappointments and my failures in life.

Saint Paul did a very good job of spelling out, in very brief words, what we should do. I'm going to turn to Romans 5, and I'm going to read verses [one] through five to close the lesson.

Paul has already said what a horrible time he had in life, with shipwrecks and snake bites and beatings and imprisonment and eventually dying. He says:

> 1 Therefore, since we are justified by faith, we have peace with God through our Lord Jesus Christ, 2 through whom we have obtained access to this grace in which we stand...

That is God's grace.

> ...and we boast in our hope of sharing the glory of God. 3 And not only that, but we also boast in our sufferings...

Which is a strange thing to say.

> ...knowing that suffering produces endurance...

An ability to survive.

...[4] and endurance produces character...

It builds us up, as far as a human being ought to be. What [are] the characteristics that comprise our nature?

...and character produces hope, [5] and hope does not disappoint us, because God's love has been poured into our hearts through the Holy Spirit that has been given to us.

So, when we do have an affliction or a disappointment or a sorrow or a failure, we should remember the words of Job, but I think also remember the words of Paul.

I've been through some bad times, and I've been through some good times, but I try to remember that my hard times should induce in me an ability to withstand difficulties because God gives me the strength to do it.

And none of us are incapable of facing any kind of difficulty in our life, no matter how bad it might be. A problem with somebody you love most dearly, an early death, even, or an affliction that all of us are going to face before we are through with this life. And in building up that character, we can have hope for the future based on the knowledge that we are saved by the grace of God, the love of God, through our faith in Jesus Christ.

We should remember, too, that as a human being, we not only have life; we not only have freedom, but we have the bountiful gift of being able to form a partnership with our Creator, who knows everything and can do anything! How could you have a better partner than that? And all we have to do is to be humble enough to do what Job said: revere God, turn away from evil, and ask God to be our source of strength.

It's a beautiful lesson and a reminder to us of the fact that regardless of our connections with our wives, our husbands, our children, our pastor we can go directly to God Almighty in a quiet moment of prayer and say, "God, I've got this problem. I don't understand why I'm having to face what I am, but I know with you I'll have the strength and ability to survive it. And out of that survival, endurance, and character-building, I'll have hope and trust and confidence that I can live the rest of my life, maybe off and on, with the presence of the Holy Spirit in my heart," through our faith in Jesus Christ.

The Last Year

And death shall have no dominion.
Dead men naked they shall be one
With the man in the wind and the west moon;
When their bones are picked clean and the clean
    bones gone,
They shall have stars at elbow and foot;
Though they go mad they shall be sane,
Though they sink through the sea they shall rise
    again;
Though lovers be lost love shall not;
And death shall have no dominion.

—Dylan Thomas
from "And Death Shall Have No Dominion"

June 9, 2019. At ninety-four years old, Jimmy Carter returns to Maranatha Baptist Church to teach Sunday School only weeks after falling and breaking his hip. A special chair that raised and lowered Carter while seated was made to accommodate his age.

Courtesy *The Atlanta Journal-Constitution*; photograph by Curtis Compton

June 9, 2019. Jimmy Carter engages with a capacity Sunday School crowd at Maranatha Baptist Church. Classes often included visitors from around the world with different religious beliefs.

Courtesy *The Atlanta Journal-Constitution*; photograph by Curtis Compton

Visitors line up to have their picture taken with Jimmy Carter following the morning class and worship service at Maranatha. Carter handcrafted the wooden cross hanging above the choir loft behind where he is seated.

Courtesy *The Atlanta Journal-Constitution*; photograph by Curtis Compton

2019. Carol Anderson, organist at Maranatha Baptist Church, and Jimmy Carter await the beginning of the Sunday School hour together. Carol began playing the organ for the church in the late 1970s and continues to provide music for Maranatha today.

Courtesy Jill Stuckey

The bulletin board hanging in the back hallway at Maranatha Baptist Church is lined with photos of the Carters and other members of the congregation fellowshipping with visitors and one another.

Courtesy Madison Hernandez Photo + Art

His Bible had been beat up a bit. The small leatherbound copy resembled any ole Good Book you might see cradled in the hand of a churchgoing deacon in the South on any given Sunday. Church bulletins—the orders of worship that Maranatha printed on creamy, off-white paper and folded in half to present as small folios for congregants to follow during services—were sandwiched between the onionskin pages, providing a simple solution for bookmarking important passages of Scripture. This Bible was taken care of, but well used. And along the lower right-hand edge, gently embossed into the soft, black leather cover, was the name of that volume's main readership

—JIMMY CARTER.

If a person's Bible reflected his life, Jimmy's Bible was on target. Having lived a very full life, he was wearing out, too. In the time that transpired between Sunday, January 6, 2019, Carter's first Sunday school lesson taught at Maranatha that year, and Sunday, November 3, 2019, the last time he approached the lectern to lead, his usually brisk stamina slowed from a visible shift in age.

In May of that year, Jimmy, at the age of ninety-four, fell at home in Plains and broke his hip. The Carters' family and friends and a concerned public were apprehensive. Understandably so. The statistics are undeniable: for persons over ninety, fracturing a hip often commences the beginning of the end.

Of course, this is Jimmy Carter we're talking about. The man was already a legend, but with such high levels of continued engagement at home and around the world into his nineties, and seeming to defy his advanced age at every turn, Carter was becoming a myth. As his longtime close spiritual friend Andrew Young, who Carter appointed ambassador to the United Nations, remarked, "He's a pure Calvinist. The kind of man who's got to wake up every morning with a full schedule."

True to his mythical form, a few Sundays after undergoing hip surgery, Jimmy was back in the saddle at Maranatha. His speech was paced and his appearance was a touch tentative, but he was behind his familiar pulpit once again, exerting one of his life's constants—teaching the Bible. He opened the lesson with his customary query, "Do we have any visitors here?" Laughter ensued. Then, as he surveyed the crowd, asking where they had come from to attend church that day, someone hollered out "DC!" With a twinkle in his eye, and that trademark toothy grin, he replied, "I used to live there." The crowd erupted, and, only if for a moment, the world let out a collective sigh.

Even before falling, Carter had become increasingly unsteady on his feet. He was adamant that he was most comfortable and effective teaching his lessons standing. He liked to pace the floor, lecturing in a conversational, thinking-out-loud manner and often engaging the crowd with questions about what a certain text or particular parable from Scripture might mean. He often recalled scenes from his own life at home in Plains his own life at home in Plains or in his work with communities around the globe through The Carter Center as a way to share how his own faith found expression in daily life.

But the Carters' longtime friend Jill Stuckey was concerned about his health. So, after inviting Jimmy and Rosalyn over for dinner and a heart-to-heart conversation, a design for a motorized chair was agreed upon and within weeks implemented at the church. Though he hardly wanted to be relegated to an electric stool, Carter's humor remained intact.

At the beginning of each class, as he sat down, he mentioned his "special chair" that the church made for "old people." At the same time from across the room, a church member raised the chair with a remote control. The room swelled with good-natured laughter as the former president of the free world was gently lifted to the height of the lectern so he could be seen by all. The antic added whimsy to the seriousness of advancing age, drawing a big laugh and setting the crowd, and their teacher, at ease.

In the twilight of his life, the thrust of President Carter's lessons became more and more focused. Less about mining for some untapped theological insight or rousing a religious debate, Carter's messages centered on themes of seeking justice, cultivating peace, measuring success by God's standards, and loving our neighbors without condition. As the Carters' second son, Chip, shared, in a tribute to his parents as a part of the couple's seventy-fifth wedding anniversary in Plains in 2021, "They taught us their values. Christian values. Plains, Georgia, values. They taught us that every person deserves our respect, regardless of their wealth, their race, their age, their politics, their sex, their sexual orientation, or the amount of power that they had. They taught us to love our neighbors and to help them when needed."

That same year, in a recorded conversation I shared with President Carter, one of the last formal interviews of his life, I asked the former leader, with a lifetime of experiences under his belt, "If you were to leave this world with one single message, what would that message be?" He replied simply: "My religious faith is very important to me, and I would just like for the teachings of Jesus Christ to be implemented in the whole world. To love one another and have a complete equality and treatment of all the people and treat each other the way we would like for them to treat us."

Perhaps all the wisdom gained over a lifetime—even one as extraordinary as Jimmy Carter's—can be summed up by a single truth: "and the greatest of these is love."

March 3, 2019

A New Way of Life

Maranatha Baptist Church
Plains, Georgia

Lesson Scripture

Ephesians 4:25–32 (NRSV)

[25] So then, putting away falsehood, let all of us speak the truth to our neighbors, for we are members of one another. [26] Be angry but do not sin; do not let the sun go down on your anger, [27] and do not make room for the devil. [28] Thieves must give up stealing; rather let them labor and work honestly with their own hands, so as to have something to share with the needy. [29] Let no evil talk come out of your mouths, but only what is useful for building up, as there is need, so that your words may give grace to those who hear. [30] And do not grieve the Holy Spirit of God, with which you were marked with a seal for the day of redemption. [31] Put away from you all bitterness and wrath and anger and wrangling and slander, together with all malice, [32] and be kind to one another, tenderhearted, forgiving one another, as God in Christ has forgiven you.

This morning we're going to be talking about Saint Paul. What do you know about Saint Paul? What's one thing you know about him?

He was a Hellenic Jew.

He was a Jew, but he was also a Roman citizen. What else do we know about him?

He was an apostle.

He wasn't one of the twelve apostles, but he was a great evangelist.

He wrote most of the New Testament.

He wrote a lot of the New Testament. He wrote ten books in the New Testament. When did he write his letters that became books?

In prison.

He wrote some of them when he was still traveling on one of his missions, but he wrote the last letters while he was in prison. What timeframe?

A.D. 60.

The middle of the first century.

I would say about 50 A.D. When was the first Gospel written?

Later than that. [*Congregation laughs*]

Either ten or twenty years later, the first Gospel, which was Mark, was written. So, the Gospels with which we begin the New Testament were all written long after Paul died—at least ten or twenty years later. We don't know exactly the timeframe.

Paul was a great evangelist, and Paul, more than anybody else, was a theologian who explained to the various churches, and therefore to us through his letters, exactly what Christianity was and what Jesus meant by his words and his actions. So, Paul was a great writer.

I've got a book at home that I've had for a long time called *The 100.* It lists the one hundred most influential people who ever lived on earth. It's a very interesting book. I have never agreed with it because it lists Jesus as number three, [*congregation laughs*] and it lists Mohammed as number one, although there are twice as many Christians in the world as there are those who believe in Islam. But why do you think that is?

I actually have the book, and one difference between Mohammed and Jesus is that Mohammed had the time to implement political and economic differences. As opposed to Jesus, where his word was more spiritual and about the religion.

Jesus had the basic commitment to represent God on earth and explain how we should live and also the character of God, but Mohammed did more to implement his religion by military action and otherwise political action throughout the world than Jesus did with Christianity, because Jesus didn't go beyond what's presently the Holy Land in his ministry. But Paul took up and went to other places—went all the way to Rome and to Ephesus and to Turkey and to Greece, Corinth, and so forth. So, Paul and Jesus, together, are looked upon as the founders of Christianity, although Jesus was the spiritual leader of it. And Paul defers completely to Jesus, but Paul came in quite early and took over after Jesus died.

As you know, Paul was saved and became a Christian when? On the road to what?

Damascus.

And in a miraculous way, Paul became a Christian after Jesus was dead, but he was converted and became a very fiery and aggressive and successful missionary, in effect, to spread the word about Jesus Christ and to interpret Jesus' words and his actions. So, Paul was really the foundation of the spread of Christianity.

So, Jesus is ranked number three and Paul is ranked number six.... I would say that Jesus was the foundation of Christianity, of course, and the son of God. Paul interpreted Jesus and spread the word about Jesus and was responsible for the spread of Christianity.

What Kind of Christian Am I?

More than any other letters that Paul wrote, the book to the Ephesians explains the gamut, the real meaning of Christianity. In the fourth chapter of Ephesians, which is our lesson for today, we will study about Jesus' teachings concerning our relationship to other human beings or other people. And Paul takes the fourth chapter of the book of Ephesians to the church in Ephesus and explains this is what Jesus meant for us to do.

Why do you think we're studying that at this time of year? We've just begun a Christian era leading up to Easter. What is that?

Lent.

What are we supposed to do during Lent?

Reflect.

Reflect! That's a very good word. Lent is when we're supposed to sit back, just for a few minutes, or a few hours, and look at ourselves, and say to ourselves, "What kind of Christian have I become?"

I'm sure that's why all of you came to church this morning [*congregation laughs*]—to think about what kind of Christian you are.

For some of you, Christianity's kind of a distant concept. For me, it's a way of life. I've been a Christian ever since I was a little baby almost. My daddy was a Sunday school teacher in the church where I was later baptized, and Rosalynn's been a Christian all her life. So, Christianity's the most important thing in my life. But for some people, I know it's not.

This morning, I want all of us, no matter what kind of person you are, to take a look, not at other people, but at yourself—not at your husband or wife, not at your mama or daddy, not at your children, but at yourself. And let's all together take a look and use Jesus' words, primarily, in Paul's fourth chapter of Ephesians and decide, "What kind of Christian am I?"

I think the most important sermon I ever heard when I grew up was in Plains Baptist Church. We had a very good preacher named John Simmons, and one Sunday, John Simmons preached a sermon—I don't remember anything he said, but I remember the name of the sermon. And the name of the sermon was "If You Were Arrested for Being a Christian, Would There Be Enough Evidence to Convict You?"

Just for a moment, ask yourself that question. Say you moved to another country, or something like that: if you were arrested for being a Christian, could you talk your way out of it? Would there be enough evidence against you to convict you for being a Christian?

I have thought about that a lot, and many people could probably say, "I've been to church a lot. I've been to church all my life. But I really went to church not because I was a real good Christian, but it helped my business. Because I ran a grocery store, or I had a little practice, and I knew that most of my clients or customers were Christians, and I wanted to be attractive to them." Or maybe, "I would've been better off financially in my hometown if I was a Christian," and so forth. So, you can think of reasons for being a Christian, but would there be enough evidence about you to convict you of being a Christian? That's a profound thing to think about.

Facing the Truth About Ourselves

Let me just read a few verses of Ephesians 4. And I'm going to start with the twenty-fifth verse. These are "Rules for the New Life," it says in my Bible.

25 So then, putting away falsehood, let all of us speak the truth...

That's the first thing—"all of us speak the truth." Why do we do that?

...for we are members of one another.

Our lives relate to one another. If you were an officer in the navy or a political leader or something else, you would want to tell the truth because you'd want your subordinates to believe things you say in a crisis. So, telling the truth is advantageous for you, but you have to be able to tell yourself the truth, too, about yourself. And that's what we're trying to do this morning. We're trying to look at ourselves this morning and to see, among other things, if you were arrested for being a Christian, could you talk your way out of it, or would there be enough evidence to convict you?

Let's read on.

26 Be angry...

It's okay to be angry

...but do not sin; do not let the sun go down on your anger.

How many of you practice that? [*Congregation laughs*] You know, Rosalynn and I had an interview not long ago. Who was it with, Rosalynn? Up at The Carter Center where we had the interview about our marriage?

Phil Donahue and Marlo Thomas.

Phil Donahue and Marlo Thomas are writing a book, and they wanted to interview me and Rosalynn because we've been married longer than they have; they've only been married, I think, forty years, and we've been married seventy-two and a half years. Anyway, they wanted to talk to us about our marriage, and one of the things that we told them was that we try not to ever go to sleep still mad with each other. We get mad with each other a lot. [*Congregation laughs*] But we pretty well stick to that; we never go to sleep without being reconciled.

And that's what Jesus tells us to do as a practical way to get along with everybody else, not just your wife or your husband. "Don't let the sun go down," it says, "on your anger." It's okay to get angry. We know Jesus got angry and turned over the tables in the temple and that sort of thing. But don't let anger stick with you.

Let's read on a few more verses.

28 Thieves must give up stealing; rather let them labour and work
honestly with their own hands, so as to have something to share with
the needy. 29 Let no evil talk come out of your mouths, but only what
is useful for building up, as there is need, so that your words may give
grace to those who hear.

How many of you, looking at your own self now, every now and then say something that is damaging to somebody else that's not there. Or might hurt their reputation? That's one of the ways to get along with your neighbors—say things that bring grace to somebody else, not try to hurt anybody. Tell the truth, but also don't say anything bad about your neighbors....

This is my favorite verse in the whole Bible—I get asked that pretty often. The thirty-second verse.

32 and be kind to one another, tender-hearted, forgiving one another, as God in Christ has forgiven you.

I think that kind of encapsulates the proper relationship between people, don't you? Be kind to one another and forgive each other, as God through Christ was kind to us and forgives us. These are just practical examples of how we should act towards other people. I'm not going to ask you to judge yourself, but I'm judging myself this morning.

A True Superpower

Let's take a few moments now and envision what you would look upon as a description of God's kingdom on earth if everybody abided with these principles. How would you describe God's kingdom?

Peaceful.

A loving community.

Filled with love and care for one another. That's enough, I think—caring for one another and peaceful. How long has the United States been a country?

Since 1776.

Well, our government wasn't established then, but a couple years later—about 242 years we've been a nation. How many of those years have we been completely at peace with other countries?

Twenty.

Four.

Forty years.

Sixteen years. [For] 226 years, the United States has been in conflict with at least one other country—226 compared to sixteen.

So, you see, our country has a long way to go, and we Americans have a long way to go, just to bring to life one facet of God's kingdom—that is peace. Not even to mention love and being kind to one another and not ever criticizing your neighbors and so forth. That makes you think, doesn't it? And what does that cost us in really practical terms?

Lately, we've been at war with Iraq. We've been at war with Afghanistan. We've been at war with Yeomen. We've been at war with

Syria. And it's estimated that we've spent about $3 trillion on those wars. That's three thousand billion dollars.

I normalized diplomatic relations with China in 1979, the first day of January. And China hasn't been at war with anybody since then—since 1979. And the United States has an enormous debt, and we are increasing the debt, I don't know how many millions of dollars every second or something like that.

But anyway, China has 18,000 miles of high-speed railroads, where the trains go more than 250 kilometers per hour. Rosalynn and I have ridden on one; they get up to about 260 miles per hour just going from downtown Shanghai to the airport. And China is building new universities every year. And all their roads, all their bridges are right up to snuff.

How many miles of high-speed railroads do we have in America? None. And our elementary and secondary schools are not all that good; our universities are very good, but I'd say the education of our children from kindergarten on up is not very good compared to other countries. Well, I'm not knocking the United States of America, but just envision if God's kingdom came to America. We would be a real superpower, I think.

How would you describe a real superpower?

Respected.

Respected, yes. By all the countries in the world.

One that takes care of its citizens.

One that takes care of its people. But let's look at—how about peaceful?

Wouldn't it be nice if every other country on earth, if they had a war or were tempted to go to war, would say, "Why don't we go to Washington, because the United States knows how to stay at peace?" Wouldn't that be great?

Or suppose somebody was being abused with human rights violations, say, being persecuted: "Why don't we go to Washington and see how they do it, because they are the number one champions of human rights?"

Or if you wanted to talk about the environment, "Why don't we go to the United States of America, because they are in the lead of all countries in making sure we have a good environment and that there's no such thing as global warming?"

Or "Why don't we go to America, because America believes in real equality among all the people—gays and straights, and African Americans and White people, and men and women, and immigrants and newcomers?"

That's what a real superpower would be if we applied in our own lives, and, as citizens, the basic principles of the kingdom of God. And that's what Paul is talking about here in the fourth chapter of Ephesians. And that's what I want you to think about this morning.

Well, what can we do about it?

A Successful Life

If you read Paul carefully, particularly if you read the book of James, which is one of my favorites—James was the half brother of Jesus, and he was kind of the head of the Christian church in Jerusalem after Jesus' death and resurrection—Paul and James said that if we don't have a clear purpose in our lives, if we don't lead a life of happiness and peace, it's our own fault. Most of us, if something's going wrong in our lives, we want to blame it on other people, on circumstances over which we didn't have any control. We don't want to accept responsibility for our own lives! But what Paul is telling us in this lesson this morning is we need to take a look at ourselves! Not somebody else—and not have somebody else be responsible for it, but we're responsible.

Every one of us receives from God—every one of you, and I, receive from God, I'd say—three or four things. One, we receive life. We are living because of God. If you doubt that, how many of you decided when you were going to be born? Or who your parents would be? Or what your native intelligence would be? Or your character? Nobody.

And so, all of us, if you assume that God is responsible for your life, we can communicate twenty-four hours a day, every day, with our Creator. We can talk directly to God through prayer. Driving an automobile or waking up in the morning or going to sleep at night, we can talk to God, and if we have a real problem in our lives, a question we can't answer or we made a bad mistake or we have a challenge we can't meet or we have a sorrow that we can't overcome, we can go to God, our Creator, and share that with him—with God.

God also gives us freedom. And that cuts both ways, because we are free to reject or you're free to accept it. It's up to you....

And God gives us another thing that we sometimes don't even think about. God gives us enough talent and ability and opportunity, every one of us, to live a completely successful life—period—as judged by God.

You might say, if you weren't in church, if I want to be successful, I want to make a lot of money. I want to live in a nice house. I want to have a good automobile. I want to have enough money, at least, for my retirement and to put my kids and grandkids through college. Nice things nothing wrong with that. I want to have friends who are loyal to me the rest of my life. I want to live to be an old person; I want to live a full life—a lot of years would be better.

How many of those things did Jesus have?

None.

None of them! Did he have a lot of money? Did he have a nice house? Did he have friends that stayed with him in his trying times? No. But Jesus led a perfect life as judged by God.

So, we have within our own capability an opportunity to live a completely successful life, and a happy life, with purpose and with peace. Every single one of us, all during every day, we make an answer to this question. What kind of person do I choose to be? Does anybody disagree with that?

Does your wife tell you what kind of person you're going to be? Does your husband? Do your parents or children? No. Every one of us decides, this is the kind of person that I choose to be. And if, at this moment, you're not satisfied with the kind of person you have chosen to be, what can you do about it? Change!

And if you want to change in a proper way, acknowledge the gifts you get from God, go to God in prayer, and every one of us has a perfect example of how we should live by looking at the life of Jesus Christ, who treated everybody the same. Samaritans, Gentiles, Jews, slaves, masters, men, women—Jesus treated everybody the same. Can we do that? No reason why we don't.

Afterword

by Jason Carter

My grandfather was one of the most famous Sunday School teachers in history. When he taught, people came from all over to hear him. As I have said before, sometimes I felt like I shared him with the world. But really, he shared the world with me. The miracle of our people and our planet. The majesty and beauty of a South Georgia pine forest. The art of a good cast and good conversation while standing in a trout stream. Spotting and naming constellations from his front yard in Plains. My grandfather's world was a world of wonder and compassion, a world filled with faith and belief in things unseen.

On Sundays, he shared this world with thousands of people who traveled from around the globe to congregate at Maranatha Baptist Church in Plains, Georgia. In many ways, this was my grandfather's home: in this tiny village in South Georgia, inside a little country church, with my grandmother, with his people, and with all those visitors, teaching from the Bible almost every weekend for nearly 40 years.

To most, Jimmy Carter was a former United States president, a determined champion of peace–a humanitarian who waged war on life-threatening diseases in the poorest communities around the world. For many, my grandfather provided an example of power that is used for good, not to dominate or control others, but to bend in service to "the least of these." (Matt. 25:40) But to my family, Jimmy and Rosalynn Carter were just "PaPa" and "Mom Carter." Regular folks. Small town folks who never forgot who they were or where they came from. In my nearly 50 years of knowing my grandfather, I never perceived a difference between his private life and his public life. No matter where he was or who he was with, he was the same person. This integrity, this honesty, was only matched by his love, and that love became the

2014. Jason Carter sits with his grandparents Jimmy and Rosalynn Carter during a Sunday service at Maranatha Baptist Church in Plains, Georgia.

Courtesy *Associated Press*; photograph by John Bazemore

substance of his faith that he lived out every day of his life.

You saw it in the way he respected people, even when he disagreed with them. He lived out the commandment "love your neighbor as yourself" (Matthew 22:39) as an ideal still worthy of commitment in our modern lives. And this love, the one you have just experienced in these Sunday School lessons, led him to preach the power of human rights, not just for some people, but for all people. That love taught him to preach an end to racial discrimination when Black people across his home state were still being deprived of basic freedoms. That love mandated him to put an end to mass incarceration. That love broke his heart for the people of Palestine and the people of Israel and moved him to spend his life trying to bring peace to that holy land. For my grandparents, "Do justice, love mercy, and walk humbly with your God" (Micah 6:8) wasn't just a Bible verse to memorize, it was a mantra they recited with their lives.

And love was the story of Jimmy Carter's life.

Forty years ago, when my grandfather first heard about Guinea worm disease, he did what Jimmy Carter does—he got to work. The disease is an ancient and debilitating condition caused by drinking contaminated water, and results in painful blisters through which a literal worm slowly and painfully emerges. When my grandfather first began tackling the problem, there were 3.5 million cases reported in humans every year. As of 2024, only 14 cases of the disease–a disease that has existed since the dawn of time–were reported worldwide. And yet, the most remarkable part of this story is that this disease is not eradicated with medicine. It's eradicated by groups of neighbors in the most marginalized villages in the world, talking and teaching each other how to safely filter and collect water.

Many times, my grandfather saw unseen people, and he respected them. He never saw them as people to pity. He saw them as a people with whom to find partnership and power in carrying out his lifelong commitment, the Book of Matthew's command "to love your neighbor as yourself."

His fellow congregants at Maranatha were also his partners. Empowered by lessons like the ones you hold in your hands, my grandfather and the people of Maranatha became a network of neighbors who, through their common belief in the teachings of Christ, talked and taught each other to love all people. People who grew up in a Christian church. People who were raised in a Jewish synagogue. People who grew up practicing Islam. People who grew up never thinking about whether God existed or not. This included people of all races. It included Yankees, Southerners, people from China, Ghana, rich people, poor people–they all came to hear a message from the Scriptures taught by my grandfather. A message of friendship with God. A message of how to live a meaningful life in the present. A message of how to love your neighbor. A message of God's love for you, and for me, and for all of us.

In a song—"Goodness of God"—we sing at my church, one of the verses says:

From the moment that I wake up
Until I lay my head
Oh, I will sing of the goodness of God.

From the moment my grandfather woke up until he laid his head, his life was singing of the goodness of his God. This book is a testament to that truth.

To have these words–his words–written down for all of us to explore in this moment in the history of our world is truly a gift. To bring people together through the preaching of love and kindness–this is the gift of my grandfather's life. This can be the gift of our lives, too.

Jason Carter
Atlanta, Georgia
May 2025

Notes

For most of the lessons President Carter taught at Maranatha Baptist Church, he read from the New Revised Standard Version (NRSV) Bible translation.. So, NRSV has been used to present the overall Lesson Scripture in each chapter. However, various translations are used when Carter or a class member reads Scripture aloud.

PREFACE

began congregating "Church Formed by Split Welcomes Carter Family," *The New York Times*, January 26, 1981.

Brown V. Board of Education *Brown v. Board of Education of Topeka,* Opinion; May 17, 1954; Records of the Supreme Court of the United States; Record Group 267; National Archives.

delivered a lesson Maranatha Baptist Church, "MBC Sunday Services," *Facebook*, December 29, 2024, www.facebook.com/MBCPlains/videos/1746693452857937.

THE 1970s

Introduction

"one of the most segregated hours" Martin Luther King, Jr, *Meet the Press* interview, April 17, 1960.

"whiskey drinking saint," "She delivered every baby," "Now, his daddy" Andrew Greer, dir. *Plainspoken*. Dace & Mohr/Narrative Productions, 2024.

"Thou shalt love" Matthew 22:39, King James Version. This is the version of the Bible Carter's father, Earl, would have read from.

"for ye are all one" Galatians 3:28, King James Version. This is the version of the Bible Carter's father, Earl, would have read from.

"faith, if it hath not works" James 2:17, King James Version. This is the version of the Bible Carter's father, Earl, would have read from.

"aura of a queen" Jimmy Carter, *Always a Reckoning and Other Poems* (New York: Times Books/Random House, 1995), p. 3.

"President Carter, you have been," "When I was a little boy" Jimmy Carter, *A Full Life: Reflections at Ninety* (New York: Simon & Schuster, 2015), p. 134.

As a prelude to Carter's inauguration The First Baptist Church of the City of Washington, D.C., "President Carter & FBC," www.firstbaptistdc.org/carter.

March 12, 1978

when Andy says Martin Luther King To read more about Andrew Young and the Civil Rights Movement, see; Andrew Young, *An Easy Burden: The Civil Rights Movement and the Transformation of America* (Waco: Baylor University Press, 2008).

April 29, 1979

the Jubilee Year To explore more about the Jubilee Year, see Enter the Bible, "Leviticus 25–The Sabbatical Year and the Year of Jubilee," www.enterthebible.org/passage/leviticus-25-the-sabbatical-year-and-the-year-of-jubilee.

THE 1980s

Introduction

Sermon on the Mount: Matthew 5-7.

"But I say to you, Love your enemies": Matthew 5:44-45, New Revised Standard Version.

"In a nation that was proud of hard work" Jimmy Carter, "Crisis of Confidence," American Experience, PBS, http://www.pbs.org/wgbh/americanexperience/features/carter-crisis.

"In rejecting Carter in favor of Reagan" Randall Balmer, *Redeemer: The Life of Jimmy Carter*, pp. xxiv-xxv.

annual Jimmy Carter Work Project To find out more about the work of Habitat for Humanity and the Jimmy Carter Work Project, see Habitat for Humanity, "Carter Work Project"; www.habitat.org/carter-work-project.

March 8, 1981

The philosopher [**Blaise**] **Pascal** Carter paraphrases a writing by French philosopher Blaise Pascal that can be found in Blaise Pascal, *Pensées* (1670), Section VII, number 534. The entire text can easily be found online.

THE 1990s

Introduction

"blessed are the poor in spirit," "those who mourn," "the meek," "the merciful" Matthew 5:3-5, 7, New Revised Standard Version.

"a table before" Psalm 23:5, New Revised Standard Version.

Their principled fashion To find out more about the work of The Carter Center, see The Carter Center home page, www.cartercenter.org

March 7, 1993

One of my favorite authors To learn more about paleontologist Stephen Jay Gould and his writings, see Stephen Jay Gould, *The Richness of Life: The Essential Stephen Jay Gould* (New York: W. W. Norton & Company, 2007).

One of my favorite theologians To learn more about Paul Tillich, one of Carter's favorite theologians whom he quoted often, see: Britannica, "Paul Tillich," www.britannica.com/biography/Paul-Tillich.

October 9, 1994

I've written a poem Jimmy Carter, *Always a Reckoning and Other Poems*, p. 81.

Reinhold Niebuhr said To learn more about Niebuhr, one of Carter's favorite theologians, see Reinhold Niebuhr, *Moral Man and Immoral Society: A Study in Ethics and Politics* (New York: Charles Scribner's Sons, 1932). Several editions are available from multiple publishers.

January 7, 1996

Millard?: When Carter calls upon Millard, he is speaking to Millard Fuller, founder of Habitat for Humanity. Millard attended Maranatha until his death in 2009.

I remember President Reagan said this Steven V. Roberts, "Reagan on Homelessness: Many Choose to Live in the Streets," *The New York Times*, December 23, 1988.

THE 2000s

Introduction

"I was infatuated with the Holy Land" Jimmy Carter, *Palestine: Peace Not Apartheid* (New York: Simon & Schuster, 2006), p. 22.

"I wanted to be able to say" Kai Bird, *The Outlier: The Unfinished Presidency of Jimmy Carter* (New York: Crown, 2021), p. 353.

"The Camp David conference should be" Jonathan Alter, *His Very Best: Jimmy Carter, a Life* (New York: Simon & Schuster, 2020), p. 416.

"for their contribution to the two-frame agreements on peace" The Nobel Prize, "Award Ceremony Speech," www.nobelprize.org/prizes/peace/1978/ceremony-speech.

"for his decades of untiring effort to find peaceful solutions" The Nobel Prize, "Nobel Peace Prize 2002," https://www.nobelprize.org/prizes/peace/2002/summary.

"Israel's continued control" Jimmy Carter, *Palestine: Peace Not Apartheid*, p. 208.

"unbecoming of a former President" Simon Wiesenthal Center, "Wiesenthal Center Re: Carter Center Resignations: 'President Carter Has Only Himself To Blame'," www.wiesenthal.com/about/news/wiesenthal-center-re-carter.html.

"abandoned your historic role" The Wall Street Journal, "Letters Sent by Carter Board Members," www.wsj.com/articles/SB116852926782473918.

"We will not learn how to live together" Jimmy Carter, *The Nobel Peace Prize Lecture*, p. 20

"Blessed are the peacemakers" Matthew 5:9, World English Bible.

December 9, 2007

We have a special law program To learn more about the impact of the Carter Center's Rule of Law program in Liberia and other countries, see The Carter Center, "Rule of Law Program," www.cartercenter.org/peace/ati/index.html.

Ten years ago, there was a tremendous crusade Richard N. Ostling, "Handmaid or Feminist?," *TIME,* December 30, 1991, pp.62-66.

August 24, 2008

Ruth Carter Stapleton was a famous evangelist A simple online search on "Ruth Carter Stapleton," President Carter's sister, will lead to more information about her life and ministry and books.

"had to accommodate changing times" Jimmy Carter, *The Nobel Peace Prize Lecture* (New York: Simon & Schuster, 2002), p. 13.

What's the Great Commission The Great Commission is outlined in Matthew 28:16-20.

THE 2010s

Introduction

"The spirit is willing" Matthew 26:41, New International Version.

the disturbing news that Jeremy Josh Carter, "Rest in Peace Dear Brother Jeremy. I Love You.," *JC Woodworking*, December 20, 2015, www.jcwoodworking.com/rest-in-peace-dear-brother-jeremy-i-love-you.

"I've had a wonderful life" The Carter Center, "President Carter Discusses Cancer Diagnosis," https://www.cartercenter.org/news/pr/carter-press-conference-082015.html

"My soul magnifies the Lord" Luke 1:46-47, 49, New Revised Standard Version, Anglicised.

"Sorry I'm late," "Jeremy was a special" Jimmy Carter Sunday School class, 20 December 2015, JCSSL778, JC Sunday School, Jimmy Carter Presidential Library, Atlanta, GA.

"But where shall wisdom be found" Job 28:12-13, New Revised Standard Version.

June 22, 2014

My number one opponent A History of Racial Injustice, "Lester Maddox Threatens Black Students; All-White Jury Acquits Him," calendar.eji.org/racial-injustice/apr/20.

THE LAST YEAR

Introduction

"He's a pure Calvinist" Kai Bird, *The Outlier: The Unfinished Presidency of Jimmy Carter*, p. 607.

"Do we have any visitors," "DC!", "I used to live there" Jimmy Carter Sunday School class, 9 June 2019, JCSSL895, JC Sunday School, Jimmy Carter Presidential Library, Atlanta, GA.

"special chair," "old people" Jimmy Carter Sunday School class, 3 March 2019, JCSSL890, JC Sunday School, Jimmy Carter Presidential Library, Atlanta, GA; Andrew Greer, dir. *Plainspoken*. Dace & Mohr/Narrative Productions, 2024.

"They taught us their values" Andrew Greer, dir. *Plainspoken*. Dace & Mohr/Narrative Productions, 2024.

"My religious faith" Andrew Greer, dir. *Plainspoken*. Dace & Mohr/Narrative Productions, 2024.

"and the greatest of these" 1 Corinthians 13:13, New Revised Standard Version.

March 3, 2019

I've got a book at home Michael H. Hart, *The 100: A Ranking of the Most Influential Persons in History* (New York: Hart Publishing Company, 1978). The book has been revised and updated and translated into multiple languages since its original publication.

As you know, Paul was saved Carter is referring to Saul's (Paul) conversion to Christianity on the Road to Damascus, chronicled in Acts 9:1-19.

Rosalynn and I had an interview Marlo Thomas and Phil Donahue, "President Jimmy Carter and Rosalynn Carter," June 14, 2021, in

Double Date with Marlo Thomas and Phil Donahue, Pushkin Industries, podcast, 22:05, www.pushkin.fm/podcasts/double-date-with-marlo-thomas-phil-donahue/president-jimmy-carter-rosalynn-carter.

"Goodness of God" Songwriters: Ben Fielding / Brian Johnson / Edward Martin Cash / Jason Ingram / Jenn Johnson. © ALLETROP (Capitol CMG)/Alletrop Music/Bethel Music Publishing/Bethel Music Publishing/Capitol CMG Paragon/Fellow Ships Music/Shout! Music Publishing/So Essential Tunes/So Essential Tunes.

Acknowledgments

I can't think of a better combination than Jimmy Carter and the Bible. I am a lifelong reader of the scriptures, and a longtime admirer of Carter, so to be entrusted with a collection of lessons that were taught by one of my greatest heroes about my very closest Friend, well, it must be a dream. Which makes Marc Jolley and the fine folks at Mercer University Press dream makers.

When I shared the idea about this book with Jill Stuckey, a long-time friend of the Carters and mine in Plains, she said, "You need to meet Marc Jolley." Marc is the Director of Mercer University Press and after vetting me over the course of several emails, Marc agreed to meet with me—and here we are. Thank you, Marc, for caring about and helping to preserve this part of our favorite president's legacy, and for letting me be me (which includes being perpetually late) throughout the entire process of creating this book. You are not just a fine editor; you are a friend.

Speaking of good people at Mercer, Director of Marketing Mary Beth Kosowski, Client Service Assistant Kelley Land, and Jenny Toole in the business office work day in and day out to wrestle manuscripts out of writers' hands like mine and release them as books like this for the world to read. And Publication Specialist Marsha Luttrell is always a happy encourager; whenever I hear from her, I believe that I really can do this.

All I can say to Mary Pearson is, "I'm sorry." As the copy editor for this book, Mary endured a very rough first draft and then suffered through piles of comments scrawled throughout the margins of the manuscript. She has dedicated her immense expertise and lots of time to make this the best book possible, and to honor President Carter's words with the utmost care. Thank you, Mary.

Burt & Burt Studio is the designer who brought this cover artwork to life—a cover that beautifully expresses Carter's spirit of welcome to the world. Major kudos to John Bazemore for capturing this wonderful photo during a Sunday school class in 2014. Judge this book by its cover!

There are plenty of other photos sprinkled throughout the book. I hope they help you place yourself "in the room" thanks to the keen eyes and superb skills of photographers Jen Bates, Grant Blankenship, Curtis Compton, Calvin Cruce, Ben Gray, Madison Hernandez, Todd Stone, Jill Stuckey, and the White House photographers during Carter's presidency. Extra gratitude goes to Grant for the time he invested in tracking down pictures I would not have otherwise known about and the people who took them; and Staton Breidenthal at the Arkansas Democrat-Gazette, Allison Schein at the Atlanta Journal-Constitution, the Norman Vincent Peale Family and Guideposts, Nelle, Robin and Danny Arial, Jeremy and Valarie Shoulta, Chris and Faith Fuller, and the staff at the Jimmy Carter Library and Museum for providing access and permissions to your photos included here.

Oh, and about the Jimmy Carter Library and Museum—if there is research to be done on the life of Carter it begins here. Archivist Sara Mitchell provided lots of expertise and support (with kindness and a smile!) as I dug through the Library's trove of Carter treasures.

It can be nearly impossible to license, much less afford to license, the use of poetry. But I'm stubborn and had made up my mind that I wanted to feature verses from President Carter's favorite poet, Dylan Thomas, as well as highlight one of Carter's own poems in these pages. Chris Wait at New Directions Publishing kindly provided access to Thomas' poetry. And Chip Carter and Lauren Gay generously granted permission to use President Carter's poem, "With Words We Learn to Hate" from his collection entitled *Always a Reckoning and Other Poems*; Donnie Roland with the Carters' estate helped pave that path. I am grateful for all of these kindnesses.

The Carter Center's Chief Operating Officer Beth Davis and Corporate Secretary Lauren Gay Barber are dynamic people and professionals who for decades worked alongside President Carter in his pursuit of peace and human rights and now continue that legacy in his name. I can't imagine proceeding with a project that involves or represents President Carter without their go-ahead. So, before I committed this book to a publisher, I drove up to Atlanta to meet with them at the center's headquarters in Atlanta where they not only gave me their blessing but also provided expert opinions and helpful advice and pledged me their friendship throughout the process.

The Carter Center's office in Plains is held down by Ruth Sanders and Polly Martin. Housed in Miss Lillian's old home, just across the street and caddy-corner from my house, Ruth and Polly's office serves as an occasional break room during my work-from-home days and our conversations are always full of their humorous stories and unique insights from working closely with President Carter for years. And they were always kind to connect me with the right contact to help me finalize various details in this book.

If it had not been for my dear friends Barry and Amanda Howard, I wouldn't have found myself in the middle of all of this! While visiting Plains several years ago, they encouraged me to attend church at Maranatha where their friends, George and Jan Williams, were waiting for me. I fell in love with the whole thing–the church and the community–and moved to Plains a few years later. George and Jan are now my backyard neighbors now (Hey neighbors!) and Maranatha Baptist Church is now my home church. So to Maranatha–thank you for saying "Yes" to a president teaching Sunday school and to all the visitors who showed up as a result. And thank you for saying "Yes" to me.

On most Sunday mornings these days, Kim Carter Fuller, President Carter's niece, shares her uncle's love of the Bible and knack for teaching from it by leading our adult Sunday school class. Thank you, Kim, for being faithful to the tradition your uncle began and for your loyal friendship to me. Reverend Tony Lowden was Maranatha's pastor when I first started attending. He soon "prophesied" my moving to Plains, and though I would have never thought it would come true, he stayed on me until it did. He continues to be a good friend and counselor; I am proud to know him. Reverend Ashley Guthas is our current pastor; she has the heart of a lioness and from her I am learning to relax in the inevitable discomfort that results from our fumbling attempts to follow Jesus. Thankful that we all get to try together. I never knew Reverend Dan Arial, but his decades of leadership at Maranatha made Jimmy Carter's Sunday School possible. Your family is a treasure to me and many others, Dan.

Later in his life, President Carter often confessed that in his early years equality between men and women was not on his radar. But once he caught on (with the encouragement of Rosalynn, I'm certain), he was all in. At the beginning of most of the classes he taught at Maranatha, he would ask a visiting female pastor to lead the class in an opening prayer. So, it felt fitting to ask Barbara Brown Taylor, an Episcopalian priest and one of my all-time favorite authors opining on spiritual life today to write the Foreword. Barbara, I think President Carter would be really pleased that this book begins with your voice. I know I am. And to end the book as good as it began, President Carter's oldest grandchild, Jason Carter, provided a poignant Afterword. Thank you, Jason, for sharing your "PaPa" with us and bookending his words with some of your own.

Many on both sides of the aisle of American government share Carter's faith. Two of those individuals offered words of endorsement for this book; former Ambassador to the United Nations Andrew Young, who began his career as a minister and a civil rights activist, and former Vice President Mike Pence, whose respect for Carter is obvious in his blurb. President Carter once called renowned author Philip Yancey his "favorite modern author," and now Philip is reciprocating the praise by offering a few words in support of the content of this book. Friends of Jimmy Carter Executive Director Kim Carter Fuller also contributed her praise to these pages. I am honored to attach their names, and words, to these pages.

The Plains townsfolk are a quirky bunch–down home people with a fascinating history. They are in a period of tender transition after the passing of the town's guiding lights, Jimmy and Rosalynn. I'm in it with them. I hope this book is one of many reminders that the spirit of the Carters will forever be reflected throughout their hometown. To the people of Plains, my heart is wide open again because of you. Thank you for taking me in.

Through their faith, the Carters understood they were loved, and they sure tried hard to love others well. So, Jimmy and Rosalynn–here's to our memories of you. We will try our very best to care for others with the same love and dignity with which you cared for us.

And finally, to my family. Especially to my parents, Tim and Jane Greer (who also helped proof these pages!)–I am so happy to be your son. Thank you for sharing your unconditional love with me, and for teaching me to look for Jesus everywhere.

Selected Bibliography

Though this is not a complete catalog of the resources used to write the introductions to Jimmy Carter's lessons featured in this book, all of the following works provide a good start to learning more about the life and legacy of the Sunday school teacher from Plains.

Alter, Jonathan. *His Very Best: Jimmy Carter, a Life.* New York: Simon & Schuster, 2020.

Ariail, Dan and Cheryl Heckler-Feltz. *The Carpenter's Apprentice: The Spiritual Biography of Jimmy Carter.* Grand Rapids: Zondervan Publishing House, 1997.

Balmer, Randall. *Redeemer: The Life of Jimmy Carter.* New York: Basic Books, 2014.

Bird, Kai. *The Outlier: The Unfinished Presidency of Jimmy Carter.* New York: Crown, 2021.

Brinkley, Douglas. *The Unfinished Presidency: Jimmy Carter's Journey Beyond the White House.* New York: Viking, 1998.

Carter, Jimmy. *Always a Reckoning and Other Poems.* New York: Times Books/Random House, 1995.

Carter, Jimmy. *The Blood of Abraham: Insights into the Middle East.* Fayetteville: The University of Arkansas Press, 1993.

Carter, Jimmy. *A Full Life: Reflections at Ninety.* New York: Simon & Schuster, 2015.

Carter, Jimmy. *An Hour Before Daylight: Memories of a Rural Boyhood.* New York: Simon & Schuster, 2001.

Carter, Jimmy. *Living Faith.* New York: Times Books/Random House, 1996.

Carter, Jimmy. *The Nobel Peace Prize Lecture.* New York: Simon & Schuster, 2002.

Carter, Jimmy. *Palestine: Peace Not Apartheid.* New York: Simon & Schuster, 2006.

Kucharsky, David. *The Man from Plains: The Mind and Spirit of Jimmy Carter.* London: Collins, 1977.

Other Selected Sources

The Carter Center home page: www.cartercenter.org

Jimmy Carter Presidential Library. JC Sunday School Files.
Carter, Jimmy. Interview conducted by the author, May 17, 2021.
Carter, Jimmy. Personal Sunday school lesson notes, 1977-1991.
Demme, Jonathan. dir. *Jimmy Carter, Man from Plains.* Sony Pictures, 2007.
Greer, Andrew. dir. *Plainspoken.* Dace & Mohr/Narrative Productions, 2024.
Maranatha Baptist Church home page: www.mbcplains.org

To plan a visit to Maranatha Baptist Church in Plains, Georgia, or to listen and watch more lessons from Jimmy Carter's Sunday school class, please visit MBCPlains.org.